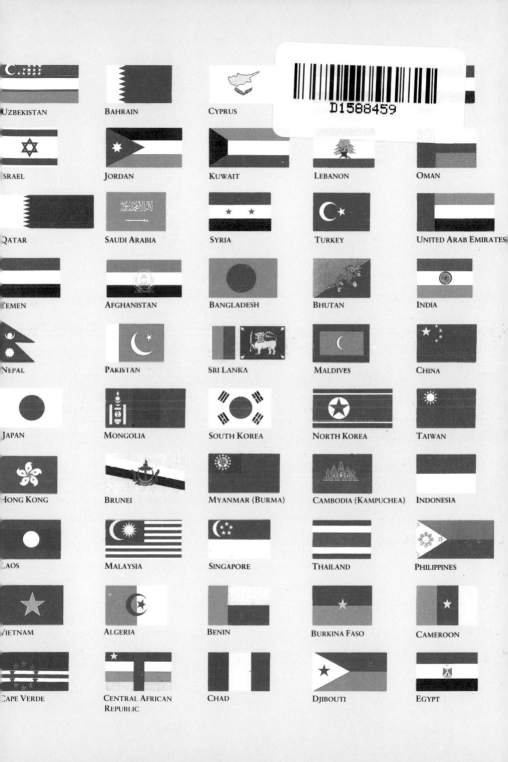

UZBEKISTAN	BAHRAIN	CYPRUS		
ISRAEL	JORDAN	KUWAIT	LEBANON	OMAN
QATAR	SAUDI ARABIA	SYRIA	TURKEY	UNITED ARAB EMIRATES
YEMEN	AFGHANISTAN	BANGLADESH	BHUTAN	INDIA
NEPAL	PAKISTAN	SRI LANKA	MALDIVES	CHINA
JAPAN	MONGOLIA	SOUTH KOREA	NORTH KOREA	TAIWAN
HONG KONG	BRUNEI	MYANMAR (BURMA)	CAMBODIA (KAMPUCHEA)	INDONESIA
LAOS	MALAYSIA	SINGAPORE	THAILAND	PHILIPPINES
VIETNAM	ALGERIA	BENIN	BURKINA FASO	CAMEROON
CAPE VERDE	CENTRAL AFRICAN REPUBLIC	CHAD	DJIBOUTI	EGYPT

EVERY GIRL'S HANDBOOK

ROGER COOTE

Mammoth

EVERY GIRL'S HANDBOOK

Produced by Roger Coote Publishing
Gissing's Farm, Fressingfield, Eye, Suffolk IP21 5SH

Research and additional text contributions by Lynda Lines and Steve Setford
DTP by Roger Coote, using Apple Macintosh and QuarkXPress.
Typeset in ITC Century Condensed, News Gothic Condensed, Symbol and Agfa
General Symbols 4. (Company and product names are trademarks or registered
trademarks of their respective owners.)
Printed in Slovenia

Illustrators (t = top, m = middle, b = bottom, l = left, r = right): Fred Anderson (Bernard
Thornton Artists) 206-214, 216-217, 220-225, 226 (l), 227 (t, ml, br), 228 (br), 229 (b), 231
(tl), 232; Ann Baum (Linda Rogers Associates) 2-25, 58-69; Peter Bull Art Studio 26-27,
28 (tl, mr), 29 (tr), 30-36, 39-63, 70-73, 74 (tl, tr), 76 (br), 82 (bl, tr, br), 83-96, 104-110, 112-
127, 161-163, 165, 166 (t), 167 (t), 168, 170-173, 177, 202 (t), 205, 233 (m, b),
237 (t), 246-253; William Donohoe 169 (br, bl), 175 (t), 191, 198; Terry Hadler (Bernard
Thornton Artists) 156 (t), 158 (b), 160 (t); Hayward Art Group 98-103; Andy Miles
(Maggie Mundy) 238-239; Michael Posen 128-129; Steve Seymour (Bernard Thornton
Artists) 80-81, 82 (tl, ml). Remaining illustrations have appeared previously in other
titles published by Hamlyn Children's Books.
Photographs on pages 226 and 227 were supplied by Zefa.

First published in 1994 by Hamlyn Children's Books
Reprinted 1994, 1995, 1996, 1997, 1998, 1999
This edition published in 2000 by
Egmont Children's Books Limited
239 Kensington High Street, London W8 6SA

ISBN 0 7497 4457 X

A CIP catalogue record for this book is available at the British Library.

Contents

LOOK GOOD, FEEL FINE

Looking and feeling good is not just about how other people see you – your 'outer' self. It's also to do with how you feel about yourself – the 'inner' you.

The first step towards feeling good inside and out is getting to know yourself. Come to terms with the things you can't change and find out about those aspects of yourself that you can change if you wish.

Perhaps the most important factor you can change is your lifestyle - especially what you eat, what exercise you take, the amount of sleep and fresh air you have. How much or how little you have of all these will affect not only your general well-being but

◁ Skipping is great exercise and you don't need expensive equipment. Just 10 minutes morning and evening will strengthen legs and arms and improve stamina. Don't skip on hard surfaces as this could injure your back.

your body shape, skin, eyes, hair and teeth.

However, it is important that you have a sensible approach to changing your lifestyle. Going on crash diets or trying to do too much exercise before you are fit, can be just as damaging to your health and looks as living on a diet of sweets, and spending all your leisure time sitting in front of the TV.

Looking after yourself doesn't have to take up hours of your time every day or cost you a great deal of money, but the rewards can last you all your life.

Healthy eating

The first step to looking good and feeling fine is eating healthily. It will ensure that you grow properly and your skin, hair and teeth stay in good condition. It also helps to protect you against illness.

For your body to work well, it needs a supply of vitamins, proteins, carbohydrates, fibre, minerals, fats and water every day. A healthy, well-balanced diet is one that provides all of these.

Vitamins

Vitamin A is needed for growth, skin, hair, nails and good eyesight. Found in oily fish, liver, butter, carrots, milk and dark green vegetables.

Vitamin B is needed for vitality, nervous system, muscle tone, blood circulation, skin and hair. Found in wholemeal bread, cereals, meat, eggs, milk, nuts and green vegetables.

Vitamin C is needed to help fight infections, for healing, good circulation, teeth, gums and bones. Found in fresh fruit and vegetables.

Vitamin D is needed for healthy bones, teeth and skin. Found in oily fish, fish liver oils and dairy products.

Vitamin E is needed for blood circulation, the nervous system and muscles. Found in liver, wheatgerm, vegetables, eggs, fish and wholemeal bread.

Vitamin K is needed to help blood to clot after a cut. Produced naturally in the stomach but also found in green leafy vegetables, liver and cereals.

Vitamins

The word 'vita' means life, and we need vitamins to stay healthy. We only need small amounts of them, but if we don't have enough this can cause stunted growth, low resistance to infection, nervous diseases, skin problems, anaemia and weakened bones and teeth. Foods containing vitamin C should be eaten every day, as the body cannot store this vitamin.

▽ Fish is a great source of protein. Oily fish – such as mackerel, salmon, trout and pilchards – is also rich in what are called Omega-3 fatty acids, which can reduce the amount of cholesterol in the blood and help to prevent heart disease in later life.

Proteins

You need proteins for growth, to build and repair body tissue and to protect you from disease. They also supply you with heat and energy.

You can get a good supply of proteins from meat, fish, poultry, butter, cheese, eggs, vegetable fats, rice, nuts, beans, lentils and other pulses.

Carbohydrates

Carbohydrates provide us with heat and energy. In some foods, they also give us roughage, or fibre, which helps us to digest food.

Most foods, except for meat, fish, poultry and cheese, contain some carbohydrates, in the form of either starch or sugar. Try to eat more foods containing starch carbohydrates and less containing sugar carbohydrates such as sweets, cakes and jams, apart from the natural sugars found in fruits. Too much sugar in your diet can cause tooth decay.

Fibre

Fibre helps your digestive system work properly and helps get rid of body wastes. It is found in beans, nuts, brown rice and pasta, whole-meal bread, fruit and vegetables.

◁ Good sources of starch carbohydrates: pasta, potatoes, wholemeal bread, lentils and pulses are all high in fibre and low in fats and sugars.

7

Water
You need water to build and repair body tissues and to dissolve and digest food. It also helps to keep your temperature steady and to get rid of body wastes.

◁ Your body needs at least 3 litres of water a day. Some of this will come from the food you eat.

Minerals

To keep healthy you need to take in various minerals.

Calcium is essential for healthy bones, teeth and nails and can be found in milk, cheese, bread, green vegetables, pulses and canned fish. Phosphorus works with calcium to give teeth and bones their strength and hardness and is present in yeast extracts, cheese, eggs, meat, wholemeal bread, fish and nuts.

Iron is an essential mineral because it helps carry oxygen through the body. It can be found in meat, especially liver, wholegrain cereals, dark leafy vegetables such as spinach and potatoes. Sodium and potassium help to regulate the salt levels in your body and these minerals can be found in milk, meat, vegetables, cheese, fruit, fish and nuts.

Other minerals, such as iodine, magnesium, zinc, copper and selenium, are found in most foods.

Fats and oils

You need fat in your diet as it is the main provider of energy, and is one of the components from which all your body cells are made. It also helps to carry vitamins A, D, E and K through the bloodstream.

There are three main types of fat – saturated, monounsaturated and polyunsaturated – and our bodies use each one differently. Try to eat less foods containing saturated fat (as too much of this type of fat can lead to health problems in later life) and more foods containing polyunsaturated and monounsaturated fats.

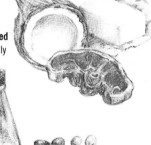

▷ **Polyunsaturated fat** is most commonly found in sunflower oil and margarines, nuts, fish and avocado.

▷ **Saturated fat** is usually found in high quantities in butter, cream, meat and coconut.

▽ **Monounsaturated fat** is found especially in olive oil and peanuts.

Foods for energy and warmth

Foods for growth and repair

▷ The wheel of health shows the types of food you need for a balanced diet.

Foods for general good health

How your body uses food

When you eat, your body takes from the food all of the nutrients it needs to make it work properly and stay healthy. Foods containing carbohydrates and fats are usually high in calories but they also give you energy. Some fat is also required for keeping you warm and helping your blood flow around your body. Carbohydrates in food are used by the body to produce essential sugars such as sucrose or glucose which also provide energy.

Body-building foods contain protein which the body breaks down into molecules called amino acids. These are vital for growth and cell renewal. Your body needs only tiny amounts of vitamins and minerals but they are essential because they help the body absorb proteins, fats and carbohydrates.

Your body's digestive system breaks down the food you have eaten into tiny particles and these are absorbed into your bloodstream.

What is a calorie?

A calorie is a unit to measure the energy value of food. Some foods contain more calories than others. Any calories you don't use up are stored in your body as fat.

The speed at which food is processed by the body is known as the 'metabolic rate'. Different people have slightly different metabolic rates.

9

How much food?

When you are young you need plenty of food to give you energy and help you grow. This is especially true during adolescence – when you change from a child into a young adult.

As this happens, your body changes shape, which can be hard to come to terms with at first. Don't worry though; many young people find that they put on a little weight but then slim down again as they get taller. It's important to make sure you have a healthy, balanced diet – and not to worry about your weight.

It's also worth remembering that people come in all shapes and sizes. There's no point in comparing yourself with friends who might be taller or shorter than you or have a different build. However, if you do think you are overweight or underweight, go and talk to your doctor. Don't be tempted to go on crash diets – they can damage your health and, in the long term, they rarely work.

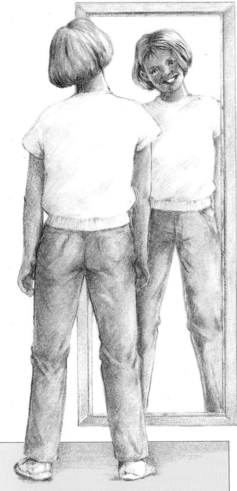

▽ During adolescence, your body goes through many changes. Being fit and healthy during this time can help you to feel more confident and take the changes in your stride.

Eating disorders

Most people can judge when they are overweight or not eating enough but some illnesses can seriously affect eating habits.

- **Anorexia nervosa** makes sufferers believe they are grossly overweight and need to eat almost nothing. They can become dangerously underweight and their health is severely affected.

- **Bulimia nervosa** leads sufferers to repeatedly overeat and then force themselves to be sick.

If you think you might be suffering from either of these illnesses, it is important to see a doctor as soon as possible.

Exercise

Heart becomes stronger and blood circulation improves

Skin benefits from improved blood circulation

Lungs have larger capacity and work better

Arteries stay in good condition and are less likely to become narrowed in later life

Energy and vitality increase. Posture improves and figure is more balanced

What happens when you exercise?

In order to work properly, your muscles need oxygen. When you breathe in, oxygen from the air is absorbed into your blood through your lungs. The oxygenated blood travels to your heart, which pumps it all around the body to your muscles. When you exercise, your muscles – including your heart – have to work harder, so they need more oxygen. In order to get this extra oxygen, you have to breathe faster and more deeply.

Why do it?

Exercise is good for you – it burns up calories, keeps your body strong and flexible, protects you from illness, gives you more energy and at the same time helps you relax.

Muscles become stronger, more supple and less liable to be damaged

Bones and joints become stronger and heal faster if injured

Getting started

Exercise helps you to stay fit because it improves your stamina, strengthens your muscles and helps keep you supple. The exercises on these pages will help to tone the muscles in various parts of your body. But before you start, remember to be sensible.

Start gently, build up gradually and do it regularly. If you have any illnesses or breathing problems, it is essential to consult a doctor first.

Wear clothes that allow you to move freely, and exercise to music to keep a rhythm going. Don't ignore pain – it's your body saying 'stop!'

Tummy toners

Tummy muscles can very quickly get out of condition, so be careful not to overstrain them when you start exercising. Once the muscles are conditioned, your tummy will be firmer and flatter.

△ **1** Lay flat on your back, knees slightly bent and hands behind your head. Slowly lift your head and shoulders off the floor.

▽ **2** Keeping the base of the spine pressed into the floor, hold for a count of three, then slowly lower yourself back down. Repeat 10 times.

▽ In the same position, slowly lift your head and shoulders off the ground. Stretch your right arm out to touch your left knee and hold for a count of three. Lower yourself back down and repeat the exercise, this time with your left arm touching your right knee. Repeat 20 times.

Warm up

Before exercising, you need to warm up your muscles to avoid injury. Stretch your arms above your head and gently circle your hips 15 times in each direction.

Bust up

Exercise won't change the size of your bust, but will strengthen and tone the muscles that support it.

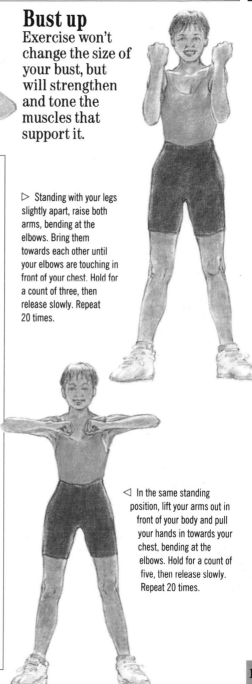

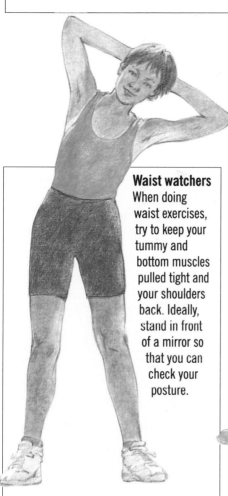

Waist watchers

When doing waist exercises, try to keep your tummy and bottom muscles pulled tight and your shoulders back. Ideally, stand in front of a mirror so that you can check your posture.

▷ Standing with your legs slightly apart, raise both arms, bending at the elbows. Bring them towards each other until your elbows are touching in front of your chest. Hold for a count of three, then release slowly. Repeat 20 times.

◁ In the same standing position, lift your arms out in front of your body and pull your hands in towards your chest, bending at the elbows. Hold for a count of five, then release slowly. Repeat 20 times.

△ Stand with your feet slightly apart and hands behind your head. Slowly bend over to the side, taking care not to lean forward or back. Bend down until you feel yourself stretching out and hold for a count of five. Raise yourself back up slowly to your original position. Repeat 10 times. Now do the same on your other side.

In the same standing position but legs further apart and hands on hips, bend your knees and bounce down for a count of ten. Repeat 5 times.

Swivelling your hips in wide circles is another good waist exercise.

The bottom line

This exercise will help to strengthen your leg muscles as well as firm up and flatten your bottom.

△ Lie on your stomach, legs straight and arms in front of you, bent at the elbow. Raise one leg, squeezing your buttocks as you lift and keeping your leg straight. Hold for a count of five, then lower your leg. Now do the same with your other leg. Repeat 20 times each leg.

Thighs right

Thighs can be the most flabby part of the body, but with exercise they can soon firm up. However, go easy on the inside thigh muscles at first, because they can tear when out of condition.

▷ Stand side on, one foot slightly in front of the other, hands on your waist. Now slowly lower your body into a kneeling position using your thigh muscles. Return to the starting position. Repeat 10 times, then switch to your other side.

▷ Lie on your side with one arm propping up your head, the other arm supporting your body. Raise your leg as high as you can, keeping your hip bone on the floor. Hold for a count of five then slowly lower. Repeat 20 times. Change sides and repeat with your other leg.

▽ Now, lying on your original side, slowly lift both legs off the ground, keeping them together. Hold for a count of five then slowly lower. Repeat 10 times. Change sides and repeat another 10 times.

◁ Yoga is a form of mental and physical exercise. There are eight different types of yoga and 200 standing and sitting positions, so it is important to learn from a qualified yoga teacher. Yoga keeps your muscles flexible and toned, and the regular breathing exercises make you feel calm and relaxed.

▽ Jogging is great all-round exercise and particularly good for toning up your legs and building up stamina. Don't be too ambitious — start off with a gentle jog around your local park and then gradually build up the distance. Aim to jog three or four times a week, but if you find yourself getting too tired or if you're in any pain, stop and rest. Wear proper running shoes to absorb the impact when running on hard surfaces and to prevent damaging your spine.

What else?

With exercise, like everything else, varying your activity helps to keep you motivated and makes it more fun. For example, cycling, swimming and walking are good, all-round forms of exercise that increase your stamina, too.

Look in at your local sports centre and see what is available. Taking up a new sport such as squash or volleyball is a good way of improving your social life as well as keeping you fit.

Try to include some exercise in your daily routine. Use the stairs instead of the lift, and walk or cycle whenever possible instead of taking a bus.

Aim to make exercise an enjoyable 'habit' so that it becomes a regular part of your life.

Beauty basics

Keeping clean and fresh is an essential part of basic beauty care. Ideally, you should have a bath or shower once a day, but if that is not possible, have an all-over wash to remove dirt and perspiration. Set aside a couple of hours a week to have a relaxing bath and a top-to-toe beauty treatment.

△ Treat yourself to a face mask every few weeks to refresh your skin. You can buy gels, creams or mud-based masks. Choose one which is recommended for your skin type and follow the instructions on the packet for what to do. You can put thin slices of cucumber on your eyes to soothe them.

Hot	43°C Too hot
Warm	38°C Ideal for a relaxing soak or to warm you up
Tepid	29°C Refreshing in hot weather
Cool	24°C A good pick-you-up in the morning
Cold	18°C Keep it short!

Bath temperature

△ Do not spend more than 20 minutes soaking, or your skin will start to wrinkle. Make sure the water temperature is no more than 38°C as very hot water can dry your skin. Add some moisturising bath oil, or bubble bath and after washing with soap or body shampoo, massage yourself all over with either a loofah, textured bath mitt or body scrub – these are all designed to rub off any dead skin and leave your body feeling soft, smooth and invigorated. After your bath, massage your whole body with moisturising lotion.

Unwanted hair

Everyone has hair on their legs, but there is no need to remove it unless you really want to. Depilatory cream is the easiest way of removing unwanted hair. It is safer than shaving and less painful than waxing your legs. Read the instructions carefully before you start. Squeeze some cream into the palm of your hand, then spread it thickly over your legs.

Leave for as long as the instructions tell you. Wipe off gently with a wet cloth, rinse and pat dry with a towel.

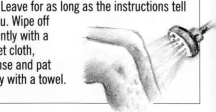

Hands and nails

Get into the habit of using a hand cream to keep your hands soft and to encourage your nails to grow faster and stronger.

▷ Cut your toenails straight across with nail clippers.

▽ Use an emery board to file your nails. File from the edges towards the centre of each nail.

Avoid biting your nails as it can be very painful as well as making your hands look very unattractive. But don't grow your nails too long as they will easily break. When you come to manicure your hands, start by filing your nails. Then soak your fingertips in warm water for a few minutes, dry them and apply some hand cream. Push back the cuticles and apply nail varnish.

△ To push back your cuticles, first rub some cuticle cream into the skin at the base of the nail. Then gently push back the cuticle with a cotton bud.

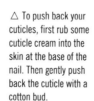

◁ Carefully paint on a thin coat of nail varnish. When it is dry, apply a second coat.

Feet

Make sure you always dry properly between your toes to avoid fungal infections. Trim your toenails, then file them from the edges inwards. Soften your cuticles and push them back carefully. Then apply two coats of nail varnish.

◁ Separating your toes with cotton wool makes it easier to put on nail varnish neatly.

Five steps to healthy teeth

- go for a dental check-up twice a year
- brush your teeth at least twice a day, working from the gum to the biting edge
- use dental floss daily to remove food particles between your teeth
- use a toothpaste with fluoride, which helps fight decay
- cut down on sugar, which combines with bacteria in your mouth to form plaque, leading to tooth decay and gum disease.

Hair care

Clean, well-groomed hair can make all the difference to the way you feel about yourself. Keeping your hair in good condition isn't just about using the right shampoo; good diet and plenty of exercise are essential to give your hair shine and vitality.

Shampooing and conditioning

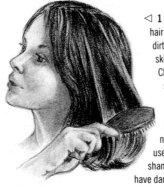

◁ **1** Brush your hair to loosen any dirt and dead skin cells. Choose a shampoo to suit your hair type – dry, greasy or normal – and use a medicated shampoo if you have dandruff.

△ **3** Pat your hair with a towel to soak up the moisture. Then massage a small amount of conditioner into your hair, combing it through to the ends.

▷ **2** Wet your hair with lukewarm water and rub a small amount of shampoo into your hair until it foams. Remember to massage your scalp, too. Then rinse your hair well to make sure all the shampoo is washed out.

▷ **4** Leave the conditioner on for the recommended time, then rinse off. Finally, rinse your hair in cold water for about 10 seconds to give it shine.

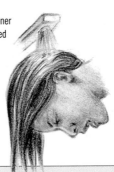

Styles to suit your face shape

Diamond-shape	Square	Long
△ Choose a style that frames the cheekbones, with fullness around the forehead.	△ A layered style will soften your jawline and a side parting will break up the symmetry of the face.	△ A short, wavy bob cut around the chin line will add width, and a fringe will make your face appear shorter.

18

Blow drying

Letting your hair dry naturally is the best way of keeping it in good condition but using a hair dryer is quicker. If you use a dryer, first dry your hair as much as you can with a towel. Hair is at its weakest when it is wet, so use a wide-toothed comb or a brush with soft, rounded bristles to avoid scalp and hair damage. For short hair styles, try finger drying – pushing your fingers through your hair as you blow dry. For curly or layered hair, scrunching the hair with your hand as you dry it will produce a bulkier look.

▷ **2** Hold the dryer (on a low setting) at least 15 cm from your head and keep it moving all the time.

▽ **3** Start drying at the back and work around the head, doing the front last. As you dry, pick up the hair, layer by layer, with the brush. Hold the hair in that position until it is dry. This will give it volume and body.

△ **1** Divide your hair into sections. It's best to dry the lower sections first, so clip the rest out of the way.

Heart-shaped

△ Try a short cut with fullness at the crown but lying flat around the cheeks. A fringe will also add balance.

Round

△ Choose short styles which give your hair height, and go for a layered fringe rather than straight and 'heavy'.

Oval

△ Most styles flatter an oval face but short styles or hair off the face will emphasize the cheekbones.

Skin care

To make sure that your skin looks at its best, you need to take good care of it.

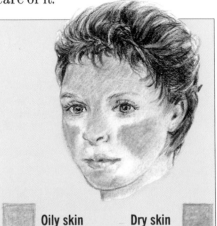

Oily skin   Dry skin

Know your skin
- **Oily skin** Overall shiny look, especially on nose, chin and forehead.
- **Dry skin** Flaky patches, especially on cheeks. Skin feels tight after washing.
- **Normal skin** A mixture of dry and oily. Often called combination skin.

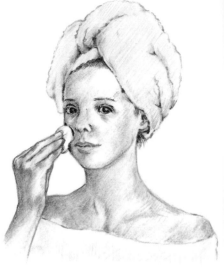

△ **Cleansing** Smooth a little cleanser over your face and neck. Wipe off with a tissue, using gentle, upward movements to tone muscles and help circulation. If you prefer to use a facial wash, ensure you rinse thoroughly with clean water.

A healthy diet, regular exercise and lots of fresh air and sleep are essential. But your skin is exposed to dirt, pollution and weather so it is important to know how to keep it clean and moisturised.

▷ Choose skin products that are recommended for your skin type. The basics you will need are: cleanser to remove dirt and make-up, or a cleansing bar if your skin is oily; eye make-up remover, either liquid or pads; toner to close the pores after cleansing; and moisturiser to protect the skin. Use cotton wool or tissues to put on and wipe off.

◁ **Toning** Soak a cotton wool pad in toner and gently wipe over your face. Avoid downward movements as this will stretch the skin and facial muscles.

Problem skin

- **Spots and acne** often occur in early teenage years, when the body's hormones are changing and the skin becomes oily. Keep your face thoroughly clean with medicated soap or lotion. Get plenty of exercise. Never squeeze your spots as this will spread the infection.
- **Sensitive skin** tends to be blotchy and prone to allergic rashes. Use only the mildest, unperfumed skin products.

▷ **Moisturising** Put small blobs of moisturiser over your face and neck and gently massage into your skin using upward movements. Apply extra moisturiser to the dry areas, such as your cheeks.

You should cleanse, tone and moisturise morning and night. Avoid using strong astringents if you have dry skin. Moisturisers help to replace lost moisture and keep the skin smooth and supple.

▷ When you're in the sun, apply suntan cream liberally to all exposed areas and re-apply it regularly – especially after swimming. Try to avoid the sun between noon and 3pm when it is at its hottest.

Tanning safely

Some sunlight is good for the skin but too much of the sun's ultraviolet rays (UVA and UVB) can lead to sunburn and skin damage. Always use a suntan cream with the right SPF (sun protection factor) for your skin type (see below) and don't spend too long in the sun at first.

Skin type	Moderate sun (UK, northern Europe) SPF Week 1	Then	Hot sun (Mediterranean) SPF Week 1	Then	Very hot sun (Tropics, Africa) SPF Week 1	Then
Sun-sensitive (pale, freckled skin; fair or red hair)	10-15	8-10	15-20	10-15	25-30	20-25
Fair (mid to pale skin; fair hair, blue eyes)	8-10	6-8	10-15	8-10	15-20	10-15
Normal (mid to pale skin; dark hair and eyes)	6-8	4-6	8-10	6-8	10-15	8-10
Dark/black (olive or black skin; dark hair and eyes)	4-6	4	6-8	4-6	8-10	6-8

Make-up

Make-up can enhance your 'best' features and tone down those you are less happy with. Wear make-up that suits you, is right for the occasion and looks natural.

Make-up kit

▷ **Concealer** Cover-up cream to hide spots and blemishes

◁ **Foundation** Skin-coloured cream that gives even colour and texture

▷ **Face powder** Stops your face looking shiny

▽ **Lip colour** Adds colour and moisture

◁ **Blusher** Red or pink powder to add colour to your face and shape to your cheekbones

▽ ▷ **Eye shadow** Coloured powder, cream or pencil to shade your eyelids

▷ **Mascara** Darkens and lengthens eyelashes

△ **Eye pencil** To outline eyes

◁ **Brush** To apply blusher

Techniques

△ **1** Put a little concealer over any spots, blemishes or dark shadows and blend it in with your fingertips.

△ **2** Dot foundation over your face, but not your eyelids, and spread evenly with your fingertips or a damp sponge making sure you smooth it in well under your chin.

△ **3** Pat powder firmly but gently all over your face, and use a large, soft brush to remove any loose powder.

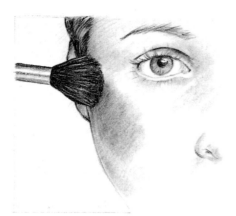

△ **4** Stroke blusher along your cheekbones. Use a deeper shade below the cheekbones to add shape to your face.

△ **7** Brush mascara on to your top and bottom lashes. Leave to dry and then put on a second coat.

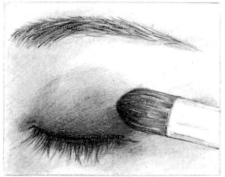

△ **5** Gently brush eye shadow over your eyelids and into the socket line. Blend evenly to avoid a solid block of colour.

△ **8** Draw an outline around the edge of your mouth with a lip pencil. Then fill in with lipstick, using a lip brush.

△ **6** Draw a fine line next to your upper and lower lashes. Then smudge with a damp cotton bud to soften the effect.

Experiment with colours and ranges of make-up to see which best suits your skin colouring and personality. Use softer shades during the day. At night, especially if you're going to a party, you can have more fun with bright, dramatic colours.

Don't try to change your looks by using a lot of make-up. Instead, use a little wisely, and bring out the best in your face.

Choosing colours

Trying out new colours can be fun but whichever 'look' you want to achieve, choose colours or shades that flatter your hair and skin colouring. Here are some ideas.

Fair skin and blonde hair

Foundation – pinky beige

Fair skin and brown hair

Foundation – light beige
Blusher – dark pink or golden peach
Eyes – grass green, light brown, apricot, gold or mid-blue
Lips – pale pink, coral pink or crimson red

Freckled skin and red hair

Foundation – light beige
Blusher – golden amber or dusky pink
Eyes – russet, sage green, deep pink, wine red or rust brown

Blusher – beige pink or peach
Eyes – sky blue, lilac, soft brown, dark mauve or grey
Lips – light pink, peachy brown or warm pink

Lips – light peach, burgundy or dark pink

Black skin and dark hair

Foundation – skin tone
Blusher – brownish red or wine red
Eyes – autumn brown, light yellow, dark blue, orange or rose pink
Lips – burgundy, bright red or bright pink

24

Fashion

Like make-up, clothes and accessories are prone to fashion changes. What's in vogue now may well be out of date very soon. If you like to be fashionable, or just enjoy wearing clothes, here are a few golden rules worth remembering:

- Wear clothes that suit your body shape and height.
- Choose colours and textures that suit your colouring and personality.
- Buy clothes in styles and colours that you will be able to mix and match.

△ Accessories are great for the 'finishing' touches. Bangles, necklaces and earrings will 'dress-up' a plain outfit for parties. Big, chunky belts look good with jeans and T-shirts.

Clothes are expensive and fashions change. If you are on a tight budget, don't rush out and buy all the latest styles. Search charity shops, jumble sales and car-boot sales for cheap, good-quality clothes and jewellery, especially when past fashions are back in vogue.

The basics

Fashions change but some types of clothes are almost timeless. Here are a few examples:

- Jeans – good for leisure wear and can also be dressed up with glamorous tops and jewellery for evening wear.
- Little black dress or slinky trousers/skirt and top – ideal for parties and special occasions.
- T-shirts – cheap and colourful and good for wearing with jeans in the summer.
- Sweatshirt – wear over your T-shirt when the weather turns cold.
- Crew- or polo-neck sweater – also good for wearing with jeans in colder weather.
- Casual jacket – can be worn with almost anything.

◁ Classic style; a glamorous look for parties.

▷ Jeans and a sweatshirt; rarely out of fashion and practical, too.

SPORT

The main reason why people take up a sport is to enjoy themselves. We all feel a sense of achievement as we become better at a sport, and we also get fitter and stronger.

There is an enormous range of sports to choose from. Some, like hockey and netball, are team games. Others, including tennis, squash and table tennis, are played by two or four players. And there are sports in which you can compete as an individual – swimming, athletics, gymnastics, showjumping and archery, for example. You now have a greater choice than ever, as girls can take part in sports such as football, cricket and rugby, which were once played only by boys.

Whatever sport you try, remember you don't have to be good at it to enjoy it; taking part is fun. Sport also gives you lots of opportunities to meet people and make new friends. The following pages will introduce you to some of the sports available. You will find even more on offer at your local sports centre.

◁ Sports such as skiing and horseriding have always been quite expensive, but they are gradually becoming more affordable.

Ice skating

△ Free-skating performances have become more athletic in recent years, with competitors attempting more complicated jumps and spins to impress the judges.

There are two main sports in ice skating, apart from ice hockey.

Figure skating

This is reputed to be the oldest Winter Olympic sport. There are singles contests – men's and women's – and others for male/female pairs. In singles competition, skaters are judged on a free-skating programme which tests their abilty to perform jumps, spins and spirals and co-ordinate skating with music.

◁ An ice skate consists of a lace-up boot made of sturdy leather with stiffening supports at the heel and under the arch. A metal blade is fitted to the sole of the boot for gliding over the ice.

Pairs competitions are also judged on free-skating, which may include lifts and partner-assisted jumps. In singles and pairs skating, a panel of judges awards marks out of a maximum of six for both technical merit and artistic impression.

Ice dancing

This is derived from pairs figure skating, but certain lifts are not allowed. All competing couples dance to set pieces of music – such as a waltz or a rhumba – and then to two pieces of their own choosing.

Speed skating

Speed skating events are held on outdoor circuits, usually 400 m long with two lanes in which skaters race against each other. Both men and women compete in the Winter Olympics and the World Championships, at distances from 500 m to 10 000 m for men and 500 m to 5000 m for women. Short-track skating is raced on an indoor circuit with four to six skaters in a race.

◁ Speed skaters can maintain speeds of about 48 km/h.

Skating feats
• The highest number of maximum six marks awarded (29) went to Jayne Torvill and Christopher Dean of Great Britain in 1984.
• American speed skater Eric Heiden won a record 5 gold medals at the 1980 Winter Olympics.

Showjumping

Showjumping is a competition to test the ability of the horse to jump over obstacles and the rider to control. Men and women compete against each other, individually and in teams.

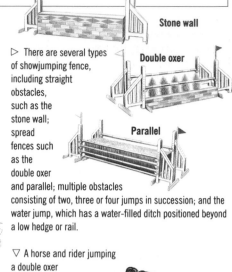

Stone wall

▷ There are several types of showjumping fence, including straight obstacles, such as the stone wall; spread fences such as the double oxer and parallel; multiple obstacles consisting of two, three or four jumps in succession; and the water jump, which has a water-filled ditch positioned beyond a low hedge or rail.

Double oxer

Parallel

▷ Banks like this are some of the most difficult obstacles in showjumping.

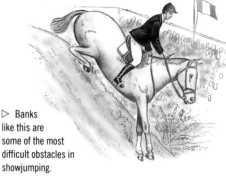

▽ A horse and rider jumping a double oxer

Depending upon the type of competition, the winner is the individual or team with either the lowest number of faults, the highest number of points, or the fastest time with fewest faults.

In all events, faults are given for knocking down or refusing to jump an obstacle, falling by the horse or rider, and failure to clear a water jump cleanly.

▷ The position of the rider and the action of the horse when jumping an upright fence.

Approach

Take-off

Three-day eventing

Showjumping forms the final phase of what are called three-day events. The first two phases are dressage and endurance competitions.
In dressage, horse and rider perform set, precise movements to demonstrate the horse's co-ordination, training and obedience. The endurance section consists of two 16- to 20-km road-and-track races, a 3-km. steeplechase and a cross-country course of about 7 or 8 km with obstacles including steep banks, water obstacles, wooden fences and stone walls.

△ A competitor tackles a water obstacle in the cross-country section of a three-day event. These obstacles are often quite wide and, unlike in showjumping, horses are not given faults for putting their feet in the water.

Puissance events are ones in which jumping ability alone is judged. In other competitions, time is an important factor in deciding the winner. In some, the horse is faulted for errors in the first rounds and the final rounds are against the clock; the winner is the rider with the fewest faults and the fastest time. In other competitions, faults are converted into time penalties in seconds, which are added to the time taken to complete the course; the winner is the rider with the fastest time.

The major championships are the Olympics, the World Championships and the Nations Cup.

Suspension

Landing

Olympic Champions, 1996

Showjumping Individual – Ulrich Kirchhoff of Germany riding Jus de Pommes
Team – Germany
Three-day event Individual – Blyth Tait of New Zealand riding Ready Teddy
Team – Australia

Netball

Netball is a seven-a-side team game, usually played by women. It was developed from basketball, and goals are scored in the same way –

◁ A netball court is 30.5 m long by 15.25 m wide, with a hard surface. Lines divide it into three equal areas – two goal thirds and a centre third. The ball is a size 5 soccer ball, of leather or rubber, weighing between 400 and 450 g. The playing positions are: goal shooter (**GS**), goal attack (**GA**), wing attack (**WA**), centre (**C**), wing defence (**WD**), goal defence (**GD**), and goalkeeper (**GK**).

by shooting the ball through a ring, 3.05 m above the ground, at the opponents' end of the court. Unlike basketball, players must not run with the ball, and they have to stay in certain areas of the court.

A game is divided into four quarters of 15 minutes each. There are intervals, between the first and second, and third and fourth quarters, and at half-time. Injury time is added to each quarter in which the injury occurs.

◁ Only the goal shooter or goal attack can shoot at goal, and they must be within the goal circle. The opponents' goalkeeper and goal defence can attempt to intercept the ball within the circle. However, no player may come closer than 90 cm to the player with the ball, or she will be penalized for obstruction.

Passing and catching

The game starts with a pass made by the centre, standing in the centre circle. The ball must be passed within 3 seconds of the starting whistle, and must go to a player who moves into the centre third to receive it.

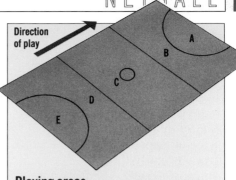

Direction of play

△ When passing the ball, a player may throw it, or bounce it once, but they must not roll it, run with it or throw it in the air and catch it again. Players can catch the ball in one or two hands or deflect it to another player. Once in possession, the ball must be passed to another player within 3 seconds.

When a ball is passed, it must cover a distance that would allow a third player to move between the hands of the thrower and receiver. A pass may not be thrown over a whole third of the court unless it has been touched by a player in that third.

Playing areas

Depending upon their playing position, players are only allowed in certain areas of the court. The areas are:

- Goal shooter – **A** and **B**
- Goal attack – **A**, **B** and **C**
- Wing attack – **B** and **C**
- Centre – **B**, **C** and **D**
- Wing defence – **C** and **D**
- Goal defence – **C**, **D** and **E**
- Goalkeeper – **D** and **E**.

If a player moves into another area she is offside, and the opposing team is awarded a free throw from that point. A player can catch the ball outside her own playing area, but her feet must not cross the line.

Once a player catches the ball, the first foot to land on the ground must stay in the same place, but she may pivot on it, moving her other foot in any direction.

Each player in a team marks her opposite number – goal defence marks the opposing goal attack, wing defence marks wing attack, and so on. A player can take possession of the ball from an opponent by intercepting a pass, but she must not deliberately kick the ball, or grab it or punch it from the opponent's hands.

World Championships

- The first netball World Championships were in 1963, and they are held every four years. Australia won in 1995, for a record seventh time.
- The highest score in a match was 120–38 by Australia against Vanuatu at the 1991 World Championships.

31

Hockey

Hockey is played by two teams of 11 men or women, on grass or on a synthetic indoor pitch.

A game is divided into two halves of 35 minutes each, and teams change ends at half-time.

The object of the game is to hit the ball into the opponents' goal, and the winning team is the one that scores the most goals. To score a goal, a player must be inside the striking circle.

There are various 'set piece' moves, including a free hit awarded when an offence is committed, a corner hit

Goal line

Penalty spot

Striking circle

Half-way line

25-yard line

▷ A hockey pitch is 100 yards (91.5 m) long and 60 yards (54.9 m) wide. There are lines across the pitch at half-way and 25 yards (22.87 m) in front of each goal line. The goals are 4 yards (3.66 m) wide and 7 ft (2.13 m) high.

▷ No physical contact is allowed, and players are penalized for dangerous play, such as raising the stick above shoulder height or hitting the ball too high in the air.

◁ The stick has a flat face on one side and the head is made of wood. The ball is hard, usually white, and weighs between 5½ and 5¾ ounces (156–163 g). The ball can only be played by pushing or hitting with the flat side of the stick; touching or hitting with any other part of the stick or with the body is a foul. The goalkeeper may touch the ball with her feet or her pads, but only within her own striking circle.

Olympic Champions, 1996
Women – Australia
Men – Netherlands

taken by the attacking side when a defender unintentionally hits the ball behind the goal line, and a penalty corner given for an offence by a defender in the striking circle or a deliberate foul inside the 25-yard line. A penalty stroke is given for a deliberate foul in the circle.

Archery

Olympic Champions, 1996
Individual Men – Justin Huish (USA)
Women – Kim Kyung-Wook (Korea)
Team Men – USA   Women – Korea

There are three types of archery – field, crossbow and target. In field archery, the targets are set out over two courses in natural terrain. Crossbow archery is similar to target but a crossbow is used instead of a longbow.

In target archery, competitors shoot a set number of arrows at targets set at different distances – 90 m, 70 m, 50 m, and 30 m for men, and 70 m, 60 m, 50 m, and 30 m for women. Usually, the archer with the highest total score is the winner, but at Olympic and World Championship level, archers compete on a knock-out basis. Archery is a sport for individuals and teams, both male and female. National teams normally consist of three archers.

▷ An archer's kit may include a quiver (a holster that holds the arrows), an armguard to protect the arm from the bowstring, and a glove or finger tab to protect the drawing hand. If you plan to take up archery, it is important to have expert tuition before using a bow.

Dacron string

Carbon fibre limbs

Magnesium handle

Bowsight

Nock Plastic fletching

Aluminium or carbon fibre shaft

Metal tip

V-bar stabilizer

△ The main parts of a modern target archery bow and arrow.

Longrod stabilizer

▽ Archery targets are made of straw ropes stitched together. Each target is fixed to a buttress or stand, so that the centre is 1.3 m above the ground. The target face is usually made of paper and is divided into five concentric coloured rings. Each colour is divided into an inner and an outer zone. The outer white zone scores one point, the inner white scores two, and so on, up to the inner gold which scores a maximum ten points.

Table tennis

Table tennis is normally an indoor game, for two players (singles) or four (doubles), either men, women or mixed. The game is played by hitting a small, light ball using a bat, back and forth across a table divided by a low net. The aim is to win points by making shots that an opponent is unable to return.

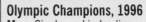

Olympic Champions, 1996
Men Singles – Liu Luoliang (China); Doubles – Liu Luoliang and Kong Linghui (China)
Women Singles – Deng Yaping (China); Doubles – Qiao Hong and Deng Yaping (China)

△ A full-size table measures 2.74 m long by 1.52 m wide, and stands 76 cm high. The net is 1.83 m long and 15.25 cm high, and is suspended across the middle of the table. The playing surface should be about 2 cm thick, and dark coloured with 2-cm wide white marking lines.

◁ Most Western and European players hold the bat using the 'shakehand' grip (above), while many Asian players prefer the 'penhold' grip (below).

When serving, a player must rest the ball on the flat palm of the hand and then throw it at least 16 cm into the air before striking it. It must bounce once on the server's side of the net and once more on the other side before it is returned.

The ball must be hit back over the net so that it lands on the server's side. It must not bounce twice in a row on the same side of the net, and volleying is not allowed.

A game is won by the first player or pair to reach 21 points or, if the score is 20-all, the first to achieve a difference of two clear points. A match is either the best of three or the best of five games.

▷ The time when a ball is in play is called a rally. Each rally continues until one player makes a fault and loses the point. The most common faults are: missing the ball, failing to hit it over the net, missing the opponent's side of the table, and volleying.

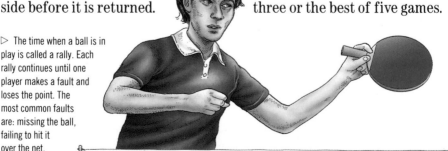

Tennis

Tennis can be played by individuals – singles – and by pairs – doubles – using rackets and a ball.

The aim is to hit the ball over a net so that an opponent cannot return it. Play begins with a service from the baseline. The ball is hit over the net to land in the opponent's right-hand service court. The opponent must let the ball bounce once and return it into any part of the court on the server's side of the net.

The ball can then be played after one bounce or on the volley, and the rally continues until one player fails to return the ball correctly.

◁ Tennis shoes should be light and comfortable, and have soles that give a good grip. Rackets must not be more than 32 in (81.3 cm) long or 12½ in (31.75 cm) wide. Tennis balls must be white or yellow and weigh between 56.7 and 58.5 g.

▽ Tennis can be played outdoors or inside, on courts which are usually made of grass, asphalt, clay, concrete or artificial grass. For singles, the playing area is 23.77 m long by 8.23 m wide. The side areas used in doubles add an extra 2.74 m to the width.

Service court

Service line

Side area

Doubles sideline

Singles sideline

Centre line

Server

Baseline

▷ A forehand volley. 'Forehand' means that the palm of the racket hand is facing the ball; a volley is a shot that is hit before the ball bounces.

35

Scoring

The player who wins a rally – the last one to return the ball successfully – scores a point. The points go from 0, or 'love', to 15, 30, 40 and then 'game', and so a player has to score at least four points to win a game. A score of 40-40 is called 'deuce'; one player must then go two points clear to win the game – the first point after deuce is called 'advantage' and the second, 'game'.

A player needs at least six games to win a set, and must be at least two games ahead – 6 games to 4, for example. If a set reaches 6 games each, a tie-breaker is played. The player who wins the tie-break game wins the set 7 games to 6.

Matches are decided on the best of five sets for men and the best of three for women.

▷ To serve, first stand behind the baseline, side-on to the court. Throw the ball into the air above your head and draw the racket back behind you. Bring the racket up, with its head back and down. As the ball drops, 'throw' the racket head at it, hitting it when your arm is fully extended and the ball is slightly in front of you. Follow through and move into position for your next shot.

Shots

Most shots in tennis are groundstrokes – played after the ball has bounced and usually just as it is starting to drop again. Examples are drives, in which the racket is swung 'through' the line of the ball in a full arc with a smooth follow-through. It is vital to get into the right position first and watch the ball on to the racket.

Volleys are mostly played close to the net, and so a quick eye and fast reactions are needed. The backswing for a volley is shorter than for a groundstroke, and the action is more punchy.

A strong, accurate serve can win quick points, but it requires a great deal of practice. The overhead smash is a volley shot that is played in a similar way to the serve. Both shots need good timing and correct positioning of the feet.

Other useful shots include the lob, in which the ball is lifted over an opponent to drop behind him, and the half-volley, hit just after the ball bounces. By angling the racket, groundstrokes can be given topspin to send the ball deep into an opponent's court, or backspin to drop it just over the net.

Wimbledon Women's Singles Champions

1884	Maud Watson (UK)	1924	Kathleen McKane (UK)	1970	Margaret Court (Aus)
1885	Maud Watson (UK)	1925	Suzanne Lenglen (Fra)	1971	Evonne Goolagong (Aus)
1886	Blanche Bingley (UK)	1926	Kathleen Godfree (UK)	1972	Billie Jean King (USA)
1887	Lottie Dod (UK)	1927	Helen Wills (USA)	1973	Billie Jean King (USA)
1888	Lottie Dod (UK)	1928	Helen Wills (USA)	1974	Chris Evert (USA)
1889	Blanche Hillyard (UK)	1929	Helen Wills (USA)	1975	Billie Jean King (USA)
1890	Helen Rice (UK)	1930	Helen Moody (USA)	1976	Chris Evert (USA)
1891	Lottie Dod (UK)	1931	Cilly Aussem (Ger)	1977	Virginia Wade (UK)
1892	Lottie Dod (UK)	1932	Helen Moody (USA)	1978	Martina Navrátilová (Cs)
1893	Lottie Dod (UK)	1933	Helen Moody (USA)	1979	Martina Navrátilová (Cs)
1894	Blanche Hillyard (UK)	1934	Dorothy Round (UK)	1980	Evonne Cawley (Aus)
1895	Charlotte Cooper (UK)	1935	Helen Moody (USA)	1981	Chris Evert Lloyd (USA)
1896	Charlotte Cooper (UK)	1936	Helen Jacobs (USA)	1982	Martina Navrátilová
1897	Blanche Hillyard (UK)	1937	Dorothy Round (UK)		(USA)
1898	Charlotte Cooper (UK)	1938	Helen Moody (USA)	1983	Martina Navrátilová
1899	Blanche Hillyard (UK)	1939	Alice Marble (USA)		(USA)
1900	Blanche Hillyard (UK)	1946	Pauline Betz (USA)	1984	Martina Navrátilová
1901	Charlotte Sterry (UK)	1947	Margaret Osborne (USA)		(USA)
1902	Muriel Robb (UK)	1948	Louise Brough (USA)	1985	Martina Navrátilová
1903	Dorothea Douglass (UK)	1949	Louise Brough (USA)		(USA)
1904	Dorothea Douglass (UK)	1950	Louise Brough (USA)	1986	Martina Navrátilová
1905	May Sutton (USA)	1951	Doris Hart (USA)		(USA)
1906	Dorothea Douglass (UK)	1952	Maureen Connolly (USA)	1987	Martina Navrátilová
1907	May Sutton (USA)	1953	Maureen Connolly (USA)		(USA)
1908	Charlotte Sterry (UK)	1954	Maureen Connolly (USA)	1988	Steffi Graf (FRG)
1909	Dora Boothby (UK)	1955	Louise Brough (USA)	1989	Steffi Graf (FRG)
1910	Dorothea Lambert	1956	Shirley Fry (USA)	1990	Martina Navrátilová
	Chambers (UK)	1957	Althea Gibson (USA)		(USA)
1911	Dorothea Lambert	1958	Althea Gibson (USA)	1991	Steffi Graf (Ger)
	Chambers (UK)	1959	Maria Bueno (Bra)	1992	Steffi Graf (Ger)
1912	Ethel Larcombe (UK)	1960	Maria Bueno (Bra)	1993	Steffi Graf (Ger)
1913	Dorothea Lambert	1961	Angela Mortimer (UK)	1994	Conchita Martinez (Spa)
	Chambers (UK)	1962	Karen Susman (USA)	1995	Steffi Graf (Ger)
1914	Dorothea Lambert	1963	Margaret Smith (Aus)	1996	Steffi Graf (Ger)
	Chambers (UK)	1964	Maria Bueno (Bra)	1997	Martina Hingis (Sui)
1919	Suzanne Lenglen (Fra)	1965	Margaret Smith (Aus)	1998	Jana Novotná (Cz Rep)
1920	Suzanne Lenglen (Fra)	1966	Billie Jean King (USA)	1999	Lindsay Davenport (USA)
1921	Suzanne Lenglen (Fra)	1967	Billie Jean King (USA)	2000	Venus Williams (USA)
1922	Suzanne Lenglen (Fra)	1968	Billie Jean King (USA)		
1923	Suzanne Lenglen (Fra)	1969	Ann Jones (UK)		

Wimbledon Mixed Doubles Champions (from 1981)

1981	Frew McMillan (SA) & Betty Stove (Hol)	1991	John Fitzgerald & Elizabeth Smylie (Aus)
1982	Kevin Curren (SA) & Anne Smith (USA)	1992	Cyril Suk (Cs) & Larisa Savchenko (Lat)
1983	John Lloyd (UK) & Wendy Turnbull (Aus)	1993	M Woodforde (Aus) & M Navrátilová (USA)
1984	John Lloyd (UK) & Wendy Turnbull (Aus)	1994	M Woodforde (Aus) & H Suková (Cs)
1985	P McNamee (Aus) & M Navrátilová (USA)	1995	John Stark & Martina Navrátilová (USA)
1986	Ken Flach & Kathy Jordan (USA)	1996	Cyril Suk & Helena Suková (Cz Rep)
1987	Jeremy Bates & Jo Durie (UK)	1997	Cyril Suk & Helena Suková (Cz Rep)
1988	Sherwood Stewart & Zina Garrison (USA)	1998	Max Mirnyi (Bls) & Serena Williams (USA)
1989	Jim Pugh (USA) & Jana Novotná (Cs)	1999	Leander Paes (Ind) & Lisa Raymond (USA)
1990	Rick Leach & Zina Garrison (USA)	2000	Donald Johnson & Kimberly Po (USA)

Wimbledon Women's Doubles Champions

1913	Winifred McNair & Dora Boothby (UK)	1978	Kerry Reid & Wendy Turnbull (Aus)
1914	Agnes Morton (UK) & Eliz. Ryan (USA)	1979	BJ King & Martina Navrátilová (USA)
1919	Suz. Lenglen (Fra) & Eliz. Ryan (USA)	1980	Kathy Jordan & Anne Smith (USA)
1920	Suz. Lenglen (Fra) & Eliz. Ryan (USA)	1981	Martina Navrátilová & Pam Shriver (USA)
1921	Suz. Lenglen (Fra) & Eliz. Ryan (USA)	1982	Martina Navrátilová & Pam Shriver (USA)
1922	Suz. Lenglen (Fra) & Eliz. Ryan (USA)	1983	Martina Navrátilová & Pam Shriver (USA)
1923	Suz. Lenglen (Fra) & Eliz. Ryan (USA)	1984	Martina Navrátilová & Pam Shriver (USA)
1924	Hazel Wightman & Helen Wills (USA)	1985	Kathy Jordan (USA) & Eliz. Smylie (Aus)
1925	Suz. Lenglen (Fra) & Eliz. Ryan (USA)	1986	Martina Navrátilová & Pam Shriver (USA)
1926	Mary Browne & Elizabeth Ryan (USA)	1987	C Kohde-Kilsch (FRG) & Hel. Suková (Cs)
1927	Helen Wills & Elizabeth Ryan (USA)	1988	Steffi Graf (FRG) & Gab. Sabatini (Arg)
1928	Peggy Saunders & Phyllis Watson (UK)	1989	Jana Novotná & Helena Suková (Cs)
1929	Peggy Mitchell & Phyllis Watson (UK)	1990	Jana Novotná & Helena Suková (Cs)
1930	Helen Moody & Elizabeth Ryan (USA)	1991	Larisa Savchenko & Natalya Zvereva (USSR)
1931	Dorothy Barron & Phyllis Mudford (UK)	1992	Gigi Fernandez (USA) & Nat. Zvereva (Bls)
1932	Doris Metaxa (Fra) & Josane Sigart (Bel)	1993	Gigi Fernandez (USA) & Nat. Zvereva (Bls)
1933	Simone Mathieu (Fra) & Eliz. Ryan (USA)	1994	Gigi Fernandez (USA) & Nat. Zvereva (Bls)
1934	Simone Mathieu (Fra) & Eliz. Ryan (USA)	1995	Jana Novotná (Cz Rep) & Arantxa
1935	Freda James & Kay Stammers (UK)		Sanchez Vicario (Spa)
1936	Freda James & Kay Stammers (UK)	1996	Martina Hingis (Sui) & Helena
1937	Sim. Mathieu (Fra) & Billie Yorke (USA)		Suková (Cz Rep)
1938	Sarah Fabyan & Alice Marble (USA)	1997	Gigi Fernandez (USA) & Nat. Zvereva (Bls)
1939	Sarah Fabyan & Alice Marble (USA)	1998	Martina Hingis (Sui) & Jana
1946	Louise Brough & Margaret Osborne (USA)		Novotná (Cz Rep)
1947	Doris Hart & Pat Todd (USA)	1999	Lindsay Davenport & Corina Morariu
1948	Louise Brough & Margaret Du Pont (USA)		(USA)
1949	Louise Brough & Margaret Du Pont (USA)	2000	Venus Williams and Serena Williams
1950	Louise Brough & Margaret Du Pont (USA)		(USA)
1951	Shirley Fry & Doris Hart (USA)		
1952	Shirley Fry & Doris Hart (USA)		
1953	Shirley Fry & Doris Hart (USA)		
1954	Louise Brough & Margaret Du Pont (USA)		
1955	Angela Mortimer & Anne Shilcock (UK)		
1956	Ang. Buxton (UK) & Althea Gibson (USA)		
1957	Althea Gibson & Darlene Hard (USA)		
1958	Maria Bueno (Bra) & Althea Gibson (USA)		
1959	Jean Arth & Darlene Hard (USA)		
1960	Maria Bueno (Bra) & Darlene Hard (USA)		
1961	Karen Hantze & Billie Jean Moffitt (USA)		
1962	Billie Jean Moffitt & Karen Susman (USA)		
1963	Maria Bueno (Bra) & Darlene Hard (USA)		
1964	Margaret Smith & Lesley Turner (Aus)		
1965	M Bueno (Bra) & Billie Jean Moffitt (USA)		
1966	Maria Bueno (Bra) & Nancy Richey (USA)		
1967	Rosemary Casals & Billie Jean King (USA)		
1968	Rosemary Casals & Billie Jean King (USA)		
1969	Margaret Court & Judy Tegart (Aus)		
1970	Rosemary Casals & Billie Jean King (USA)		
1971	Rosemary Casals & Billie Jean King (USA)		
1972	Billie Jean King (USA) & Betty Stove (Hol)		
1973	Rosemary Casals & Billie Jean King (USA)		
1974	Ev. Goolagong (Aus) & Peggy Michel (USA)		
1975	A. Kiyomura (USA) & Kaz. Sawamatsu (Jap)		
1976	Chris Evert (USA) & Mart. Navrátilová (Cs)		
1977	Helen Gourlay (Aus) & Joanne Russell (USA)		

Squash

Squash is a racket game played in a court enclosed on four sides.

Out-of-court line

Service line

Tin

Service box

Half court line

It is normally played by two people, although doubles can be played on a larger court. When serving, a player must have one foot in the service box. The server hits the ball so that it strikes the wall above the service line and bounces back far enough to land behind the short line on the opposite side of the court. The other player must then return it before it bounces twice, and so that it hits the wall between the tin and the out-of-court line. Play continues until one player fails to make a good return. If the server wins the rally, he or she gets a point.

△ A singles court measures 9.75 m long by 6.4 m wide. The out-of-court line is 4.57 m above the floor at the front of the court, and slopes down to 2.15 m high at the back. The walls must be completely smooth. The floor is usually made of hardwood planks.

◁ A squash racket should be 68.5 cm long and 21.2 cm wide.

▷ In many squash strokes, the power comes not from swinging the arm but from the action of the wrist. As squash courts are quite small, it is important that players do not obstruct each other. Each player must try to give his or her opponent a clear sight of the ball and enough room to reach and play it.

▽ The ball is made of rubber or rubber and butyl, and must weigh between 23.3 and 24.6 g. Some balls bounce higher than others, and the degree of bounce is shown by a coloured spot marked on the ball.

▽ Shoes must have soles that don't mark the court.

If not, the other player becomes the server. The game is won by the player who first gains 9 points. A match is the best of five games.

Swimming

Swimming
as a sport
is for both
individuals
and teams. Competitors race
against each other over a set
distance, and the first swimmer to
touch the end of the pool at the
finish of the race, is the winner.

△ The most popular stroke chosen in freestyle is the front crawl, because it is also the fastest. Some swimmers kick their legs very fast, with as many as six or eight beats to one arm stroke – this is known as the flutter kick. Others prefer to kick their legs in time with their arm movements.

Competitive events are held in four categories – freestyle, breaststroke, butterfly and backstroke. Apart from freestyle events, in which a swimmer may use any stroke he or she chooses, other strokes are governed by regulations and judges are used at some competitions to ensure that swimmers comply with the rules.

Competitions are held in pools of varying sizes, but in the Olympics, the pool measures 50 m long and is divided into eight lanes. Each swimmer must remain in his or her own lane during a race.

Swimming World Records – Women (in 50-m pool)

Event	Record	Holder/nationality	Date set
50 m freestyle	24.51 sec	Jingyi Le (Chn)	11 Sep 1994
100 m freestyle	54.01 sec	Jingyi Le (Chn)	5 Sep 1994
200 m freestyle	1 min 56.78 sec	Franziska Van Almsick (Ger)	6 Sep 1994
400 m freestyle	4 min 03.85 sec	Janet Evans (USA)	22 Sep 1988
800 m freestyle	8 min 16.22 sec	Janet Evans (USA)	20 Aug 1989
1500 m freestyle	15 min 52.10 sec	Janet Evans (USA)	26 Mar 1988
4 x 100 m freestyle relay	3 min 37.91 sec	China (Jingyi Le, Ying Shan, Ying Le, Bin Lu)	7 Sep 1994
4 x 200 m freestyle relay	7 min 55.47 sec	GDR (Stellmach, Strauss, Möhring, Friedrich)	18 Aug 1987
100 m backstroke	1 min 00.16 sec	Cihong He (Chn)	10 Sep 1994
200 m backstroke	2 min 06.62 sec	Krisztina Egerszegi (Hun)	25 Aug 1991
100 m breaststroke	1 min 07.02 sec	Penelope Heyns (RSA)	21 Jul 1996
200 m breaststroke	2 min 24.76 sec	Rebecca Brown (Aus)	16 Mar 1994
100 m butterfly	57.93 sec	Mary T Meagher (USA)	16 Aug 1981
200 m butterfly	2 Min 05.96 sec	Mary T Meagher (USA)	13 Aug 1981
200 m individual medley	2 min 09.72 sec	Yanyan Wu (Chn)	17 Oct 1997
400 m individual medley	4 min 34.79 sec	Yan Chen (Chn)	17 Oct 1997
4 x 100 m medley relay	4 min 01.67 sec	China (Cihong He, Guohong Dai, Limin Liu, Jingyi Le)	10 Sep 1994

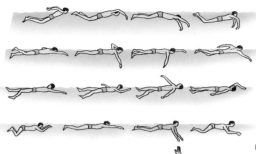

◁ **Swimming strokes** In the butterfly stroke, the arms are brought forward together and scooped backwards under the water, while the legs do a double kick called a dolphin leg kick. In the front crawl, the swimmer uses the left and right arm alternately and the legs kick up and down. In the backstroke, the swimmer is face up in the water. The arms rotate alternately and the legs are kicked up and down as in the front crawl. The breaststroke is the slowest stroke of all. The arms are pushed straight out in front and then the hands are pulled back to the side, moving the swimmer through the water. At the same time, the legs are kicked out backwards and then brought together, pushing the swimmer forward.

Butterfly

Front crawl

Backstroke

Breaststroke

In all events, except the backstroke, swimmers begin a race by diving in from starting blocks.

Swimmers compete at various distances ranging from 50 m to 1500 m. One of the events which tests a swimmer's all-round ability is the individual medley. Competitors swim an equal distance in all four strokes, starting with the butterfly, followed by the backstroke, then breaststroke, and finishing with freestyle. As well as the freestyle relay, there are also medley relays in which each member of the team swims a different stroke.

▷ When diving from a highboard, the entry into the water is vitally important; the legs must be straight and the feet together with the toes pointed. A diver, when entering the water head-first, must punch a hole in the water for his or her head to follow. A bad entry can result in the diver being badly injured.

Diving

There are two main types of diving events: springboard and highboard.
- Springboards are flexible boards at heights of 1 m and 3 m.
- Highboards are solid platforms at 3 m, 5 m, 7.5 m and 10 m.

In competitions, divers must perform four or five compulsory dives followed by four, five or six of their own choosing (the number depends upon the event). Judges give each dive marks according to its level of difficulty – the number of twists, somersaults and so on – and how well it is performed. The winner is the diver with the highest total of marks.

Olympic Champions, 1996
Springboard
Men – Ni Xiong (China)
Women – Fu Mingxia (China)
Highboard
Men – Dmitri Sautin (Russia)
Women – Fu Mingxia (China)

Athletics

▽ The layout of a typical athletics stadium, with a 400-m running track surrounding an area in which field events take place. Modern tracks are made of synthetic materials and can be used in all types of weather.

The sport of athletics is as old as the ancient Olympic Games, and provided the inspiration for the modern Olympics.

Shot put

5

6

Triple jump

7

Hammer and discus

8

Pole vault

Long jump

Water jump for steeplechase

1

2

Javelin

4

High jump

3

Finish line for all races

Key to track event starts
1 110 m hurdles, 2 100 m and 100 m hurdles, 3 800 m and 10 000 m, 4 400 m and 400 m hurdles (staggered start), 5 1500 m, 6 3000 m steeplechase, 7 3000 m and 5000 m, 8 200 m (staggered start).

◁ Track athletes are allowed to run in bare feet, but most wear tight-fitting, lightweight shoes with spiked soles that help grip the track.

It comprises a wide range of events demanding many different skills.

Modern athletics is divided into two main categories – track (running and walking) and field

(jumping and throwing). All events are held in a stadium, except for long-distance running and walking, which take place outside on the roads and finish in the stadium.

▽ Starting blocks are used for races up to and including 400 m and for the first runner in a relay race. They provide a firm base for the feet to push against at the start of the race and can be connected to a device that detects any false starts. Races are started by an official firing a starting pistol into the air.

△ The Olympic steeplechase is a men's event run over 3000 m. It comprises 28 hurdle jumps and 7 water jumps and is considered to be the most gruelling of all endurance events. When clearing the water jump, the athlete steps on the hurdle and lands with one foot in the water.

Most athletes concentrate on one or two events, but some choose to compete in a variety of track and field events. The heptathlon is a seven-event competition for women, and the men's decathlon consists of ten different events.

The relays are the only events in which teams race against each other. A baton is passed between four team members, who each run a 'leg' of either 100 or 400 m.

Olympic events – who does what?

Track events	Men	Women
100 m	✓	✓
200 m	✓	✓
400 m	✓	✓
800 m	✓	✓
1500 m	✓	✓
3000 m	✗	✓
5000 m	✓	✓
10 000 m	✓	✓
4 x 100 m relay	✓	✓
4 x 400 m relay	✓	✓
100 m hurdle	✗	✓
110 m hurdle	✓	✗
400 m hurdle	✓	✓
3000 m steeplechase	✓	✗
Marathon (42.295 km)	✓	✓
10 km walk	✗	✓
20 km walk	✓	✗
50 km walk	✓	✗

Field events	Men	Women
Javelin	✓	✓
Shot put	✓	✓
Discus	✓	✓
Hammer	✓	✓
High jump	✓	✓
Pole vault	✓	✓
Long jump	✓	✓
Triple jump	✓	✓
Heptathlon	✗	✓
Decathlon	✓	✗

△ The high jump is made over a crossbar which is raised after each round. Competitors remain in the contest until eliminated by three consecutive failures at clearing the bar. Today, most high jumpers use the Fosbury flop technique (above), in which they jump the bar backwards. This style of jumping is named after the American athlete Dick Fosbury.

43

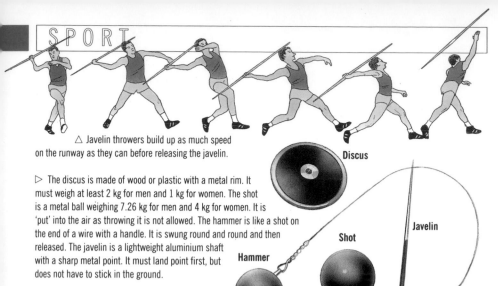

△ Javelin throwers build up as much speed on the runway as they can before releasing the javelin.

▷ The discus is made of wood or plastic with a metal rim. It must weigh at least 2 kg for men and 1 kg for women. The shot is a metal ball weighing 7.26 kg for men and 4 kg for women. It is 'put' into the air as throwing it is not allowed. The hammer is like a shot on the end of a wire with a handle. It is swung round and round and then released. The javelin is a lightweight aluminium shaft with a sharp metal point. It must land point first, but does not have to stick in the ground.

Discus

Javelin

Shot

Hammer

Athletics World Records – Women

Event	Record	Holder/nationality	Date set
100 m	10.49 sec	Florence Griffith-Joyner (USA)	16 Jul 1988
200 m	21.34 sec	Florence Griffith-Joyner (USA)	29 Sep 1988
400 m	47.60 sec	Marita Koch (GDR)	6 Oct 1985
800 m	1 min 53.28 sec	Jarmila Kratochvílová (Cs)	26 Jul 1983
1000 m	2 min 28.98 sec	Svetlana Masterkova (Rus)	23 Aug 1996
1500 m	3 min 50.46 sec	Qu Yunxia (Chn)	11 Sep 1993
1 mile	4 min 12.56 sec	Svetlana Masterkova (Rus)	14 Aug 1996
2000 m	5 min 25.36 sec	Sonia O'Sullivan (Irl)	8 Jul 1994
3000 m	8 min 06.11 sec	Wang Junxia (Chn)	13 Sep 1993
5000 m	14 min 28.09 sec	Jiang Bo (Chn)	23 Oct 1997
10 000 m	29 min 31.78 sec	Wang Junxia (Chn)	8 Sep 1993
Marathon	2 hr 20 min 43 sec	Tegla Loroupe (Ken)	26 Sep 1999
3000 m steeplechase	9 min 48.88 sec	Yelena Motalova (Rus)	31 Jul 1999
100 m hurdles	12.21 sec	Yordanka Donkova (Bul)	20 Aug 1988
400 m hurdles	52.61 sec	Kim Batten (USA)	11 Aug 1995
High jump	2.09 m	Stefka Kostadinova (Bul)	30 Aug 1987
Pole vault	4.62 m	Stacy Dragila (USA)	27 May 2000
Long jump	7.52 m	Galina Chistyakova (USSR)	11 Jun 1988
Triple jump	15.50 m	Inessa Kravets (Ukr)	10 Aug 1995
Shot	22.63 m	Natalya Lisovskaya (USSR)	7 Jun 1987
Discus	76.80 m	Gabriele Reinsch (GDR)	9 Jul 1988
Hammer	76.07 m	Michaela Melinte (Rom)	29 Aug 1999
Javelin	67.09 m	Mirela Manjani-Tzelili (Gre)	28 Aug 1999
Heptathlon	7291 pts	Jackie Joyner-Kersee (USA)	23-24 Sep 1988
4 x 100 m relay	41.37 sec	GDR (Gladisch, Rieger, Auerswald, Göhr)	6 Oct 1985
4 x 200 m relay	1 min 28.15 sec	GDR (Göhr, Müller, Wöckel, Koch)	9 Aug 1980
4 x 400 m relay	3 min 15.17 sec	USSR (Ledovskaya, Nazarova, Pinigina, Bryzgina)	1 Oct 1988
4 x 800 m relay	7 min 50.17 sec	USSR (Olizarenko, Gurina, Borisova, Podyalovskaya)	5 Aug 1984
5000 m walk	20 min 13.26 sec	Kerry Saxby-Junna (Aus)	25 Feb 1996
10 000 walk	41 min 56.23 sec	Nadezhda Ryashkina (Rus)	24 Jul 1990
20 000 walk	1 hr 37 min 19.1 sec	Ailing Xue (Chn)	18 Sep 1999

Gymnastics

Gymnastics is an artistic sport which combines exercise, dance, strength and skill to perform movements either on the floor or on various pieces of apparatus. Competitive gymnastics is divided into four disciplines – men's and

Olympic Champions, 1996 – Women
Floor exercises Lilia Podkopayeva (Ukr)
Beam   Shannon Miller (USA)
Vault   Simona Amanar (Rom)
Asymmetric bars   Svetlana Chorkina (Rus))
Rhythmic gymnastics   Ekaterina Serebryanskaya (Ukr)
Individual   Lilia Podkopayeva (Ukr)
Team   USA

▷ Floor exercises allow gymnasts self-expression, but compulsory exercises and acrobatic, gymnastic and dance elements have to be included in the performance.

▽ The pommel horse exercise calls for perfect balance and strength.

women's artistic gymnastics, rhythmic gymnastics (for women only) and sports acrobatics.

In the Olympic Games there are individual and team competitions. In artistic gymnastics, the events for men are floor exercises, pommel horse, rings, vault, parallel bars and horizontal bar. For women, the events are vault, asymmetric bars, balance beam and floor exercises.

Rhythmic gymnastics consists of floorwork performed to music, with or without small hand apparatus, such as ropes, hoops, balls and ribbons. Sports acrobatics, which combines tumbling and balancing routines, is not included in the Olympic Games.

As gymnastics demands great suppleness, young people can be very successful. For example, Nadia Comaneci was the youngest ever Olympic Champion at the age of 14 and Pasakevi Kouna was only 9 when she represented Greece at the Balkan Games in October 1981.

The Olympic Games

◁ The Olympic symbol of five interlocking rings represents the five continents of the world.

▷ An important part of the opening ceremony of the Olympic Games is the lighting of the Olympic flame from a burning torch. Teams of runners carry the torch from Olympia, Greece, to the stadium where the games are to be held. The flame is a symbol of the revived Olympic spirit.

The inspiration for the modern Olympic Games came from the games held in ancient Greece over 2000 years ago. These games, held at Olympia in honour of the Greek god Zeus, were a regular event from 776 BC until AD 393.

◁ This Greek statue of a discus thrower has come to symbolize the ancient Olympic Games.

It was the determined efforts of a young French nobleman, Baron Pierre de Coubertin, that led to the beginning of the modern Olympic Games. The first modern Olympiad was held in the Greek city of Athens in 1896.

Since then, the Olympics have generally been held every four years, except during the First and Second World Wars. The number of events and competitors has grown dramatically over the years.

At the 1992 Olympics held in Barcelona, Spain, a record 9369 competitors (6659 men and 2710 women) from 169 nations strove for medals in 31 sports.

▽ Baron Pierre de Coubertin, founder of the modern Olympic Games. It took him 3 years to gain support for the revival of the games, but he finally succeeded in 1896.

Olympic venues

1896	Athens
1900	Paris
1904	St Louis
1906	Athens
1908	London
1912	Stockholm
1920	Antwerp
1924	Paris
1928	Amsterdam
1932	Los Angeles
1936	Berlin
1948	London
1952	Helsinki
1956	Melbourne
1960	Rome
1964	Tokyo
1968	Mexico City
1972	Munich
1976	Montreal
1980	Moscow
1984	Los Angeles
1988	Seoul
1992	Barcelona
1996	Atlanta
2000	Sydney

Olympic events

Archery • Athletics
(track and field)
• Badminton
• Baseball • Basketball
• Boxing • Canoeing • Cycling
• Diving • Equestrian events • Fencing
• Field hockey • Gymnastics • Handball
• Judo • Modern pentathlon (comprises
horseriding, fencing, shooting, swimming
and running) • Rowing • Shooting
• Soccer • Swimming • Synchronized
swimming • Table tennis • Tennis
• Volleyball • Water polo
• Weightlifting
• Wrestling • Yachting

At each Olympiad, one or
more 'provisional' sports are tried. In 1996
in Atlanta, USA, the provisional sport
was softball.

◁ Volleyball became an
Olympic sport for both men and
women in 1964.

However, the main
theme of the
Olympics is still
individual skill
and courage, team
spirit and friendship
among all the
competing athletes. No
one nation wins, and it
is cities rather than
countries that are
chosen by the
International
Olympic Committee
(IOC) to host the
Games. The athletes do not
compete for money but for medals
that signify their talents – gold for
first place, silver for second
and bronze for third.

Many people would now agree
that the Olympic ideal held by
Coubertin, of 'the most important
thing in the Olympic Games is not
winning but taking part' has been
somewhat 'lost' over the years.
The Games are now watched
on TV by millions of people
all around the world, and
Olympic champions become
household names and are able to
earn vast amounts of money from
sponsorship and advertising.

Also, political boycotts, protests
and acts of terrorism – such as the
murder of 11 Israeli athletes at
Munich in 1972 by Palestinian
terrorists – has tarnished the spirit
of the Games.

◁ There are
Olympic events for two-
man and four-man bobsleighs.

Winter Olympic events

These include: Alpine skiing (downhill,
slalom and giant slalom) • Biathlon
(cross-country skiing and rifle shooting)
• Bobsleigh • Curling • Freestyle skiing
• Ice hockey • Ice skating (figure skating
and ice dance) • Luge (toboggan)
• Nordic skiing (cross-country and
ski-jumping) • Speed skating.

Winners and losers

Over the years, some Olympic sportsmen and women have become legendary winners – and losers.

◁ The young gymnast Olga Korbut, delighted the world with her displays of originality at the 1972 Games. She came seventh overall, after falling from the asymmetric bars, but she won two individual gold medals on the beam and the floor exercises.

△ Near the end of the 1908 Marathon, the race leader, Dorando Pietri of Italy, staggered into the stadium and ran the wrong way around the track. He collapsed from exhaustion and was helped across the finish line, only to be disqualified for not running the entire race unaided. Even so, he was given a special trophy for his bravery.

▽ In some sports, technology is as important as athletic ability – Chris Boardman won an Olympic gold medal and set a new world record for the 4000 m individual pursuit on the revolutionary Lotus bike at the 1992 Games.

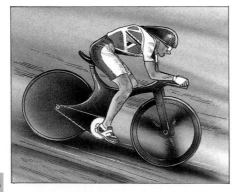

△ Bob Beamon's leap of 8.90 m in 1968 set a long jump world record that stood for 23 years.

▷ Jesse Owens won four gold medals at the 1936 Berlin Olympics. Despite this, the German Chancellor, Adolf Hitler, refused to shake his hand at the medals ceremony – because he was furious that a black athlete had beaten Germany's best runners and long jumpers.

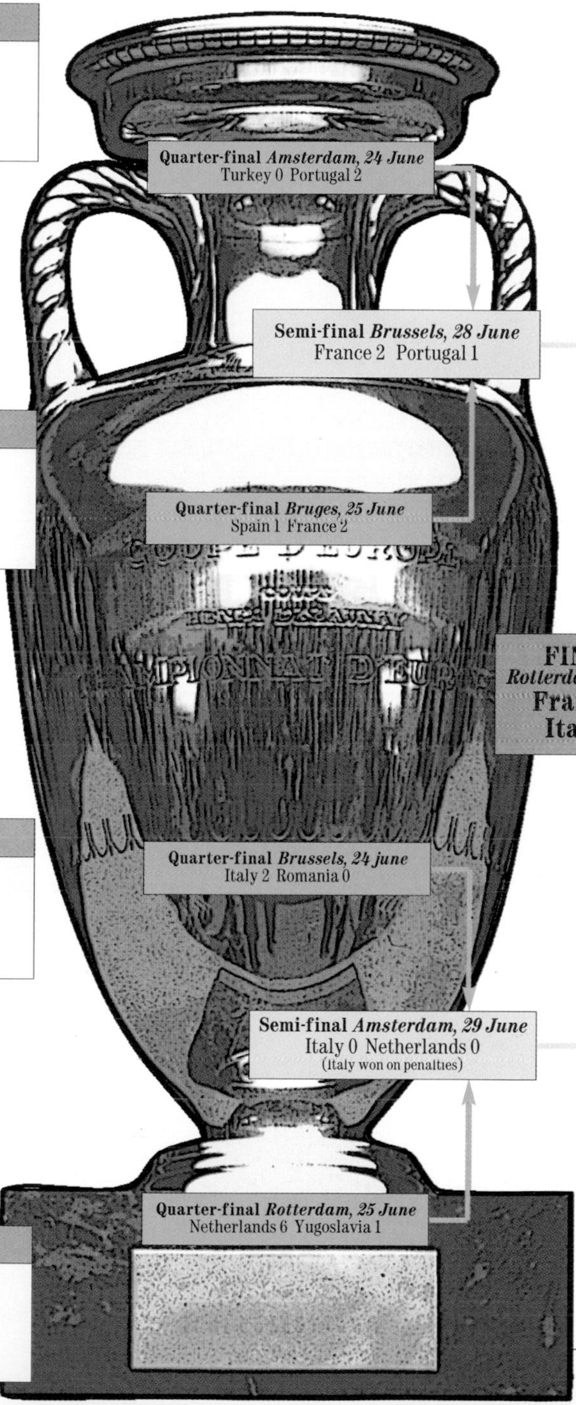

Group A *12-20 June*

Germany 1 Romania 1
Portugal 3 England 2
Romania 0 Portugal 1
England 1 Germany 0
England 2 Romania 3
Portugal 3 Germany 0

Quarter-final *Amsterdam, 24 June*
Turkey 0 Portugal 2

Semi-final *Brussels, 28 June*
France 2 Portugal 1

Group B *10-19 June*

Belgium 2 Sweden 1
Turkey 1 Italy 2
Italy 2 Belgium 0
Sweden 0 Turkey 0
Turkey 2 Belgium 0
Italy 2 Sweden 1

Quarter-final *Bruges, 25 June*
Spain 1 France 2

FINAL
Rotterdam, 2 July
France 2
Italy 1

Group C *13-21 June*

Spain 0 Norway 1
Yugoslavia 3 Slovenia 3
Slovenia 1 Spain 2
Norway 0 Yugoslavia 1
Slovenia 0 Norway 0
Yugoslavia 3 Spain 4

Quarter-final *Brussels, 24 june*
Italy 2 Romania 0

Semi-final *Amsterdam, 29 June*
Italy 0 Netherlands 0
(Italy won on penalties)

Quarter-final *Rotterdam, 25 June*
Netherlands 6 Yugoslavia 1

Group D *11-21 June*

France 3 Denmark 0
Netherlands 1 Czech Rep. 0
Czech Rep. 1 France 2
Denmark 0 Netherlands 3
Denmark 0 Czech Rep. 2
France 2 Netherlands 3

Sporting greats

Muhammad Ali Boxer (17 Jan 1942–)
Ali first gained fame as Cassius Clay when
he won the light-heavyweight gold medal at
the 1960 Rome Olympics. In 1964 he beat
Sonny Liston to win the heavyweight
championship. Shortly afterwards he
became a Muslim and changed his name to
Muhammad Ali. Throughout the rest of the
1960s, he was unbeaten. In 1967 he
was stripped of his title for refusing
to be drafted for the Vietnam War
and, after his return, was beaten
by Joe Frazier in 1971. Ali
regained the heavyweight
championship in 1974, lost it 4 years
later and regained it once more. He
was the only man to hold the title three
times. He called himself 'The Greatest' –
and he probably was.

▷ Muhammad Ali

**Severiano
Ballesteros** Golfer
(9 Apr 1957–)
'Seve' Ballesteros is
perhaps the finest golfer
Europe has ever produced,
and for a number of years in
the 1980s he was regarded as
the best in the world. He first
rose to prominence in 1979,
when he won his first 'Major',
the British Open; he also won it
in 1984 and 1988. In 1980 he
became the first European ever to
win the US Masters, and he won it
again three years later. Ballesteros
has also won five World Matchplay
titles and has been Europe's best
Ryder Cup golfer.

▷ Severiano
Ballesteros

Serge Blanco
Rugby Union player
(31 August 1958–)
Blanco played 93 times for France and scored 38 international tries – a French record. Although he was a full back, he was a brilliant attacking player and scored some of the best individual tries ever seen. However, he was somctimes inconsistent in defence and goal kicking.

△ Serge Blanco

▷ Ian Botham

Ian Botham
Cricketer
(24 Nov 1955–)
Botham began playing one-day cricket for Somerset in 1973, and made his first-class début the following year.

Björn Borg lennis player (6 Jun 1956–)
During his peak years, Borg dominated the world of tennis. Between 1976 and 1980, hc won the men's singles at Wimbledon five times in succession. He also won the French Open six times and the Italian Open twice. However, he never managed to win the US Open, even though he reached the final four times. Borg had a strong serve and powerful topspin attacking shots, both on the forehand and on his two-handed backhand.

He played his first Test match for England in 1977 and, within just 2 years and 9 days, he took his first 100 Test wickets. It took him only 21 Tests to reach the 'double' of 1000 runs and 100 wickets, 42 Tests for 2000 runs and 200 wickets and 71 Tests for 3000 runs and 300 wickets – all three are unbeaten records. In 1978 against Pakistan, he scored 108 runs and took 8 wickets in one innings, and 2 years later against India he hit 114 and picked up 6 wickets in one innings and 7 in the other. Among his finest batting achievements were two thrilling centuries against Australia in 1980 and a double century against India in 1982.

◁ Björn Borg

◁ Steve Davis

Steve Davis
Snooker player
(22 Aug 1957–)
After winning
the British
junior billiards
title, Davis became a
professional snooker player
in 1978. Just 3 years later, he
won his first World Championship. He
went on to become the most successful
player of the 1980s, taking 22 major
tournaments compared with the five won by
his nearest rival. Davis' titles included five
World Championships, four British Opens
and six UK Opens. After a lean time in the
early 1990s, he won the European Open and
his seventh Irish Masters title in 1993,
which gave him a total of 66 professional
tournament victories.

◁ David Campese

David Campese Rugby Union
player (21 Oct 1962–)
Campese won his first
Australian cap in 1982,
at the age of 19.

He was
one of the
most exciting
players of the 1980s
and early 90s, with great
speed and agility that helped
him to avoid tackles. He scored
well over 50 tries – a record in
international matches. He was an
unorthodox player, and was not the
most effective defender, but his
scoring abilities more than
made up for his
shortcomings. He had
many offers to play for
Rugby League clubs but
turned them all down,
preferring to appear for
Mediolanum in Milan, Italy,
during the Australian close season.

Nadia Comaneci Gymnast
(12 Nov 1961–)
In Montreal in 1976, at the age of 14,
Comaneci became the first Olympic
gymnast ever to be awarded a
perfect score of 10.0. She won gold
medals in both the asymmetric bars
and the beam, bronze in the floor
exercises and gold in the combined.
She was also part of the Romanian
squad which won silver in the team
competition. At the 1980 Moscow
Olympics, she won two more gold
medals and one silver.

◁ Nadia Comaneci

▷ Kornelia Ender

and four golds at the Montreal Olympics 4 years later. Then, at the age of 18, she announced her retirement from competitive swimming.

▷ Don Bradman

Don Bradman
Cricketer
(27 Aug 1908–)
In a career that lasted from 1927 to 1949, Bradman came to be regarded as the greatest batsman of all time, and no one has surpassed him since then. He averaged a century (100 runs) every 2.9 innings, scoring over 200 runs a record 37 times, and over 300 six times. In his 52 Test matches for Australia, he scored 29 centuries and achieved an average of 99.94 runs per innings – an unbeaten record. He was knighted in 1949 for his services to cricket.

Kornelia Ender Swimmer
(25 Oct 1958–)
Ender took her first world record at the age of 14, and went on to break a total of 23 in her career – more than any other female swimmer. She won three silver medals at the 1972 Munich Olympics and a further silver

Johan Cruyff
Footballer (25 Apr 1947–)
Cruyff was a fine attacking forward with excellent ball control and fast acceleration. When Pelé retired in 1974, Cruyff was acknowledged as the world's finest player. He helped his club, Ajax, to win many honours, including the European Cup three times, and played a vital part in making Holland one of the world's best international teams during the mid-1970s.

◁ Johan Cruyff

Nick Faldo Golfer
(18 Jul 1957–)

Faldo was a gifted amateur player, and he won the English championship just after his 18th birthday.

▷ Nick Faldo

In 1978, 2 years after turning professional, he won his first important title, the PGA. In the mid-1980s he decided to change his swing, and this affected his game for 3 years. But, by the end of that decade, he had become the best golfer in the world. He won the US Masters three times, the British Open three times, the World Matchplay twice and the Johnnie Walker World Championship once.

Steffi Graf Tennis player (14 Jul 1969–)

After winning her first major championship – the French Open – in 1987, Graf went on to become the world's best female tennis player during the late 1980s. In 1988 she completed the Grand Slam, winning the Open Championships in England, France, Australia and the USA. Her strong serve and powerful forehand have helped her to win Wimbledon seven times and to become the second highest money-winner in women's tennis, after Martina Navrátilová.

◁ Steffi Graf

Sunil Gavaskar
Cricketer
(10 Jul 1949–)

Gavaskar was one of the greatest run-scorers in the history of Test cricket. He had an excellent batting technique and was able to concentrate for very long innings. He scored 10 122 runs in 125 Test matches for India, including a record 34 centuries.

▷ Sunil Gavaskar

Ruud Gullit Footballer (1 September 1962–)
After beginning his career as a sweeper, Gullit went on to become a brilliant attacking midfield player. He played for Haarlem, Feyenoord and then PSV Eindhoven in his native Holland, before transferring to the Italian club AC Milan in 1987. That year he was voted both European and World Footballer of the Year, and in 1988 he helped Milan to win the Italian League Championship and led Holland to victory in the European Championship. Despite knee injury problems, he helped Milan to take the European Cup twice and the Italian League title twice more, before moving to Sampdoria in 1993 and then to Chelsea in 1995.

▷ Ruud Gullit

Florence Griffith-Joyner
Athlete
(21 Dec 1959–21 Sep 1998)
'Flo-Jo' first came to prominence in 1984, when she took the silver medal in the 100 m at the Los Angeles Olympics.

Lucinda Green Equestrian sportswoman (7 Nov 1953–)
After making her international début in 1971, she won her first Badminton three-day event 2 years later.

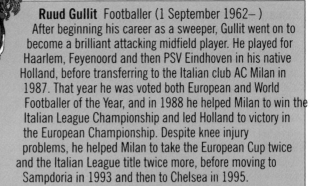

In 1988 she shattered the 100 m world record and went on to become one of the stars of the Seoul Olympics, where she won golds in the 100 m, 200 m and 4 x 100 m relay, and a silver in the 4 x 400 m relay.

△ Lucinda Green

She won at Badminton a record six times in all, as well as winning twice at the Burghley Horse Trials, twice in the European Championships and once in the World Championships.

△ Florence Griffith-Joyner

Richard Hadlee Cricketer (3 Jul 1951–)
Although he was a top-class all-rounder who batted left-handed and bowled right-handed, Hadlee is best remembered for his outstanding bowling. Between 1973 and 1990 he took 431 Test wickets at an average of 22.29 runs per wicket. He also took 10 wickets in a match 36 times – a record that looks set to stand for many years to come. His bowling helped his national side, New Zealand, to become a highly successful team, winning Test series against Australia both at home and away for the first time ever. In 1990 he was knighted.

Raimondo D'Inzeo
Equestrian
sportsman
(2 Feb 1925–)
With his brother, Piero, and two others, Raimondo D'Inzeo shares the record of competing in eight Olympics. He won six medals, including a gold in showjumping at Rome in 1960. He was also the world champion in 1956 and 1960.

Kareem Abdul-Jabbar Basketball player (16 Apr 1947–)
He began his career as Lew Alcindor, and changed his name when he converted to Islam. He was extremely tall – 2.18 m – and became one of the greatest centres in the history of the game. He led the Milwaukee Bucks to an NBA title in 1971, only his second year in the American professional league. Four years later he joined the Los Angeles Lakers, with whom he won five more NBAs. He retired in 1989 with an NBA record of 38 387 points from 1560 games. He was voted the NBA's Most Valuable Player a record six times and appeared in 18 All-Star games.

▷ Kareem
Abdul-Jabbar

◁ Richard Hadlee

◁ Raimondo
D'Inzeo

Billie Jean King Tennis player (22 Nov 1943–)
Between 1961 and 1979, Billie Jean King won a record 20 Wimbledon titles in the singles, doubles and mixed doubles. On two occasions – in 1967 and 1973 – she won all three Wimbledon titles at the same championships. In 1967 and 1968 she took the Grand Slam by holding all four major tournament titles at one time. During her career she won a total of 39 Grand Slam events.

△ Billie Jean King

Miguel Induráin Cyclist (16 Jul 1964–)
As an amateur, Induráin was Spanish Champion in 1983 and competed for Spain in the 1984 Los Angeles Olympics. He turned professional in 1985 and entered his first Tour de France. He failed to finish the gruelling race both that year and the next, but from 1987 onwards he steadily improved his performance. He won the Tour de France five times in succession, from 1991 to 1995. In the 1992 race, he set a record average speed of 39.504 km/h.

Jahangir Khan Squash player (10 Dec 1963–)
The most successful squash player of all time, Jahangir won six World Open titles and 10 successive British Opens. From April 1981 to November 1986, he played over 500 matches and won every one. In 1982 he won a major title – the ISPA Championship – without losing a single point, by beating his opponent 9-0, 9-0, 9-0 in the final.

△ Miguel Induráin

◁ Jahangir Khan

Carl Lewis Athlete (1 Jul 1961–)
Lewis is possibly the finest athlete of all time, and has won eight Olympic gold medals and one silver in the 100 m, 200 m long jump and sprint relay. He has also set nine world records in his career, although all of them have since been beaten.

▷ Carl Lewis

His graceful sprinting style combined speed, grace, power and technique. Lewis remained at the top for over 10 years.

▷ Nigel Mansell

Olga Korbut
Gymnast
(16 May 1955–)
Although not one of the greatest gymnasts, Korbut was certainly among the most popular.

△ Olga Korbut

With her elfin looks and original, lively performances, she won the spectators' hearts at the 1972 Munich Olympics, and took three gold medals.

Nigel Mansell Racing driver (8 Aug 1953–)
Mansell was Britain's most successful racing driver of the 1980s and early 1990s, coming second in the World Drivers' Championship in 1986, 1987 and 1991 and winning it in 1992. In his winning season, he started in pole position 14 times and won a record 9 Grand Prix races. In 1993 he switched to Indy Car racing in the USA and won the PPG World Series in his first season.

◁ Sugar Ray Leonard

Sugar Ray Leonard Boxer (17 May 1956–)
After winning the light-welterweight gold medal at the 1976 Montreal Olympics, Leonard turned professional. Three years later he won his first world title – the WBC welterweight championship. During the next 9 years, he took four more world titles and retired from boxing four times – once with a detached retina that threatened his eyesight. In his professional career, he won 33 fights and lost only one.

Gary Lineker Footballer (30 Nov 1960–)
Lineker, a fast, stylish, high-scoring forward, played for Leicester, Everton, Barcelona and Tottenham Hotspur before joining Grampus Eight of Nagoya, Japan, in 1992. By that time he had scored 322 goals in 631 senior games. His tally of 48 goals for England is just one short of Bobby Charlton's record. He won the European Cup-Winners' Cup with Barcelona in 1989, and the FA Cup with Tottenham in 1991. He stopped playing professional football in 1995.

▷ Gary Lineker

Marita Koch Athlete (18 Feb 1957–)
Koch was an elegant runner whose sprinting career is unequalled by any other female athlete. In all she set 16 world records – at 200 m, 400 m, 4 x 100 m relay, 4 x 200 m relay and 4 x 400 m relay – along with 17 world indoor best times at distances from 50 m to 400 m. She won 17 gold medals at major championships, as well as four silvers and one bronze, and a further 15 golds and five silvers at World and European Cup finals. Although she retired in 1986, her 400 m record remains unbeaten.

▷ Marita Koch

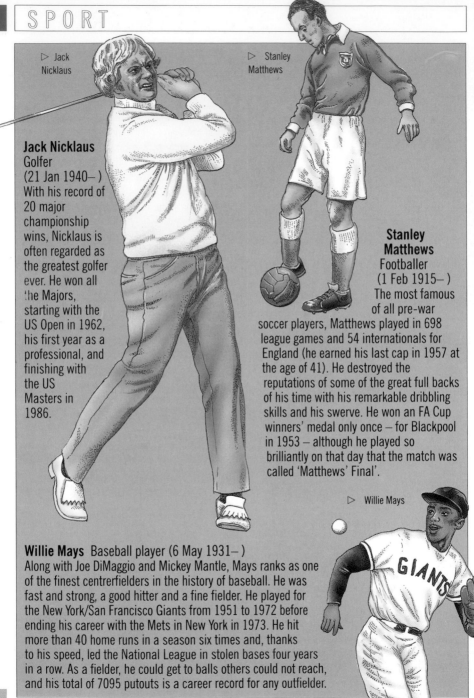

▷ Jack Nicklaus

▷ Stanley Matthews

Jack Nicklaus
Golfer
(21 Jan 1940–)
With his record of 20 major championship wins, Nicklaus is often regarded as the greatest golfer ever. He won all the Majors, starting with the US Open in 1962, his first year as a professional, and finishing with the US Masters in 1986.

Stanley Matthews
Footballer
(1 Feb 1915–)
The most famous of all pre-war soccer players, Matthews played in 698 league games and 54 internationals for England (he earned his last cap in 1957 at the age of 41). He destroyed the reputations of some of the great full backs of his time with his remarkable dribbling skills and his swerve. He won an FA Cup winners' medal only once – for Blackpool in 1953 – although he played so brilliantly on that day that the match was called 'Matthews' Final'.

▷ Willie Mays

Willie Mays Baseball player (6 May 1931–)
Along with Joe DiMaggio and Mickey Mantle, Mays ranks as one of the finest centrefielders in the history of baseball. He was fast and strong, a good hitter and a fine fielder. He played for the New York/San Francisco Giants from 1951 to 1972 before ending his career with the Mets in New York in 1973. He hit more than 40 home runs in a season six times and, thanks to his speed, led the National League in stolen bases four years in a row. As a fielder, he could get to balls others could not reach, and his total of 7095 putouts is a career record for any outfielder.

Eddy Merckx Cyclist (17 Jun 1945–)
Merckx is regarded as the greatest cyclist of all time. He was the best time-trialer, the strongest climber and one of the fastest sprinters. He won more titles than any other rider in the Tour de France (5 times), Giro d'Italia (5), World Professional Road Race (3), Milan-San Remo (7), Ghent-Wevelgem (3) and Liège-Bastogne-Liège (5). In the 1969 Tour de France he achieved the unequalled feat of winning the yellow jersey (overall winner), green jersey (points winner) and polka-dot jersey (King of the Mountains).

▷ Joe Montana

Joe Montana American footballer (11 Jun 1956–)
One of the finest quarterbacks, Montana helped the San Francisco 49ers to win four Super Bowl titles and is the only player to be voted Super Bowl Most Valuable Player three times. He is rated the NFL's all-time leader for passing efficiency, and holds Super Bowl career records for 11 touch-down passes, 1142 yards gained passing and 83 pass completions.

△ Eddy Merckx

Martina Navrátilová
Tennis player (18 Oct 1956–)
Having won the Wimbledon singles a record nine times and the Grand Slam twice, Navrátilová is acclaimed as the best woman tennis player of modern times and perhaps of all time. She also won the womens' doubles at Wimbledon seven times with Pam Shriver, and the mixed doubles three times.

▷ Martina Navrátilová

61

Gary Sobers Cricketer (28 Jul 1936–)
Generally felt to be the best-ever all-rounder, Sobers made his Test
début in 1954, at the age of 17. Four years later, he scored 365 not
out against Pakistan – a record that was broken in 1994 by fellow
West-Indian player Brian Lara. He scored a total of 8032 runs in
Test matches, including 26 centuries, took 235 wickets and held
109 catches. He captained the West Indies 39 times, and was knighted
for his services to cricket in 1975.

▽ Gary Sobers

Jesse Owens Athlete (12 Sep 1913–31 Mar 1980)
Owens' marvellous career included three
outstanding achievements: he won four gold
medals at the 1936 Berlin Olympics; he
set six world records in a single day
(25 May 1935); and his long jump
record was unbeaten for over
25 years. His Olympic medals were in
the 100 m, 200 m,
4 x 100 m relay
and long jump. He
retired shortly
after his Olympic
triumph, at
the age
of 23.

△ Jesse Owens

▷ Pelé

Pelé Footballer (23 Oct 1940–)
The most famous footballer of all, Pelé was
born Edson Arantes do Nascimento. He was
a master of all footballing skills and came
to be a legendary player throughout the
world. Although a regular player for his
club, Santos, from the age of 16, he rose to
fame during the 1958 World Cup, when he
scored a hat-trick in the semi-final and two goals in
Brazil's victory in the final. In 1970 he won his
second World Cup winners' medal. He collected
many Brazilian league and cup honours with
Santos, and helped them to win the World Club
Championship in 1962 and 1963. He retired in
1974, but returned to play for the New York
Cosmos. By the time he retired finally in 1977, he
had scored 1281 goals in 1363 first-class games,
including 97 goals in his 111 matches for Brazil.

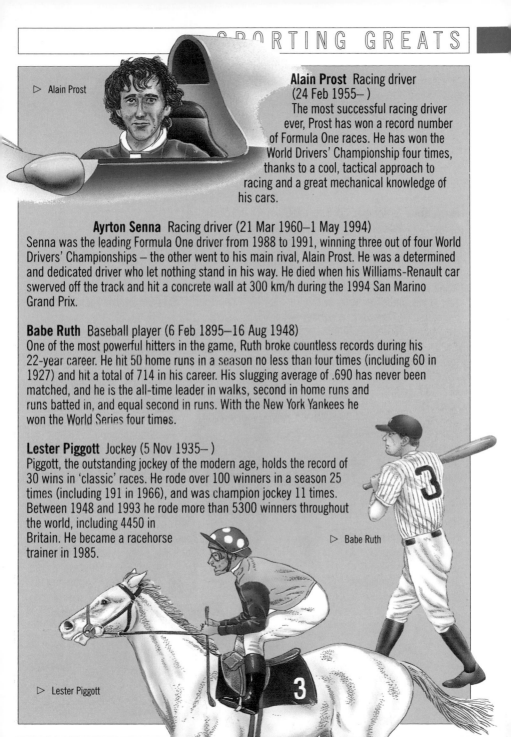

▷ Alain Prost

Alain Prost Racing driver
(24 Feb 1955–)
The most successful racing driver ever, Prost has won a record number of Formula One races. He has won the World Drivers' Championship four times, thanks to a cool, tactical approach to racing and a great mechanical knowledge of his cars.

Ayrton Senna Racing driver (21 Mar 1960–1 May 1994)
Senna was the leading Formula One driver from 1988 to 1991, winning three out of four World Drivers' Championships – the other went to his main rival, Alain Prost. He was a determined and dedicated driver who let nothing stand in his way. He died when his Williams-Renault car swerved off the track and hit a concrete wall at 300 km/h during the 1994 San Marino Grand Prix.

Babe Ruth Baseball player (6 Feb 1895–16 Aug 1948)
One of the most powerful hitters in the game, Ruth broke countless records during his 22-year career. He hit 50 home runs in a season no less than four times (including 60 in 1927) and hit a total of 714 in his career. His slugging average of .690 has never been matched, and he is the all-time leader in walks, second in home runs and runs batted in, and equal second in runs. With the New York Yankees he won the World Series four times.

Lester Piggott Jockey (5 Nov 1935–)
Piggott, the outstanding jockey of the modern age, holds the record of 30 wins in 'classic' races. He rode over 100 winners in a season 25 times (including 191 in 1966), and was champion jockey 11 times. Between 1948 and 1993 he rode more than 5300 winners throughout the world, including 4450 in Britain. He became a racehorse trainer in 1985.

▷ Babe Ruth

▷ Lester Piggott

△ Mark Spitz

Mark Spitz Swimmer (10 Feb 1950–)
At the 1972 Munich Olympics, Spitz set a
record that is unbeaten in any sport – he
won seven gold medals in a single Olympics.
Together with those he had won in Mexico
City 4 years earlier, he amassed a total of
nine golds, one silver and one bronze – a
better performance than any other swimmer.
He also set 26 world records at individual
events – the 100 m, 200 m and 400 m
freestyle, and 100 m and 200 m
butterfly – and six
others in relay
races. He
tried to
make a
comeback
in 1991, with
the aim of being
selected for the USA
team at the 1992
Barcelona Olympics.
However, despite his best
efforts, he was unable to
compete with swimmers
who were much younger
than he was.

Daley Thompson Athlete (30 Jul 1958–)
Thompson proved himself to be the best in
the world at the most demanding of all
athletics disciplines – the decathlon. This
consists of 10 individual track and field
events (100 m, 400 m, 1500 m, 110 m
hurdles, high jump, pole vault, long jump,
shot, discus and javelin) held over 2 days.
Points are awarded for each athlete's
performance in each event. Thompson
won the gold medal at both the
1980 Moscow and 1984 Los
Angeles Olympics. He was also
World Champion in 1983,
European Champion in 1982
and 1986, and Commonwealth
Champion in 1978, 1982 and
1986. He set four world
records in the
decathlon; the final
one (8847 points
at the 1984
Olympics) was
unbeaten for
over 8
years.

◁ Daley
Thompson

HOBBIES

avoided if you follow the few simple safety guidelines in the panel below. And don't forget – enjoy yourself. That's what hobbies are all about.

▷ Roller-skating and roller-blading are good fun – and good exercise. Make sure you wear the proper protective pads and helmet, and don't skate on roads.

▷ There are many different types of kite to suit both beginners and experienced flyers.

In this section you will find information on a wide range of hobbies that you can enjoy all year round. Some are quite energetic outdoor activities, such as sailing and horseriding. Others can be done quietly and indoors – cookery, chess and stamp collecting, for example. There is literally something for everyone.

In almost any hobby, accidents can happen and people can get hurt. But most accidents can be

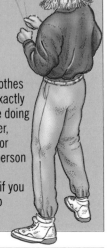

Safety guide
- Always follow the rules of the hobby or sport carefully
- Use the correct equipment and make sure it is in good order
- Wear the correct clothes
- Ensure you know exactly what you should be doing
- If you are a beginner, have an instructor or other responsible person with you
- Keep your temper; if you lose it you might do something silly.

Cookery

Cooking is not only fun and creative, it is also a useful skill to learn. Once you have mastered the basics, you will have the confidence to tackle more difficult recipes and perhaps even invent a few of your own. However, as cooking involves handling food and potential hazards, such as sharp knives and boiling water, you do need to bear in mind a few simple rules.

Cooking, like many things, is a skill that will improve with practice. You will get to know which flavours complement each other and be able to experiment with spices and herbs – although you should stick to the recipe at first.

Dos and don'ts

- Wash your hands first.
- Tie back long hair.
- Cut on a chopping board – not the worktop or table.
- Wear an apron.
- Preheat the oven to the correct temperature.
- Sift flour and icing sugar before using.
- Follow the recipe and weigh/measure ingredients accurately – don't guess.
- Keep your working area as tidy as possible and clear up as you go.
- Don't allow pets in the kitchen when you are cooking.
- Don't have saucepan handles overhanging the cooker top.
- Use a thick cloth to handle hot pans.

Weights, measures and temperatures

Many recipes list ingredients with both Imperial and metric weights and measures. The conversions are not exact, and so it is important to stick to either the metric or the Imperial quantities and not mix them.

Weights
1 ounce = 25g

Liquid measures

Imperial	Metric
¼ pint	150 ml
½ pint	300 ml
¾ pint	450 ml
1 pint	600 ml
1½ pints	900 ml
1¾ pints	1 litre

Spoons
1 level teaspoon (tsp) = 5 ml
1 level tablespoon (tbsp) = 15 ml

Oven temperatures

	°C	°F	Gas mark
Very cool	110	225	¼
	120	250	½
Cool	140	275	1
	150	300	2
Moderate	160	325	3
	180	350	4
Moderately hot	190	375	5
	200	400	6
Hot	220	425	7
	230	450	8
Very hot	240	475	9

Cooking techniques

◁ **Boiling** To cook rapidly in liquid at a temperature of 100°C (boiling point). This method of cooking is normally used for vegetables, pasta, rice, bacon joints and eggs. As a high heat is used, you need to be careful that the food does not stick and that the pan does not boil dry.

▷ **Frying** To cook in hot fat or oil. There are two types of frying – shallow frying is when only a small amount of oil is used and the food must be turned halfway through cooking. Deep frying is when enough fat is used to completely cover the food, but the pan must be only half full of fat before the food is added.

◁ **Stir-frying** To fry quickly in a little hot fat, stirring constantly. A very healthy way of cooking, especially for retaining the vitamin content and colour in vegetables. Many Chinese recipes use this method of cooking using a round-based pan called a wok, but a frying pan can be used instead.

▷ **Blanching** To immerse food briefly in boiling water to either loosen the skin from nuts, fruit and vegetables, destroy harmful bacteria in vegetables before freezing, or remove strong and bitter flavours.

▽ **Grilling or broiling** To cook under or over direct heat. This is a fast method of cooking which requires little fat. It helps to seal in flavour and browns the food.

▷ **Roasting** To cook in the oven with a small amount of fat. Used for cooking meat, poultry, game and accompanying vegetables, such as potatoes.

◁ **Basting** To moisten meat, poultry or game during roasting or grilling by brushing or spooning over it the juices and melted fat from the tin.

▽ **Steaming** To cook food in the steam rising from boiling water. This is an ideal way to cook vegetables as they remain crunchy and still full of goodness. This method is also used for cooking fish and suet dishes, such as Christmas pudding. The food must not come into contact with the water.

▽ **Braising** To fry meat in hot fat to seal in the juices and then cook slowly, in a covered pot with vegetables and a little liquid. Good for cheaper and tougher cuts of meat as the long, slow cooking tenderizes the meat and adds flavour to the liquid.

▷ **Poaching** To cook in an open pan in simmering liquid. A gentle and slow way of cooking eggs, fish and chicken.

▽ **Simmering** To cook in liquid at a temperature just below boiling point, approximately 96°C. The liquid is brought to the boil first, then the temperature is adjusted until the surface of the liquid gently bubbles. This method is used for cooking vegetables, stews and sauces, once you have brought them to the boil.

Sandwiches

◁ Chicken liver pâté, topped with coleslaw on crisp lettuce.

◁ Tuna mixed with mayonnaise and a little curry powder on cucumber slices.

◁ A slice of ham followed by a slice of cheese on crisp lettuce. Add a little mustard, if you like.

◁ Cottage cheese topped with chopped celery and apple.

◁ Sliced red pepper, fruit chutney and cold cooked chicken in that order.

◁ Strawberry jam spread thinly on crunchy peanut butter.

Sandwiches can be eaten at any time of the day and are quick to prepare when you haven't got the time to cook. But this doesn't mean they have to be boring. With a little imagination, you can combine all kinds of fillings to make delicious and interesting sandwiches. Try inventing some of your own.

When you are hungry, make a sandwich with thickly sliced wholemeal bread or cut a small French loaf lengthways.

Try toasting your sandwich under the grill to make a hot and substantial snack. Alternatively, you could use hot fillings, such as grilled bacon or a fried egg.

Pizzas

A basic pizza is simply a dough base, topped with tomatoes, cheese and herbs, and baked in a hot oven until the cheese bubbles. The topping can be made more interesting by adding other vegetables, meat and fish.

To make two pizza bases you will need:
6 g (¼ oz) dried yeast
125 ml (¼ pint) lukewarm milk or water
200 g (7 oz) plain flour
½ teaspoon salt
olive or vegetable oil to grease baking trays

Making pizza dough

◁ **1** Dissolve yeast in 2 tablespoons of warm water or milk. Leave for 10 minutes in warm room. Meanwhile, sieve flour and salt into a warm mixing bowl. Make a well in the centre and pour in yeast mixture and remaining milk or water. Mix by hand until the dough leaves the side of the bowl clean.

◁ **2** Turn dough out on to a floured surface. Knead well until smooth and not sticky. Cover with clingfilm and leave in a warm place for about 1 hour or until doubled in size.

◁ **3** Turn out and knead again for a minute or so. Divide dough in two and roll each piece into a circle 25 cm across.
Place dough on greased and floured baking trays. Pinch up edges to form a round rim.

◁ Burgers do not have to come frozen in packets. Making your own is easy, cheap and, if you use lean beef, healthy.

Burgers are traditionally served in a bun and can come with a variety of toppings. Here are a few suggestions:
- Sliced tomato and pickled dill cucumber, lettuce, tomato relish and mayonnaise.
- Hot chilli relish – as above but add a few drops of hot pepper sauce to the relish.
- Blue cheese and onion – add grated blue cheese to the mayonnaise and replace the dill cucumber with sliced onion rings.
- Barbecue bacon – grilled bacon, sliced tomato and barbecue relish.
- Nutty banana – spread a layer of crunchy peanut butter and top with sliced banana.
- Pizza burger – spread a layer of pizza topping (see below), sprinkle with grated cheese and grill until the cheese melts.

Burgers
To make 4 burgers you will need:
450 g (1lb) lean minced beef
30 ml (2 tbsp) finely chopped onion
1 teaspoon salt
¼ teaspoon pepper

Mix beef, onion and seasoning in a bowl. Shape the mixture into 4 patties each about 2.5 cm (1 inch) thick. Place on a rack and cook under a hot grill for about 8 minutes, turning once.

Pizza toppings
To make tomato and cheese topping for two 25-cm bases you will need:
45 ml (3 tbsp) oil
1 large onion, peeled and finely chopped
60 ml (4 tbsp) tomato purée
pinch of dried oregano and marjoram
salt and pepper
100 g (4 oz) cheddar cheese.

Heat oil in a saucepan and fry onion for 5 minutes. Stir in purée, herbs, salt and pepper. Cook for 2 minutes. Spread on the bases and sprinkle with the cheese. Bake in a hot oven for 20-25 minutes or until risen and golden.

▽ For variety, replace cheddar with Italian mozzarella cheese and add one or more of the following: tomato, mushroom or green pepper slices, onion rings, pitted green or black olives, tuna or anchovy fillets, sliced sausage or ham, cooked minced beef or pepperoni sausage.

Jacket potatoes
Scrub, dry and prick potato all over with a fork. Bake at 200°C (400°F), gas mark 6 for 1-1¼ hours until soft. Cut in half and top with butter.

▽ **Filled potatoes** After cooking, scoop out and mash the flesh in a bowl with a tasty filling. You could try peeled prawns and spring onion in spicy tomato dressing; sour cream and chopped chives; or sliced sausage and grated cheese. Why not experiment with fillings of your own? There is a huge range of ingredients and flavours to choose from.

Salads

Salads are not just for the summer. By using a variety of flavours and textures, you can make healthy, tasty salads at any time of year.

Always wash the ingredients well before using them. If adding fruit, such as apple, avocado or banana, cut it at the last moment and dip it in lemon juice to prevent the flesh turning brown.

Green salad Lettuce, green pepper, watercress, spring onions and cucumber tossed in French dressing (see below). You could add any of the following: sliced apple or orange, grated cheese, hard-boiled egg, olives, herbs or chopped nuts.

Waldorf salad Mix chopped celery and apple (dipped in lemon juice) with mayonnaise. Stir in chopped walnuts and serve on lettuce leaves.
Curried pasta salad Mix a little curry powder with mayonnaise. Add cooked pasta, ham, chopped red pepper, spring onion and black olives and toss until coated.
Coleslaw Mix shredded white cabbage, grated carrot, thinly sliced onion and sultanas in mayonnaise with a little lemon juice added.
Mixed bean salad Drain a can of mixed pulses. Combine with chopped tomato, green pepper, onion, parsley, unsalted peanuts and seasoning. Add French dressing and mix.

For a main meal, add egg, cooked meat and chicken, cheese or fish to your salad or serve with a baked potato or freshly baked bread.

A choice of dressings
- **French** Put 1 part wine vinegar, 3 parts olive oil, salt and pepper in a screw-top jar. Shake well to mix.
- **Yoghurt** Mix 6 parts plain yoghurt, 1 part lemon juice, 1 crushed garlic clove, salt and pepper. Beat to mix well.
- **Blue cheese** Mix crumbled blue cheese (to taste) with mayonnaise and seasoning. Beat to mix thoroughly.
- **Thousand Island** Add 1 part tomato purée to 8 parts mayonnaise. Mix in a few chopped capers, and salt and pepper. A few drops of chilli sauce will spice it up.

▽ Spoilt for choice. – a selection of salad ingredients. All kinds of vegetables, fruit, nuts and herbs can be used, along with rice, pasta, beans and pulses. It is easy to add extra flavour with an interesting dressing (see left).

Cakes

For 24 chocolate cup cakes:
75 g (3 oz) margarine
200 g (7 oz) caster sugar
2 eggs, beaten

100 g (4 oz) self-raising flour
50 g (2 oz) cocoa powder
50 ml (2 fl oz) milk
24 paper cake-cases

For the icing:
175 g (6 oz) icing sugar
30 ml (2 tbsp) warm water
2 teaspoons cocoa powder

△ 1 Blend the margarine and sugar. Gradually beat in the eggs. Sift the flour and cocoa powder together and beat into the mixture a bit at a time, alternately with the milk, until smooth.

△ 2 Place paper cases in greased patty tins and divide mixture between them. Bake at 190°C (375°F) gas mark 5 for 30-35 minutes. Place the cakes on a wire rack until cold.

△ 3 Dissolve the cocoa powder in a little of the water. Slowly add the rest of the water to the sugar, beat until smooth and add the dissolved cocoa. Dip the top of each cake in the icing.

Variations

Queen cakes

Cream-filled chocolate cakes

Cherry cakes

Chocolate brownie cakes

△ Replace the cocoa powder with 100 g (4 oz) of dried fruit and omit the icing on the top.

△ When cold, cut the cake in half. Spread bottom half with whipped cream and replace the top.

△ Replace cocoa powder with 50 g (2 oz) glacé cherries. Omit cocoa from icing. Decorate top of cake.

△ Add 50 g (2 oz) of chopped walnuts to the chocolate cup cake recipe above.

Puddings

Puddings can vary from heavy suet puddings served with thick custard to light, delicate sorbets or mousses. Whatever you choose, try to make sure it balances with the other dishes you are eating.

Fresh fruit salad (made with apples, bananas, oranges, black grapes). Make a syrup by boiling together 300 ml (½ pint) water and

◁ **Banana split** In a dish, slice a banana in half lengthways, pipe whipped cream over the top and add two scoops of ice-cream. Pour chocolate sauce over the top and serve with a wafer or, if you prefer, chopped nuts.

100 g (4 oz) sugar. When the sugar has dissolved, allow to cool. Slice or dice the fruit, pour on the syrup, and cool in a fridge for 30 minutes. Variations: use more exotic fruit, such as melons, kiwi fruit, peaches, pineapple and mango. Serve with cream, or with natural yoghurt – a healthier alternative.

Pets

◁ All puppies are small and cuddly but some grow into very large dogs that need lots of food, space and exercise.

Pets can give lots of love and companionship. But, before you decide to get one, be sure you can provide the food, exercise and care it will need. There will be extra costs, too, such as vet's bills.

There are many pets to choose from. Before you decide which to get, consider how much space it will need, whether it will upset any other pets you have and who will look after it when you are away.

need a comfortable basket, a collar and lead and separate bowls for food and water. A puppy needs four small meals a day containing a little meat, cereal and milk. Adult dogs require two meals a day and the occasional marrow bone.

▷ Grooming keeps a dog's coat in good condition. Long-haired dogs need brushing every day. Bath your dog when necessary and dry it with a towel or hairdryer.

Dogs

The most important things when choosing a dog are its size and temperament. A puppy or dog will

Puppies need to be house-trained, which demands patience. Don't give up – your puppy will learn to obey you and will be easier to train further. All dogs need walking every day – the distance will depend upon the dog's size.

▽ When training a dog, there are four important things it should learn.

1 Heel Hold the lead so that the dog is just behind your left leg. Say 'heel' and begin to walk. If it tries to overtake you or pulls away, pull back firmly, repeating 'heel'. Praise your dog when it begins to walk correctly.

3 Stay Once it has learned to sit, say 'stay' and take a few steps backwards. It will try to follow, but repeat 'stay' and make it sit. Praise your dog when it stays sitting.

4 Come Attach a long piece of string to the dog's lead and make it sit. Walk a few steps backwards and tell the dog to 'stay'. Then say 'come' and call the dog's name. At the same time, pull gently on the string. Praise the dog when it comes to you. After a few lessons, you should be able to call the dog without using the string.

2 Sit With the dog standing still say 'sit' and at the same time push down firmly on its behind until it sits. Praise the dog and repeat until the dog sits on your command only.

Cats

Cats are less dependent than dogs, you don't need to take them for walks, for example. But they do require a certain amount of care and most cats will respond with love and affection.

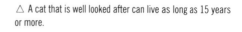

△ A cat that is well looked after can live as long as 15 years or more.

◁ Give your kitten plenty of toys; otherwise it will find its own.

▷ You could spend a lot of money on a special cat bed and then find your cat is just as happy in a cardboard box. Make it cosy by lining it with soft old clothes and place it in a draught-free corner.

Cats, especially long-haired breeds, do need to be brushed and combed regularly to remove loose hair and to keep their coats in good condition. But never attempt to bath a cat as they hate water, and are very good at keeping their own coats clean.

A young kitten should be given four small meals a day of either fish or meat – tinned catfood can be given at this stage. By the time it is six months old, meals can be cut down to two larger feeds as with adult cats. Cats have individual tastes so you should vary their food but avoid too much fish in the diet.

Kittens also have to be house-trained. At first your kitten will need a litter tray, which must be cleaned out regularly. Once the kitten is settled, you should train it to go to the toilet outside.

Kittens need to be inoculated against feline infectious enteritis – a type of 'flu that can kill very young or old cats. They will also need a booster once a year throughout their lives. Use a special pet-carrying box or basket to take your cat to the vet, to prevent it from escaping and running away in fright.

▷ Cats like to be able to come and go as they please, so a cat flap is ideal. Your cat will soon learn how to use it.

Rabbits

Rabbits should have two meals a day – one of crushed cereal, which can be bought from a pet shop, the other a mixture of green and root vegetables and fruit. Clean hay should always be available.

Never pick up a rabbit by the ears as it can be painful; support its weight when lifting it.

△ A rabbit hutch should be raised off the ground, away from damp and draughts and out of direct sun. It should have two compartments – one for sleeping and the other for eating. The sleeping area needs clean straw for bedding. Put a drip-feed water bottle in the eating area, and change the water daily. Clean the hutch once a week. Rabbits also need a safe place to exercise.

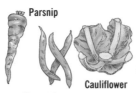

Turnips **Carrots** **Parsnip**

Runner beans **Cauliflower** **Spinach**

◁ Give rabbits fresh, raw vegetables, but not lettuce – they like it but it isn't good for them. Wild plants, such as dandelion and clover leaves, make nice treats.

Guinea pigs

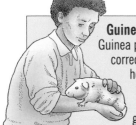

Guinea pigs or cavies – their correct name – need similar homes to rabbits. The food they eat is also similar, with lots of green vegetables and grass. They eat little and often and need plenty of fresh water.

△ When lifting a guinea pig, support its weight with both hands. Hold the animal in the palm of your hand, resting its body along your arm.

Hamsters

Hamsters are delicate and must be kept in a warm place indoors. They must be housed alone, or they will fight. A small meal of grains, seeds, nuts, vegetable or fruit will satisfy a hamster. A hamster will make a food hoard in its cage, and this must be removed regularly, or the food will go bad.

▷ An exercise wheel for a mouse or hamster should be attached to the cage wall and have a solid back to prevent the creature trapping its tail.

Mice

Mice need similar cages to hamsters, and must be kept away from dampness. They are active animals and enjoy ladders, ropes, tunnels and exercise wheels. Provide hay or newspaper for nest-making. Feed twice a day, and take out any old food. Mice will eat mouse food, bought from pet shops, and scraps of bread, fruit, vegetables and meat.

▽ A hamster cage should be made of metal or hardwood, to withstand gnawing. Put peat or sawdust on the floor. Provide hay for nesting and a drip-feed bottle for water.

Fish

Goldfish are the most popular and easiest fish to keep in either a garden pond or a coldwater tank. They can be fed twice a day on dried fish food, bought from a pet shop. Don't overfeed them.

Tropical fish are more exotic and must be kept at an even temperature of 24°C. A tropical aquarium is similar to a coldwater tank, but it needs electric heaters, a thermostat, a thermometer and a pump to aerate the water.

△ Cover the bottom of a goldfish tank with gravel and plant pondweed to provide food and shade. Keep the tank out of direct sun.

◁ An angel fish adds dazzling colour to an aquarium. The colour and markings will depend on the age of the fish.

▷ A longnose butterfly fish. Ask advice in a pet shop before stocking a tropical tank, as some fish are likely to attack and eat others.

Birds

A wide range of birds can be kept in cages, but the most popular varieties are budgerigars, canaries and mynah birds.

All cage birds can be fed on packet bird food bought from a pet shop with occasional fruit and greenstuff. Cuttlefish in the cage will provide the bird with a good source of calcium and help it to trim its beak.

All small caged birds need daily exercise out of their cage, but be sure the room is safe before opening the cage.

◁ The bottom of a budgerigar's cage should be lined with sanded paper. For feeding, the cage will need seed dispensers and a water container – a millet spray and cuttlefish will provide extra nourishment. Ladders, perches and other toys will entertain the bird but take care not to clutter up the space. Place the cage away from draughts. Once a week, the sanded paper should be renewed and the whole cage cleaned thoroughly.

△ Exotic birds like the blue-and-yellow macaw have beautiful plumage. They need a large cage and a spacious area to exercise.

Wildlife and nature

You can study plants and animals almost anywhere – in towns and in the countryside, in parks and at the seaside.

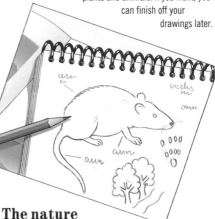

▽ Making sketches will help you to remember the things you have seen. It also trains you to look carefully at plants and animals. If you want, you can finish off your drawings later.

△ If you are going out for the day, plan your trip in advance and check the weather forecast. A map and compass will help you find your way.

▽ Some of the equipment you might find useful, and some of the things you might look out for.

The nature detective's kit

You don't need a lot of expensive equipment, but some things are very useful to have.

You should always have a notebook and pencil with you. It is hard to remember what you have seen once you get home again, so try to make notes and a few rough drawings on the spot.

Nature dos and don'ts

When you are out nature-watching, it is important to follow these guidelines – for your own safety and for the good of the environment.

- Make sure you have the right clothes to keep you warm and dry
- Always tell a responsible adult where you are going and when you expect to be back
- If you are going to be out for several hours, take food and drink with you
- Don't go on to private land unless you have been given permission
- Close field gates behind you
- Don't pick or damage plants – draw them or take photographs
- Don't harm animals or take them away with you – if you capture any creatures to study them, make sure you release them unharmed
- Don't leave any litter.

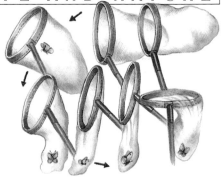

△ Catching a butterfly is not as easy as it seems. When you have swept the net through the air and caught the butterfly, turn your wrist so that the mouth of the net closes to stop the insect escaping. Butterflies are delicate and you should handle them very carefully. Always let them go unharmed.

A small hand lens or magnifying glass will help you to take a close look at small objects. You will need a good torch if you plan to go nature-watching at night.

A fishing net is useful for pond dipping and for catching flying insects. A plentiful supply of containers is essential for keeping your finds in.

Binoculars allow you to watch birds and animals without scaring them away. A new pair can be expensive, but you can often buy them cheaper second-hand. The same is true of a camera, which enables you to keep a photographic record of what you have seen.

You might want to set up a display of the things you have seen and collected. It could include specimens, such as shells and bones, as well as your notes, written up neatly and illustrated with drawings and photographs.

Nature all around

There are plants and animals almost everywhere. These pages give just a few examples of where to look and what to look for.

▽ On sandy or muddy seashores, a spade is useful for digging up buried worms or molluscs. It is a good idea to tie a string around the handle of your magnifying glass to hang it round your neck.

△ A home-made viewing box will help you to see underwater. Cut the bottom from a plastic box or bowl and glue a piece of perspex over the hole. You can use cling film instead of perspex, but you must bring it right up over the sides and fix it at the top.

On the seashore there are seaweeds, crabs, worms, birds and countless other living things. You can sometimes find fish, starfish and other creatures trapped in rockpools when the tide has gone out. Whenever you go to the seaside, try looking for interesting seashells to collect.

Ponds, rivers and lakes are good places to find interesting wildlife. A huge range of animals lives in water and around it, including fish, water beetles, frogs, voles and dragonflies. You might be able to catch quite a few pond insects just by scooping a net through the water. Put them carefully into a jar with some pond water, and don't forget to put them all back in the pond when you have finished looking at them.

▽ Different types of trees have different bark. The best way to see this is by making bark rubbings. To make a rubbing, pin a sheet of strong paper to a tree and rub all over with a thick wax crayon. You can get interesting effects by using differently coloured paper and crayons.

△ Some of the creatures you might find in a village pond (from left to right): common toad, pond skaters, great pond snail, great diving beetle, moorhens and water scorpion.

△ If you collect some frogspawn and keep it in a large jar with pondweed, tadpoles will hatch and turn into frogs. Return the frogs to the wild, near the pond where you found the frogspawn.

A pitfall trap
Bury a jar up to its rim in the soil. Put some stones around the edge and rest a piece of wood on top. Check the trap twice a day and let go any creatures you catch.

In fields and woodlands you will find all kinds of fascinating things, from tiny insects and wild flowers to trees and quite large mammals, such as deer. Most creatures are shy and you will have to keep quiet and out of sight if you are to get close enough to see them.

There is plenty to see even in towns and cities. Bats, squirrels, hedgehogs and foxes can all live there, as well as many species of birds. Most towns have a park, with trees and maybe even a lake. Finally, don't forget to look in your own garden or back yard.

Tracks and signs

Animals and birds often leave clues which, if you can read them, will tell you what species are living in an area. These clues may be in the form of footprints or other tracks, signs of feeding, droppings, or nests, burrows and other dwellings. Here are some signs left by some common creatures – and the odd rare one – to get you started.

△ Most mice live in burrows with warm nests, which they normally leave at night to feed. Neatly opened hazelnuts are a tell-tale sign. You might find footprints at the edges of ponds and streams.

△ Badgers dig underground burrows, called setts. In doing this they throw out mounds of soil which, over the years, can become very large. Their prints are quite easy to identify, as their feet have large pads. The claws on the fore-feet (above left) are longer than on the hind feet (above right).

▷ Grey squirrels are now very common and easy to find. They live in trees and their long back legs help them to leap from branch to branch. They are quite noisy animals, and you may hear their 'chuck, chuck' calls. They eat nuts by splitting open the shells, and gnaw the bark from trees to get at the wood below. Look for prints in damp ground.

△ Rabbit burrows are often found in grassland, close to woods or hedgerows which provide cover. You might find their tracks in sandy soil or in the snow. The hind feet leave tracks side by side, while the fore-feet print in a line.

▷ Foxes are found all over Europe, but they are shy and difficult to watch. At dawn or dusk you may be lucky enough to see a fox tracking and pouncing on a mouse or vole. Fox footprints appear in straight lines in soft ground or snow.

△ Some caterpillars roll leaves into a tube (left) to protect themselves from birds. Others are so small that they can live inside a leaf. (right).

△ Otters are now rare and are only found around unpolluted water. You may find tracks in estuary mud.

Casts
To make a cast of a track, first add water to plaster of Paris until the mixture is creamy. Then pour it into a cardboard ring. When it has set, lift up the plaster.

△ When watching birds, look out for different wing shapes and flight patterns.

81

Birdwatching

Birdwatching is an ideal way to enjoy natural history. There are around 9,200 species of birds and they live all over the world. This means that you can study them no matter where you are.

You can start by watching the birds in your own back garden. A simple bird table with bread, nuts, dried fruit and other food will tempt birds to stay. You could also make or buy a nesting box; be sure to put it where the birds will be safe from cats.

Basic equipment

If you want to see more species of birds, you will have to go further afield. Many birds are very timid and hard to get close to, and you will find binoculars very useful. So is a field guide to help you identify the birds you see, and a notebook and pencil for notes and drawings.

Wear warm, dry clothes and take food and drink with you if you are planning to be out for a few hours. Tell an adult where you are going and when you will be back.

▽ A bird box like this is ideal for tits to nest in. You can make one from wooden planks about 15mm thick and 150mm wide. The hole should be about 25mm in diameter for blue and coal tits, and 28mm for great tits.

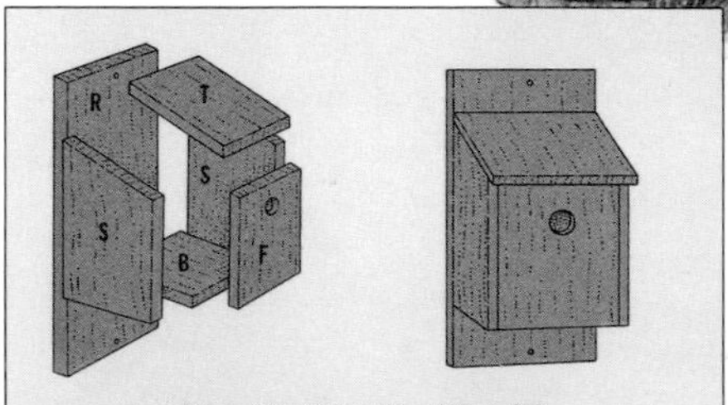

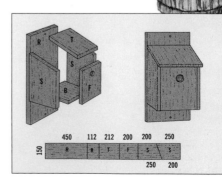

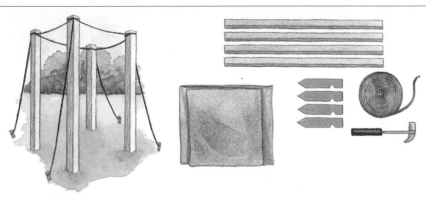

Making a hide

To construct your own hide, you will need four wooden poles, strong twine, tent pegs, a hammer and a piece of cloth, canvas or tarpaulin. Hammer the poles into the ground and tie twine around the top. Use the tent pegs and more twine to anchor the poles in position and then place the cloth over the top.

△ When you are watching birds that you don't recognize, you may not have time to look them up in a field guide. A few notes or a quick sketch in your notebook will help you to identify them later.

Hides

There are a number of clubs and societies for people interested in birds. Some of them run their own bird sanctuaries or reserves, where there are wooden hides from which birds can be studied.

It isn't hard to make your own portable hide. Set it up by a bird table to get a really close view, or take it with you when you go out into the countryside.

Photography

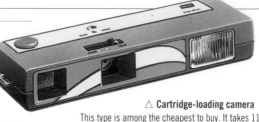

Photography is a good way of keeping a record of the places you visit, people you know and things you see. It is also an enjoyable and creative hobby – seeing a good picture that you have taken yourself gives a great sense of achievement.

△ **Cartridge-loading camera**
This type is among the cheapest to buy. It takes 110 or 126 cartridge films. Some have manual controls; others are automatic and may have a built-in close-up lens.

▽ **Disposable** These cameras have the film sealed inside and can only be used once. There is nothing to set – you only have to point and click. Some disposable cameras can now be used underwater.

△ **35 mm Autofocus**
This camera focuses for you, calculates the amount of light entering the lens, adjusts the aperture and fires a built-in flash if needed. It takes 35 mm film.

Cameras

There are various types of camera to choose from. They all work on the same principle and have many parts in common, but some operate in different ways from others. Buy the best camera you can afford, but don't worry if you can't afford very much. You can get good results from cheap, modern cameras.

▽ **35 mm Single lens reflex (SLR)** With SLR cameras, you look through the lens that takes the photograph, so you see what the camera 'sees'. They take 35 mm film. They are often of very good quality, and many are fully automatic and can make all of the settings for you. Most SLRs can be fitted with a range of lenses and other accessories. They are expensive.

How it works

1 Rays of light from an object pass through the lens of a camera. The lens changes the direction of the rays, causing them to converge.

2 A door called a shutter opens and lets the rays through. They then pass through a hole called the aperture.

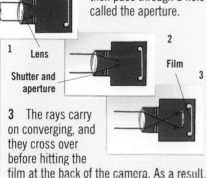

1 Lens

Shutter and aperture

2

Film

3

3 The rays carry on converging, and they cross over before hitting the film at the back of the camera. As a result, the image on the film is upside down.

Lenses

28 mm wide-angle

50 mm

70-210 mm zoom

△ These lenses are for 35 mm SLR cameras. The number in mm is called the focal length. The longer the focal length, the closer an object appears to be when seen through the lens, and the narrower the angle of view. A zoom lens is one in which the focal length can be adjusted.

▽ This is how a scene might look through a 'normal' 50-mm lens (**1**), a 28-mm wide-angle lens (**2**) and a zoom lens set at a long focal length (**3**).

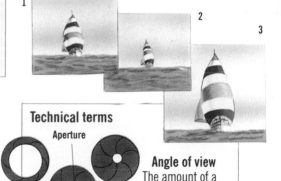

1

2

3

Film

Films are coated with chemicals that turn black when light hits them – such as when a camera shutter is opened. An image of the photographed object is imprinted on the film. It is called a negative, because the lightest areas of the object turn the film chemicals darkest, and the darkest areas appear light. Positive prints, with the correct colours or shades can then be made from the negatives.

▽ Two of the most popular film sizes. Most films produce either colour or black-and-white photos.

126 cartridge

35 mm

Technical terms

Aperture

Angle of view The amount of a scene that can fit into a photograph.

Aperture The hole that lets light into the camera. The wider the aperture, the more light reaches the film. Aperture is measured in f-stop numbers; the higher the f-stop number, the smaller the aperture.

Depth of field The distance between the nearest and furthest points in a scene or photograph that are in focus, or sharp.

Exposure The amount of light reaching the film, controlled by the brightness of the subject, the speed at which the shutter opens and closes, and the aperture size.

The Internet

The Internet is a vast network of computers, all over the world, connected together via telephone lines. With the right equipment, anyone can connect their own computer to the 'net' and swap information, pictures and sounds.

△ An external modem. This plugs into the computer and the telephone socket.

▷ Speakers like these, together with a 'sound card' inside the computer, can produce good quality, stereo sound. Many World Wide Web pages include sounds.

There are several different systems that make up the net, with names like Gopher, FTP, Telnet and IRC, and they all need different software. The most popular aspects of the net are e-mail and the World Wide Web.

E-mail

This is short for 'electronic mail'. It is a way of sending messages across the world, from one computer to another, in a matter of seconds. Each e-mail user has a unique number, or 'address'.

When you know how to use e-mail, you can send and receive computer files – such as software programs, text, pictures and sounds – as well as messages.

▽ To connect to the Internet you will need a personal computer, a modem, an account with an Internet Service Provider (ISP) and the correct computer software. The modem, which links the computer to the telephone system, may be a separate box, like the one above, or it may be built-in to the computer. There are many ISPs, which charge a monthly fee in return for unlimited access to their powerful 'host' computers that are permanently connected to the Internet. Many ISPs provide their customers with the necessary computer software free of charge.

◁ The World Wide Web has literally millions of pages, on thousands of different topics, including pop music...

▷ ...conservation and other environmental issues...

◁ ...every kind of sport you can think of...

◁ ...space, and much, much more

Searching the Web

There are Web pages that cover just about everything you can think of, and plenty of things you can't.

With so much information available, it's hard to know where to look for it. You can start with a special web site called a 'search engine'. Type in what you are looking for – say 'football' or 'pop music' or 'ballet' – and the search engine hunts for all the pages that contain that word or phrase. It lists the relevant pages on the screen as links, and a mouse-click will take you straight to any page you choose. Browsers usually have a button marked 'search' or 'net search', which will take you to a selection of search engines.

If you find a page that you think you will want to go back to, you can tell your browser to 'bookmark' it to help you find it again easily.

The World Wide Web

The Web consists of millions of documents, or 'pages', stored at Web 'sites' on thousands of 'host' computers around the world. The pages are all linked together. Clicking with your computer mouse on a highlighted 'link' on one page takes you to another page, which will have links to another, and so on. To view Web pages you need a piece of software called a 'browser' – Netscape Navigator and Internet Explorer are the most popular, but there are many others.

Internet jargon

Browser A computer programme that lets you read the computer language (called HTML) that web pages are written in.
ISP A company that provides a connection to the Internet.
Modem A device that connects a computer to the telephone system, allowing it to send and receive information.
URL Universal Resource Locator – the address of a Web page.
Web site A collection of Web pages about a particular subject.
World Wide Web A system that enables users to move from one document to another via links.

Walking and camping

If you are planning to go walking in the countryside, it is vital to be well prepared. The clothes you wear should be comfortable and suitable for the weather conditions. But bear in mind that the weather can change rapidly, especially in hilly country and always make sure you will be able to stay warm and dry if it takes a sudden turn for the worse.

△ Lightweight walking boots are fine for general use. They are flexible and fairly waterproof. In rough terrain and in cold, wet weather, stiff-soled mountain boots give more protection.

Safety points
- make sure you have the right clothing to keep you warm and dry, even if the weather becomes bad
- keep your equipment – torch, compass, rucksack and so on – in good order
- before you set out, tell a responsible person where you are going and when you expect to be back
- don't go alone; walking is often more enjoyable with a friend, and if one person has an accident the other can help or go to get help

△ Protected from the elements: a hat, gloves and several layers of clothing topped with waterproofs. Modern waterproofs are often made using 'shell' fabrics which keep rain out but don't trap sweat in.

It is best to wear several layers that can be taken off one by one if you get too warm. If you are not going to be walking anywhere rough or wet, trainers are ideal. Otherwise, get some walking boots with soles that give a good grip.

You will need a rucksack for your spare clothing and other kit. Don't get one that is far bigger than you need – you will have to carry it! Make sure it is waterproof, but pack spare clothing in plastic bags to be safe. Other useful equipment includes sunglasses, a torch, a

△ A 'Silva'-type compass like this one is ideal for walking. It comes with clear instructions on how to use it; read them and practise at home or in your local park before you venture off the beaten track. Learn how to read all the information given on maps – the scale, the contour lines and the various symbols that represent buildings, marshy ground, railway lines and so on.

Finding north
If you lose your compass, a watch can help you find north. Turn the watch until the hour hand points to the Sun. The line half-way between the hour hand and a line joining the centre of the watch to 12 o'clock points south. The opposite direction is north.

S

N

water bottle and food, sun barrier cream to prevent sunburn, a sunhat, a first-aid kit and a whistle – six blasts are a distress signal.

Finally, and perhaps most important of all, if you are going into unfamiliar territory, you must have a good map and compass and know how to use them.

Camping

In countries with a mild climate, you can go camping all year round. But if you've never done it before, it is a good idea to make your first expedition when the weather forecast is good. If possible, go with some friends who are experienced campers and learn from them.

There are two main types of camping. One involves staying on established campsites which have facilities including toilets, water, electricity, a shop and maybe even a restaurant. The alternative is for you to find places to stay, often by asking for permission from the owner of the land on which you plan to camp.

The basic equipment you will need is a lightweight tent, a sleeping bag and an insulated mat, a lightweight cooking stove, spare fuel, plastic mug and plates, cutlery, pots and pans, a can opener, water containers, waterproof matches, a first-aid kit, – and a large rucksack to put it all in. The rucksack should have lots of side pockets for

△ If the weather turns suddenly very bad while you are out walking, you will need to take shelter. If there is none nearby, you can make a temporary shelter from a lightweight groundsheet or plastic sheet secured with some suitable poles or a wall and some stones.

△ Setting up camp. This type of tent, called a ridge tent, is usually stable, weatherproof and has plenty of space inside. Ridge tents come in a variety of sizes. The boy has set up the cooking stove near the tent – but not inside it because of the risk of fire. When you leave your campsite, always leave everything clean and tidy.

Don't pitch your tent...

- so that your head lies downhill
- side-on to the wind
- on undulating or rocky ground
- downhill from a river or stream
- under trees or overhanging rocks
- on wet or marshy ground
- on ground that is too hard for you to get tent pegs into
- close to water where animals regularly drink or wallow
- on private land without first being given permission from the landowner.

things you need to get at easily. Don't forget things like your washing kit, clothes, sunglasses, sun cream and a torch. If you are walking or cycling around an area, you will need a map and compass.

This may sound like a huge amount to carry, but if you are going with friends the cooking equipment can be shared out between you.

You might want to combine camping with cycling. If not, you will have to get around on foot or by bus and train. In any case, your equipment should be light enough for you to carry it all comfortably.

The most important item is the tent. Choose one that is easy to erect and waterproof, and buy the best you can afford – a camping equipment shop can advise you.

Before you set out, practise pitching and striking the tent – putting it up and taking it down – in the garden or a nearby field, and sleep in it for a couple of nights. Try packing everything in your rucksack, too. You might find you need to leave some non-essential items behind.

Fishing

There are three main types of fishing – coarse, fly and sea fishing (see pages 94 and 95). In general, the equipment, or tackle, for each type is broadly similar, although some items are designed specifically for one type of fishing. For advice on choosing equipment, ask at your local fishing tackle shop.

The rod is the most important piece of tackle. No single rod is ideal for all uses; it is best to choose one that best suits the type of fishing you plan to do.

◁ Rods for coarse fishing. A float rod (far left) is good for learning the basic skills of fishing. Start off with a 3- or 3.3-m rod. When the weather makes float fishing impractical, or to cast long distances, a 3-m leger rod (left) is best. For large, heavy fish, such as pike and carp, you will need a specimen rod.

Line and reels

Nylon fishing line comes in different strengths, or breaking strains, according to the weight it can hold without breaking. The line is loaded on to a reel attached to the rod. A fixed-spool reel (above left) is suitable for most coarse fishing on rivers and lakes. A closed-face reel (above right) is useful when casting into the wind. Both usually hold about 100 m of line.

▷ Ask a friend to help you load line on to a reel. Your friend can keep a slight tension while you wind on the line.

▽ Here are some of the basic items of tackle, and a few of the signs that can tell you where certain types of fish may be found in a river.

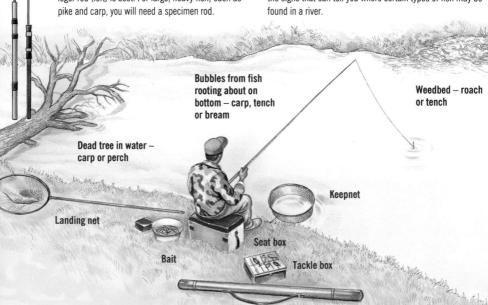

Bubbles from fish rooting about on bottom – carp, tench or bream

Weedbed – roach or tench

Dead tree in water – carp or perch

Landing net

Keepnet

Seat box

Bait

Tackle box

Hooks and knots

Hooks come in various shapes, and in sizes numbered from 1 - the largest - to 20.

Loop-to loop attachment

Spade end knot

Tucked half blood knot

△ Line is attached to hooks by means of knots. A loop-to-loop attachment is useful for connecting a hooklength to the main fishing line. (A hooklength is about 300 mm of line tied to a hook.) Use a spade end knot with spade end hooks, and a tucked half blood knot for hooks with eyes. The hooks above all have a barb – a sharp point facing away from the main tip. Barbless hooks, which can easily be removed from a fish's mouth, are now being used more widely.

Fry scattering – pike, perch or zander

Fish on surface of their feeding area – roach

Lily pads – tench

How to handle fish

Always wet your hands before handling a fish; if you don't, the layer of protective slime covering the fish will stick to your hands. A fish that has lost its coating is more likely to catch infections and diseases when returned to the water.

◁ Unhook the fish as soon as you have caught it. Hold small fish in the hand when removing the hook. Lay larger fish on a soft, damp surface.

◁ Use a weighing sling to weigh your catch. Don't weigh fish by the gills if you are going to return them to the water. Many owners now insist that coarse fish are returned alive to their river or lake.

◁ Hold large fish upright in the water until they are able to swim away.

◁ Place fish gently into a keepnet; don't drop them in. Never put too many fish in a keepnet.

◁ Don't put very large carp in a keepnet; a keep sack is much better.

◁ To release fish from a keepnet, hold the net and let the fish swim out.

Coarse fishing

All freshwater fish, except salmon and trout, are called coarse fish. They are caught by either float fishing or leger fishing.

◁ Floats suspend the hook and bait in the water, and move to indicate a bite.

If the fish are feeding a long way from the bank, or if the wind is too strong for a float, try legering. This uses a heavy weight to hold the bait near the bottom, and a bite indicator on the rod to tell you when a fish has taken the bait.

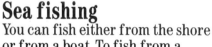

▷ There are several leger 'rigs'. This one is called the running leger with bomb.

Casting a float

1 Hold rod up and in front of you. Trap line against handle with tip of forefinger and open bale arm. Hold butt of handle slightly away from you. Lift rod tip just past vertical.
2 Punch rod forward firmly and smoothly, keeping butt close to you.
3 As float flies past rod tip, at about 45°, release line.
4 Line will spill rapidly from reel. Follow through with rod until it is about level over the water. Engage bale arm and wind in slack.

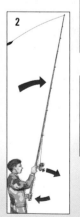

Sea fishing

You can fish either from the shore or from a boat. To fish from a beach you will need a powerful rod called a beachcaster, and a fixed-spool reel. Only go boat fishing with an adult who has experience of boats and knows the area well.

▽ As the tide rises in an estuary, fish will move in from the open sea. Mackerel can be seen chasing shoals of small fry, making the surface bubble with activity. If you see a shoal of mackerel moving up an estuary, cast and retrieve across the path of the shoal.

Cast here

Direction of shoal

Casting from the shore

This off-the-ground cast is suitable for a standard beachcaster. Always make sure no one is close to you.

◁ Trap the line with your forefinger

Direction of cast

(wear a protective finger glove). Stand almost side-on to direction of cast. Turn to hold rod behind you, with your weight on your back foot. Rest bait on ground.

◁ Pull rod forward past chest and turn forward as you do so.

◁ Begin to transfer your weight to your front foot. Push rod away from you strongly and smoothly with your upper hand and arm, and pull butt towards you with the lower hand. Release the line when rod has swung past the vertical.

Tide

Retrieve

▷ A fly fishing reel. A 27-m backing line is wound on to the reel first and the main fly line is then attached to it.

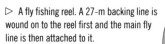

Fly fishing

In fly fishing, artificial 'flies' are used to imitate the insects and small fish that are eaten by game fish, such as trout. There are special rods, reels and line for fly fishing, and a vast array of different flies.

▷ An artificial fly designed to resemble a winged insect. So-called dry flies imitate insects floating on the surface, and wet flies behave like drowned insects or tiny fish and are used below the surface. Other types of fly are nymphs, lures and streamer flies.

Fly fishing is not as difficult as many people think. The hardest part is learning to cast properly, and it is a good idea to get an experienced fly angler or a professional teacher to give you lessons. Being able to 'present' the fly well is the secret of success.

▽ Presenting the fly. Cast the fly just upstream of a fish (trout always face upstream) and allow the fly to float with the current (red arrow). Collect slack line with your free hand, and don't strike until the fish takes the fly downward.

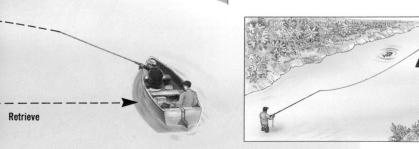

Cycling

Cycling can be a hobby, a sport or simply a way of travelling from A to B. It has lots of advantages. For example, it is cheap, good exercise, doesn't pollute the environment and enables you to see the countryside. It also gives you a degree of independence, so that you don't have to rely on other people whenever you want to go somewhere.

There are a number of different types of bike available, from BMXs for small children up to sports racing bikes. One of the most popular is the mountain bike, like the one shown below.

Safety
Cycling is great fun, but it can also be dangerous, especially on busy roads. Following these simple rules will help you to ride as safely as possible.

- Learn what the road signs and traffic signs mean and always obey them.
- Watch what other traffic is doing and make the correct signals yourself.
- Wear bright clothes so that you can be seen easily day and night.
- Wear a cycling helmet.
- Make sure that you have good front and rear lights. Always use them at night.
- Don't carry passengers on your bike or balance things on the handlebars.
- Make sure your bike is in good working order.
- Always tell someone where you are going before setting off on your bike.

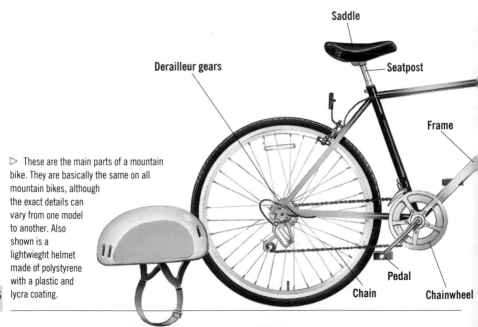

▷ These are the main parts of a mountain bike. They are basically the same on all mountain bikes, although the exact details can vary from one model to another. Also shown is a lightwieght helmet made of polystyrene with a plastic and lycra coating.

Saddle

Derailleur gears

Seatpost

Frame

Pedal

Chain

Chainwheel

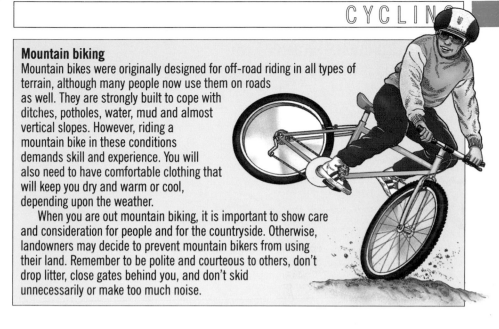

Mountain biking

Mountain bikes were originally designed for off-road riding in all types of terrain, although many people now use them on roads as well. They are strongly built to cope with ditches, potholes, water, mud and almost vertical slopes. However, riding a mountain bike in these conditions demands skill and experience. You will also need to have comfortable clothing that will keep you dry and warm or cool, depending upon the weather.

When you are out mountain biking, it is important to show care and consideration for people and for the countryside. Otherwise, landowners may decide to prevent mountain bikers from using their land. Remember to be polite and courteous to others, don't drop litter, close gates behind you, and don't skid unnecessarily or make too much noise.

Handlebars

Handlebar stem

Brake cable

Brake block

Front forks

Tyre

Rim

Spoke

Hub

Valve

Whichever style you choose, it is important to make sure the bike is the right size for you. Divide your own height by three, and this will give you the ideal frame size of the bike, from the pedal crank to the base of the saddle. When you sit on the saddle, you should be able to touch the ground with the toes of both feet.

It is useful to know how to maintain the bike yourself. The following pages show how to adjust the brakes, saddle and handlebars, and repair a puncture. You will need a few simple tools, including spanners, screwdrivers, tyre levers, puncture repair kit and pump. For more advanced maintenance, you will need other tools. But don't attempt anything you are not sure about; if you don't do it properly, you could have an accident.

Basic bike maintenance

△ **Saddle height** A badly positioned saddle can be uncomfortable and even painful. With the bicycle supported – perhaps by a friend or by using a wall to help you balance – sit on the saddle and put your heel on the pedal. With the pedal in its lowest position, you should feel a slight stretching at the back of the knee.

△ **Adjusting the height** There are two types of saddle – quick-release and bolt-on. Quick-release or QR saddles are adjusted by turning a lever and then raising or lowering the saddle. A bolt-on saddle is held in position by a binder bolt which is loosened with a spanner or an allen key. Retighten the bolt or QR lever after adjustment.

△ **Adjusting the handlebars** The handlebars should be at the same height as the saddle or up to 5 cm lower. To adjust, loosen the stem bolt at the top and tap it with a hammer and a block of wood, as shown. Raise or lower the handlebars, making sure there is at least 5 cm of stem inside the frame. Retighten the stem bolt.

△ **Adjusting brake tension 1** A cable runs from each brake lever to one of the brake units. The brake cable is fixed to the yoke of the brake with an anchor bolt. A bridge cable loops through the yoke, pushing the brake blocks on to the rim when the brake lever is pulled. If your brakes are slow to work or are rubbing on the rim, adjust the tension. First, ask a friend to squeeze the brake blocks against the wheel rim tightly.

△ **2** Loosen the main cable anchor bolt and either pull some more cable through to make the brake respond faster, or release some cable if the blocks are rubbing. Retighten the anchor bolt. Your bike may have an anchor bolt holding the bridge cable in place. If so, you can alter the brake tension in the same way as above, but using this bridge cable anchor bolt instead of the main cable anchor bolt.

△ **Replacing a brake block** Worn brake blocks don't work properly. To replace one, loosen the brake block nut and remove the worn block. Fit a new one and position it carefully before retightening the nut fully. The whole of the block should press on the rim when the brake is applied. To stop the brake squeaking, angle the block so that the front part touches the rim first – called 'toeing in' the brake.

Mending a puncture

Make sure you always carry a
puncture repair kit with you.

It is best to start by removing the
wheel. Then take out the tyre valve
to release any air left inside.

△ **1** Pinch the tyre all the way around near the rim. Using tyre levers, lift the rim of the tyre free of the wheel. Make sure you do not pinch the inner tube.

△ **2** Remove the section of the tube where you think the puncture might be and see if you can find a hole.

△ **3** If you can't see the puncture, remove the tube completely. Replace the valve and inflate the tube with a bicycle pump.

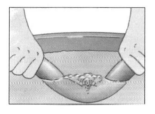

△ **4** Then put the tube in water. Do this bit by bit until you see air bubbles escaping from the tube. They will show you where the puncture is.

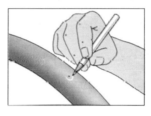

△ **5** When you have found the hole, mark it with a ballpoint pen.

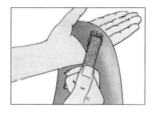

△ **6** Dry the area around the puncture. Then roughen it with some fine-grained abrasive paper. This will help the glue to stick to the tube.

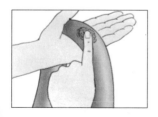

△ **7** Spread rubber solution on the tube and wait until it becomes 'tacky'.

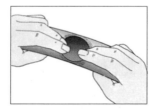

△ **8** Place the patch on the rubber solution and hold it there firmly for a minute or two. Dust the patched area with chalk to remove any stickiness. Inflate the tube slightly. Check inside the tyre for pieces of grit.

△ **9** Starting with the valve, push the tube back inside the tyre and replace the tyre inside the rim of the wheel. Don't use tyre levers. Instead, using a firm grip, roll the tyre back on to the rim. Finally, pump up the tyre until it is inflated fully.

Horseriding

Learning to ride well takes a lot of hard work and practice but it isn't simply a matter of mastering the techniques of riding.

When riding, always wear a hard riding hat that fits you correctly and has a chinstrap. If you are riding on roads when the light is poor, wear bright colours or reflective tabards. With breeches you should wear riding boots and with jodhpurs, ankle boots. Never ride in shoes without heels.

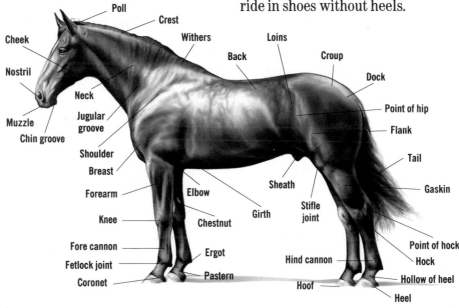

Poll, Crest, Cheek, Withers, Loins, Back, Croup, Nostril, Dock, Neck, Point of hip, Muzzle, Jugular groove, Flank, Chin groove, Shoulder, Breast, Tail, Forearm, Elbow, Sheath, Gaskin, Stifle joint, Knee, Girth, Chestnut, Fore cannon, Ergot, Point of hock, Fetlock joint, Hind cannon, Hock, Coronet, Pastern, Hollow of heel, Hoof, Heel

△ Before you start your lessons, get to know the points of a horse as these are frequently talked about in riding schools.

You also need to learn how to look after a horse – its welfare – and the tack – the equipment worn by a horse or pony.

The best way to learn to ride is to be taught by a qualified instructor at a reputable riding school. Riding a friend's horse or helping out at the local stables are cheaper options, but you might not be taught correctly.

Controlling a horse

There are various methods, or aids, for controlling a horse. Natural aids are signals that you make with your hands, seat, legs and voice, and which horses and ponies are trained to obey. Artificial aids include a stick or whip and spurs.

In your early lessons, the instructor might control your horse or pony using a long lunge rein. This will give you confidence in controlling the horse yourself.

▷ Your riding hat should fit snugly so that it does not fall off when you bend over. Always keep the hat on when you are around horses, even after you have dismounted.

◁ There are a number of types of bit. Which bit is used depends upon the style of bridle that is fitted. The bits shown here, from the top, are an eggbut snaffle, Pelham, Kimblewick, D-ring snaffle, and Weymouth with curb chain.

Tack

The basic tack is the saddle, bridle and headcollar, including the stirrups, bit and reins. It must all fit properly or it could cause pain and discomfort to the horse and be a danger to the rider.

A headcollar is used to hold the horse while putting on the bridle, and for leading and tying up the horse. Once the bridle is in place, the headcollar is removed.

The rider gives instructions to the horse using the reins, which are attached to the bit. The bit fits in the horse's mouth and is held in place by the bridle. Buckles on the bridle can be adjusted to ensure a good fit. There are five types of bridle; the snaffle, shown below, is best for an inexperienced rider.

▽ When fitting a bridle, the browband should not be so tight as to pull the headpiece on to the ears. The bit should be level in the mouth and the throat lash must not be fastened too tightly or it will cause the horse to choke.

Saddle and girth

The purpose of a saddle is to help the rider to balance on the horse's back, and to help the horse maintain its own balance. The best type for a young rider is a general-purpose saddle. The stirrup irons are attached to the saddle by leathers which are adjustable to suit the rider's length of leg. The saddle is held in place by a band called a girth, which passes under the belly and is buckled to the saddle. There are several styles of girth, made of leather, webbing or nylon.

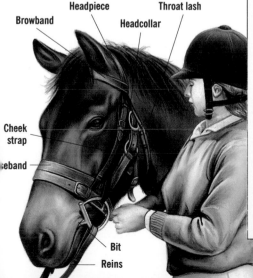

Headpiece
Throat lash
Browband
Headcollar
Cheek strap
eband
Bit
Reins

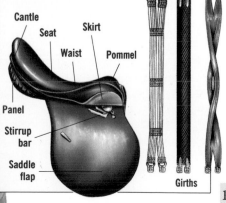

Cantle
Seat
Skirt
Waist
Pommel
Panel
Stirrup bar
Saddle flap
Girths

Cleaning and grooming

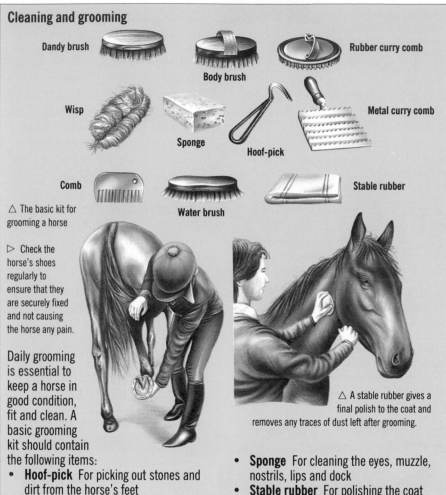

Dandy brush

Body brush

Rubber curry comb

Wisp

Sponge

Hoof-pick

Metal curry comb

Comb

Water brush

Stable rubber

△ The basic kit for grooming a horse

▷ Check the horse's shoes regularly to ensure that they are securely fixed and not causing the horse any pain.

△ A stable rubber gives a final polish to the coat and removes any traces of dust left after grooming.

Daily grooming is essential to keep a horse in good condition, fit and clean. A basic grooming kit should contain the following items:

- **Hoof-pick** For picking out stones and dirt from the horse's feet
- **Dandy brush** To remove dirt, dust and caked mud
- **Body brush** To stimulate circulation and clean off dandruff and grease
- **Metal curry comb** For cleaning the body brush while grooming
- **Rubber curry comb** To remove loose hair when the winter coat is being shed
- **Wisp** For massaging and toning the horse's muscles

- **Sponge** For cleaning the eyes, muzzle, nostrils, lips and dock
- **Stable rubber** For polishing the coat
- **Water brush and comb** To clean and comb the mane and tail after brushing.

All tack should be wiped clean after use. Once a week, take it apart and wash it thoroughly. Apply saddle soap to the leather to preserve it and keep it supple.

Walk

◁ **Mounting** Check the girth is tight and the saddle secure. Stand on the horse's left side, holding both reins in your left hand. Turn the stirrup iron towards you with your right hand. Put your left foot in the stirrup, and turn your body to face the saddle. Grasp the saddle with your right hand and swing your right leg over the horse's back and sit gently in the saddle.

▷ **Correct sitting position** The upper part of your body should be upright, not leaning towards the neck or the tail of the horse. Sit deep into the saddle – the lowest part of the horse's back – and keep your legs flat against the horse's side, alongside the girth. Rest the ball of each foot on the bar of the stirrup.

▽ **Dismounting** Holding the reins firmly, remove both feet from the stirrups. With your left hand on the horse's neck, lean forward, swing your right leg clear of the horse's back and jump off landing gently on the balls of your feet.

Starting to ride

The horse has four main paces, or gaits. The walk is the slowest, followed by the trot, the canter and the gallop, which is the fastest. As a horse accelerates, it changes from one gait to the next. In doing so, it changes the order in which its feet hit the ground. This gives each gait a distinctive beat. The walk has four beats to each stride; the trot has two; the canter, three; and the gallop has four, though much faster than those of the walk.

▽ The four gaits of the horse. The sitting position remains the same for the walk, trot and canter but changes for the gallop. The rider leans forward from the hips but still keeps his or her back straight.

Trot	Canter	Gallop

Jumping

When you have learnt to ride, you may like to try jumping. Horses are not natural jumpers but they do have good balance and, when they have been trained with a rider, seem to find it easy and enjoyable.

You might begin by trotting over a line of coloured poles spaced out evenly on the ground. This will help you learn how to sit in a well-balanced position that will enable the horse to jump easily. As you gain confidence, you can raise the poles 15 to 20 cm above the ground, and eventually progress to higher obstacles. The secret of successful jumping is to approach the jump at an even, controlled pace and with enough momentum to clear it.

△ A horse and rider jumping in perfect style. The horse's hind legs are poised to push upwards and forwards, the forelegs are neatly folded and the rider is well balanced.

A horse of your own

Owning a horse of your own is a big responsibility. One of the first things to consider is where you will keep it, especially if you live in a town. Livery stables look after horses, but they are costly. Renting a field is cheaper as the horse can be grass-kept, but it will need extra food of hay and bran in the winter. Some plants can make horses ill if they eat them; you will have to find out about these plants and remove them from the field. The horse will need a warm shelter, which must be kept clean.

Pony breeds

These are some of the most popular riding ponies.

◁ **Exmoor**
Height: 12.2–12.3 hands. A tough, hardy and independent pony which is best suited to an experienced rider as it can sometimes be wilful if not correctly handled.

▷ **New Forest**
Height: 12.2–14.2 hands. Large, intelligent and friendly. An ideal all-round riding pony for both children and adults, and very used to traffic.

◁ **Shetland**
Height: 9–10 hands. Strongest of all breeds for its size; it can pull twice its own weight. Suitable for small children.

▷ **Welsh Pony** Height: up to 13.2 hands. Gentle but courageous, this highly intelligent animal is regarded as a first-class riding pony.

When choosing a horse, size is very important. When you sit in the saddle your feet should hang just above the girth, although it is best to buy a horse slightly too big as you will grow. Horses and ponies are measured in hands, units of 10 cm. A horse is over 14.2 hands high and a pony – a small horse – is 14.2 hands or less.

Horses for sale are advertised in horse and riding magazines, but many people prefer to buy a horse they already know. When going to look at a horse, it is best to go with someone who knows about horses, or ask a vet to examine it fully. Look for a horse that has a good, even temperament, is physically fit and well, is calm in traffic and has no bad habits. It should be strong enough to carry an adult but docile enough for young children.

▽ Trekking or riding holidays combine exercise and seeing the countryside, and they help to improve your riding skills at the same time.

Windsurfing

Windsurfing is quite a recent invention – the first sailboard similar to those of today was made in 1968. Even so, the sport has caught on very quickly.

A sailboard is basically a surfboard with a mast and sail. Unlike a sailing boat, which has a rudder for steering, a sailboard must be steered by moving the sail to change its angle to the wind. This is possible because of the so-called universal joint at the base of the mast, which enables the sail to be moved in any direction.

Windsurfing is not as easy as it looks. When you start you will probably spend more time in the water than on it, so make sure you can swim first. If you want to learn windsurfing, it's best to join a club and have lessons. You will be able to use the club's equipment, too, and delay the expense of buying your own sailboard.

Wind direction

△ This diagram shows how the sail should be positioned relative to the wind.

◁ It is possible to reach quite high speeds on a sailboard – if you can stay on your feet. When windsurfing in cold water, it is best to wear a wetsuit. It will help to keep you warm even if you fall in.

Sailing

If you are planning to learn to sail, it helps if you know someone who has a boat. Otherwise, your best bet is to join a sailing club.

Boats are usually described in terms of their rig - the number, size and arrangement of masts and sails. The main picture on this page shows a dinghy - the cheapest form of sailing boat - with what is called a sloop rig. This means that it has a single mast with one sail, called the jib, in front and the larger mainsail behind the mast.

Sloops are very popular and they come in a wide range of sizes. Other types of rig include cutter, yawl, ketch and schooner.

△ An ocean-going racing yacht

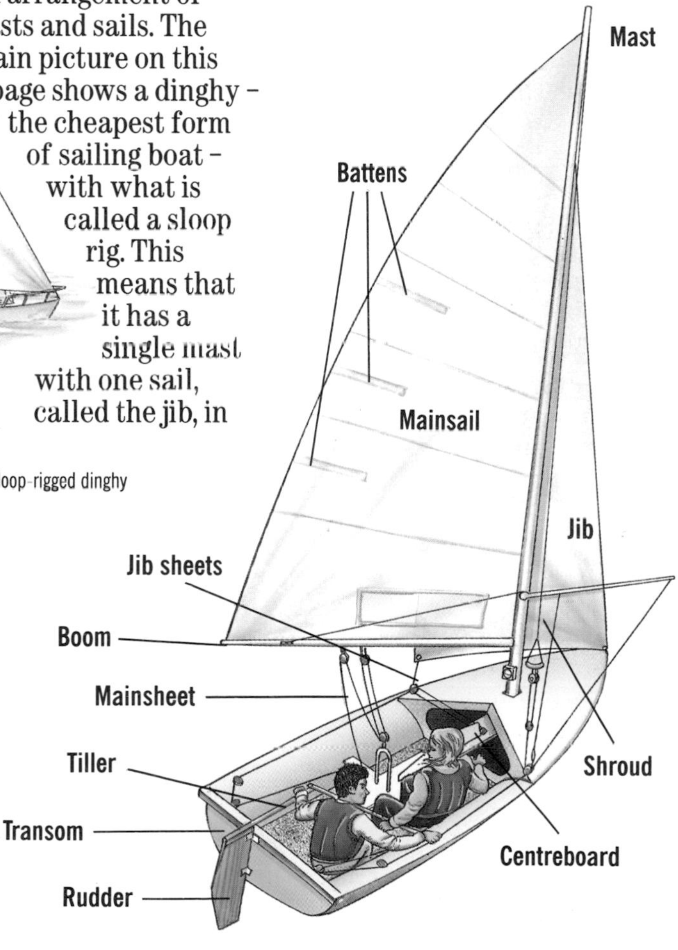

▷ The main parts of a sloop-rigged dinghy

Mast

Battens

Mainsail

Jib

Jib sheets

Boom

Mainsheet

Tiller

Transom

Rudder

Shroud

Centreboard

The direction in which a boat is moving relative to the wind is called its point of sailing. When the boat has the wind behind, it is said to be running. The mainsail is at right angles to the boat, so that the wind is pushing the boat straight ahead. If the jib is set to catch the wind on the opposite side of the mast from the mainsail called goose-winging – the boat will travel faster.

The boat is reaching when the wind is blowing from the side, and the mainsail will be at 45° to the boat. With the wind coming from ahead the boat is beating, or sailing close-hauled. It is impossible for a boat to sail head-on into the

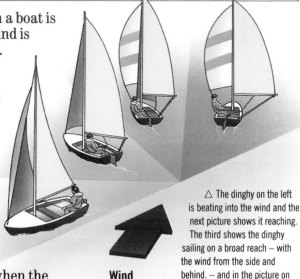

△ The dinghy on the left is beating into the wind and the next picture shows it reaching. The third shows the dinghy sailing on a broad reach – with the wind from the side and behind. – and in the picture on the right it is running.

Wind

wind, but a sloop can almost achieve this by beating, and by changing direction from one side of the wind direction to the other – called tacking. The sails must be set closer together than for reaching, as the boat is pushed forward by the air accelerating through the narrow slot between the mainsail and the jib.

Safety is of great importance in sailing. It is essential that everyone on board a sailing boat wears a life-jacket that will keep them afloat should the boat capsize. If this happens, stay with the boat until help comes.

◁ Essential safety equipment for sailing includes a bailing bucket, radio, flares, gas-propelled horn, spare line, waterproof flashlight, waterproof kitbag, bullhorn, first-aid kit, flotation cushion and, of course, a life-jacket.

Canoeing

Canoeing covers several different sports and a variety of boats, all of which are propelled by paddles. The kayak is an enclosed craft used for touring and racing.

The best way to start canoeing is to join a local club. You will find experienced people who can help you to learn in safety, and it will probably be a good source of second-hand canoes.

Before you think of getting into a canoe, make sure you can swim at least 50 m in the type of clothes you would wear for canoeing.

◁ A touring kayak. There is a foam block at each end of the hull to provide buoyancy. A spray cover is worn around the paddler's waist and stretched over the edges of the cockpit to give a watertight seal. Crash helmets are used in rough and rocky water.

It is made of plastic or fibreglass and has double-ended paddles, with the blades normally at 90° to each other. There are a number of kayak types, each designed to deal with certain water conditions.

Canoes are open boats that were originally developed from the craft used by North American Indians. They are usually made of plastic, wood or aluminium and have single-bladed paddles.

△ A leisure canoe. The raised decking at each end contains buoyancy foam. The spade-type paddles are made of wood, or have an aluminium shaft with plastic or wooden blades.

Safety points
- Make sure you can swim well.
- Always wear a life-jacket.
- Go canoeing in a group and stay together.
- Don't go in bad weather.
- If you capsize, swim for the bank, pulling the canoe with you.
- Wear a crash helmet on rough water.
- Always tell someone where you are going.

Chess

In chess, two players each have 16 pieces, arranged as on the board below. Players take turns to move, white going first, and the pieces can be moved according to the diagrams on this page. Chess was first played in India 1500 years ago, when the pieces represented the Indian army (see below). After the game was brought to Europe in the Middle Ages, the pieces changed to those we use today.

The object of the game is to capture the opponent's king. An enemy piece is captured by moving on to the square that piece occupies. Captured pieces are removed from the board. When a player's king is in a position where it could be captured on the next move, it is in 'check' and must move to a safe position. If there are no safe positions available, the king is in 'checkmate' and the game is lost.

▷ The board is ready for play to start.

◁ The bishop (elephant) can move any number of squares diagonally.

◁ The pawn (footsoldier) moves forward one square at a time, or two on its first move. It captures pieces by moving one square diagonally. If it reaches the opposite baseline, it can be exchanged for another piece, usually an extra queen.

▷ The knight (cavalry) can move two squares forward or backward and then one square to the left or right. It is the only piece that can jump over other pieces.

◁ The rook or castle (chariot) can move any number of squares forward, backward or to either side.

▷ The king (also a king in the ancient Indian game) can move in any direction but only one square at a time. When a player's king has been captured, that player loses the game.

△ The queen (vizier) is the most powerful piece. It can move any number of squares in any direction.

Draughts

Draughts is played on a chess board with two sets of 12 counters. A counter may be moved forward one square diagonally. The object is to capture all an opponent's pieces. On reaching the opponent's back line, a counter becomes a king and can move forward or back.

△ The layout of the board at the start of a draughts game.

△ A piece is captured when it is jumped over. If it is possible to capture a piece, a player must do so.

Backgammon

This is a game for two players. Each player has 15 counters, or stones, and tries to remove them from the board by moving them according to the score on two dice. The players move in opposite directions: in the picture below black moves clockwise and white anti-clockwise. If a player has one stone on a certain point on the board, it can be knocked off the board by an opponent's stone. But if a player has two or more stones on a point, no opponent's stones may land there. All 15 of a player's stones must be in a specific quarter of the board – called that player's home board – before any can be removed.

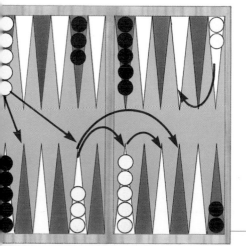

◁ The board is set up for the start of a game. To move, a player rolls both dice and may move two stones, one for each die score, or may move the same stone twice. Doubles are scored twice over. The arrows show all the possible moves White could make with a first throw of 5 and 2. White must move all his or her stones into the bottom-right corner before removing any; Black must move towards the top-right.

Stamps

Stamps are interesting to collect, as they come from all over the world and are often colourful.

▷ The world's first adhesive postage stamp was the Penny Black, first issued in 1840 in England. It showed the young Queen Victoria, and was designed to show that postage had been paid on a letter.

▽ Some equipment for stamp collectors. The perforation gauge measures the spacing of the perforations around the edges of stamps, and the tweezers are for handling stamps gently.

Album

Magnifying glass

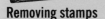

Tweezers

Perforation gauge

Removing stamps

Before putting stamps in an album, remove them from the envelopes – unless the post-mark or envelope is unusual or valuable.

1 Cut around them and carefully float them **face-up** on warm water in a bowl.
2 Allow enough time for the paper to get thoroughly wet; don't pull it too soon.
3 To remove any remaining gum, wash with a clean paintbrush and warm water. Put them on blotting paper to dry.
4 When dry, press them between sheets of blotting paper and some heavy books.

△ Stamps come in a great variety of shapes and sizes. Shown here are a triangular stamp from Mongolia, one in the shape of a map of Sierra Leone, and two 'se tenant' (joined) stamps from Kiribati which both form part of a single design.

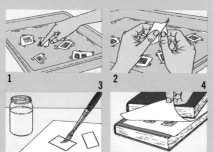

Some people collect stamps from one country, while others try to get as many as they can on a certain theme, such as animals or sports.

You can buy your own country's stamps at post offices. More exotic varieties are sold in stamp shops, by post and at stamp exhibitions and auctions.

ART AND HISTORY

Ever since humans first walked on the Earth, they have been creating art – paintings and sculptures, music and songs, dances and plays, stories and poems, and buildings.

All of these arts have changed greatly over the years, as people learned how to use different materials and new techniques, and saw the world in different ways.

▷ This solid gold funeral mask was made in Greece during the Mycenaean age, almost 3500 years ago.

The period of the past that we know most about is the time since writing was developed, when people began to make written records of their civilizations.

The first writing

The earliest types of writing were simple marks used for counting or identifying objects. The first real system of writing was developed about 5000 years ago by the Sumerian people in Mesopotamia. At first they used simple pictures of objects, called pictographs, which were scratched into the surface of clay tablets. Over hundreds of years, the pictographs were gradually simplified into a number of 'cuneiform' (wedge-shaped) marks made with a stylus.

Other civilizations, including the Egyptians, the Minoans and the Chinese, developed their own styles of writing.

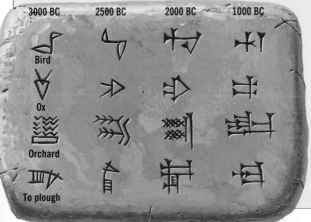

◁ How Sumerian pictographs changed into cuneiform symbols

3000 BC 2500 BC 2000 BC 1000 BC

Bird

Ox

Orchard

To plough

Books and writers

People have been writing stories and poems for many hundreds of years – and have been passing them on by word of mouth for many thousands. One of the earliest writers we know about was Homer, who lived in ancient Greece around 2700 years ago. He wrote two epic poems – the *Iliad*, about the siege of Troy, and the *Odyssey*, about the journeys of a mythical Greek hero called Odysseus.

Homer

Some of the most famous Roman writers were the poets Virgil, Ovid and Horace. Virgil's best-known work, the *Aeneid*, tells of a Trojan prince called Aeneas, who tried to found an empire in Italy. Virgil died before he finished the poem, leaving instructions that it should be destroyed. Fortunately, this did not happen. Cicero and Julius Caesar wrote about Roman history and politics.

▽ The story of Aladdin and the genie of the lamp comes from a collection of tales called the 'Arabian Nights'. The stories came originally from India and were written by several authors. They were taken from India to Persia, and were then translated into Arabic in about the eleventh century.

Until the Middle Ages, the language mainly used for writing in Europe was Latin. One of the first major works not in Latin was *The Divine Comedy*, a poem by Dante, which was written in the fourteenth century in Italian. About the same time, the English writer Geoffrey Chaucer wrote *The Canterbury Tales*. It is about a group of pilgrims travelling to Canterbury, each of whom tells a story on the way.

▽ The hare and the tortoise is one of the best known of Aesop's Fables. These originated in the sixth century BC and were brought together between 250 BC and AD 250.

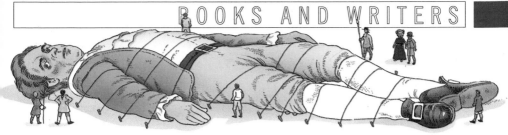

The first adventure novel was written in Spain in 1605 by Miguel de Cervantes. It describes the travels and adventures of Don Quixote and his faithful servant, Sancho Panza.

Two other important works of the seventeenth century are *Paradise Lost*, a poem by John Milton, and *Pilgrim's Progress*, a so-called moral fable written by John Bunyan.

Daniel Defoe was an English author and adventurer. He wrote more than 250 works in many different styles and is also credited as being the founder of British journalism. His most famous book, *Robinson Crusoe*, published in 1720, tells of a man marooned on a desert island after a shipwreck.

Jonathan Swift, an Irish poet and satirist, is best remembered for *Gulliver's Travels*, published in 1726. On the surface, the book seems to be a pleasant story about a man whose travels take him to various lands inhabited by strange creatures.

△ In this scene from 'Gulliver's Travels' by Jonathan Swift, Gulliver has been captured by the tiny Lilliputians.

One of the first great English novelists was Henry Fielding, who wrote *Tom Jones* in 1749. At the same time, Voltaire and Jean Jacques Rouseau were writing in France. They were both philosophers, but they wrote novels, too. Voltaire is best known for his short story, *Candide*.

The six great novels of Jane Austen all appeared in the early years of the nineteenth century. Her works include *Pride and Prejudice*, *Emma* and *Persuasion*, and are regarded as some of the greatest novels in the English language.

Jane Austen

▷ The swashbuckling heroes of 'The Three Musketeers', the best-known work of the French author Alexandre Dumas. He also wrote 'The Count of Monte Cristo' and 'The Black Tulip'.

115

There were many other great writers in the nineteenth century, including Nikolai Gogol, Ivan Turgenev, Leo Tolstoy and Fyodor Dostoyevsky in Russia; and Honoré de Balzac, Stendahl, Emile Zola and Gustave Flaubert in France. In Britain, William Thackeray's *Vanity Fair*, Charlotte Brontë's *Jane Eyre* and Emily Brontë's *Wuthering Heights* were published, along with *Middlemarch* by George Eliot and *Tess of the D'Urbervilles* by Thomas Hardy. One of the most famous of all British writers was Charles Dickens, the author of *Oliver Twist*, *David Copperfield*, *A Christmas Carol* and many other great works.

△ Charles Dickens's character Oliver Twist

The nineteenth century also saw the appearance of the first truly American authors, writing about American themes. Among them were James Fenimore Cooper, who wrote *The Last of the Mohicans*, Herman Melville, author of many stories of the sea and seafaring, including *Moby Dick*, and Samuel Clemens, who wrote under the name of Mark Twain.

▷ In his best novels, 'Tom Sawyer' and 'Huckleberry Finn', Mark Twain drew on his experiences as a boy in Missouri, USA, and as a riverboat pilot on the Mississippi river.

The great American novelists of the twentieth century include Ernest Hemingway, William Faulkner and John Steinbeck. Among the huge number of famous European writers are James Joyce, Virginia Woolf, George Orwell, Graham Greene, Franz Kafka, Thomas Mann and Marcel Proust.

During this century, writers from Australia, South America, Asia and Africa have also become well known in Europe and North America.

▽ A scene from 'Moby Dick', Herman Melville's book about the whaling industry in the USA.

Famous writers

Aesop (629–560 BC) A Greek slave who collected a large number of fables, each of which had a moral.

Austen, Jane (1775–1817) An English novelist whose six most famous works are 'Sense and Sensibility', 'Pride and Prejudice', 'Northanger Abbey', 'Mansfield Park', 'Emma' and 'Persuasion'.

△ The Brontë sisters – Charlotte, Emily and Anne

Balzac, Honoré de (1799–1850) A French writer best known for his studies of the society of his time.

Brontë, Charlotte (1816–1855), **Emily** (1818–1848) and **Anne** (1820–1849) Three English sisters most famous for 'Jane Eyre' (Charlotte), 'Wuthering Heights' (Emily) and 'Agnes Grey' (Anne).

Chaucer, Geoffrey (c.1340–1400) One of the greatest English poets, writer of the 'Canterbury Tales'.

Dickens, Charles (1812–1870) A novelist who wrote mainly about urban society in Victorian Britain.

Faulkner, William (1897–1962) American novelist who developed new writing techniques in works including 'As I Lay Dying'.

Golding, William (1911–1993) An English writer who first became famous for 'The Lord of the Flies', published in 1954.

Greene, Graham (1904–1991) One of the greatest English novelists, whose books include 'The Power and the Glory' and 'The Third Man'.

▷ William Golding was awarded the Nobel prize for literature in 1983.

Grass, Günter (1927–) A German novelist, author of 'The Tin Drum'.

Hemingway, Ernest (1899–1961) American writer whose works include 'For Whom the Bell Tolls'.

Joyce, James (1882–1941) Irish author who wrote 'Dubliners' and 'Ulysses'.

Naipaul, V.S. (1932–) Trinidadian author of 'A House for Mr Biswas'.

Orwell, George (1903–1950) English writer of 'The Road to Wigan Pier', 'Animal Farm' and 'Nineteen Eighty-Four'.

Salinger, J.D. (1919–) American author, most famous for 'The Catcher in the Rye'.

Scott, Sir Walter (1771–1832) Scottish author of 'Waverley' and 'Ivanhoe'.

Shelley, Percy Bysshe (1792–1822) English poet who wrote 'Prometheus Unbound' and 'To a Skylark'.

Stevenson, Robert Louis (1850–1894) Scottish novelist and poet who wrote 'Treasure Island' and 'Kidnapped'.

Swift, Jonathan (1667–1745) Irish satirist, author of 'Gulliver's Travels'.

Tolstoy, Leo (1828–1910) Russian author of 'War and Peace' and 'Anna Karenina', regarded as two of the world's greatest novels.

Wells, H.G. (1866–1946) English author of 'The Time Machine' and 'The War of the Worlds'.

Woolf, Virginia (1882–1941) English writer, best known for works such as 'Mrs Dalloway', 'The Waves' and 'To the Lighthouse'.

Wordsworth, William (1770–1850) English poet known for his mastery of language in poems including 'Intimations of Immortality'.

Theatre

The first dramas developed from religious festivals in Greece, held in honour of the god Dionysus about 3000 years ago. The Greeks built amphitheatres, with seats cut into hillsides so that people could see. Later, the Greek playwright Sophocles began using stage scenery. Other Greek playwrights included Aeschylus, Euripides and Aristophanes. Most dramas in ancient Greece were either tragedies – emotional plays with unhappy endings – or comedies.

Different forms of drama later emerged in India, China and Japan, and they, too, developed from religious ceremonies and rituals.

Stages

In a Greek theatre (1), the audience sat in a stepped amphitheatre around a circular orchestra – a space for singing and dancing. The rectangular stage was low down. The stage in a Roman theatre (2) was raised above the ground and was sometimes sheltered by a wooden roof. Modern theatres sometimes have an open stage (3) with no curtain. This allows the actors and audience to feel closer together. In theatre-in-the-round (4), the stage is surrounded on all four sides by the audience. There are aisles at the corners through which the actors can enter and leave the stage.

◁ Greek actors wore masks designed to tell people about the characters they played, and to help amplify their voices so that the audience could hear them.

The Romans, who came after the Greeks, enjoyed plays with plenty of action, as well as farces and pantomimes. After Roman times, theatres in Europe were destroyed or allowed to fall into ruins.

◁ An open-air theatre in ancient Greece about 2300 years ago. One of the most famous Greek theatres of the time was at Epidaurus. It was large enough to hold an audience of 14 000 people.

Entertainment was provided by acrobats, minstrels and jugglers who travelled from place to place, performing for feudal lords in their castles.

In the Middle Ages, theatre grew again in Europe. People were able to watch mystery plays (about the creation of the world and Adam and Eve), miracle plays (on the miracles of Jesus Christ) and morality plays (about good and evil). They were performed on stages built in market places in towns and villages.

The first theatres to be built in Europe after Roman times were in Italy in the fifteenth century. England's first theatre was built in about 1576. Some 10 years later, William Shakespeare moved from his birthplace at Stratford-upon-Avon to London and joined a company of actors. He acted in and directed plays, and wrote more than 30 great plays of his own, most of which are still performed regularly all over the world.

By the seventeenth century, theatres looked rather like they do today, with a horseshoe-shaped auditorium, a platform stage, a proscenium arch separating the stage from the audience, and curtains that could be drawn across the stage.

△ The famous Globe theatre in London, where William Shakespeare acted and wrote. It could hold an audience of 2000 people, who stood in the open courtyard in front of the stage or sat in the galleries, out of the rain.

Famous playwrights

Chekhov, Anton (1860–1904) Russian writer of 'The Seagull' and 'Three Sisters'.
Goethe, Johann (1749–1832) German playwright, best known for 'Faust'.
Ibsen, Henrik (1828–1906) Norwegian who wrote 'Peer Gynt' and 'Hedda Gabler'.
Molière (1622–1673) French writer of 'Tartuffe' and 'Le Misanthrope'.
Osborne, John (1929–1995) Welsh playwright of social drama 'Look Back in Anger'.
Shakespeare, William (1564–1616) The greatest English playwright. His works include 'Othello', 'Macbeth', 'As You Like It' and 'Richard III'.
Sophocles (496–406 BC) Early Greek playwright who wrote 'Oedipus Rex'.

William Shakespeare

119

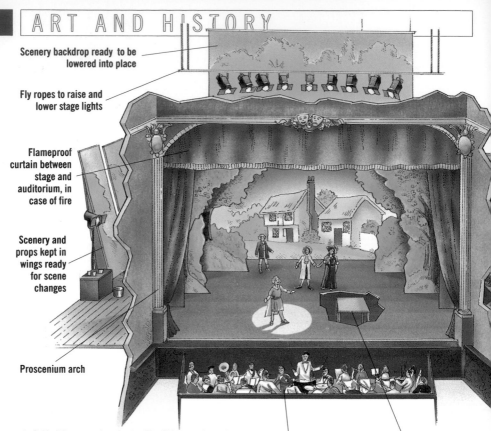

Scenery backdrop ready to be lowered into place

Fly ropes to raise and lower stage lights

Flameproof curtain between stage and auditorium, in case of fire

Scenery and props kept in wings ready for scene changes

Proscenium arch

△ Behind the scenes in a theatre. The 'fly' space above the stage is where scenery and equipment hang, ready to be lowered into place by ropes and pulleys. Some stages can be angled or raised to change the view of the audience.

Musicians in orchestra pit

Actors or props can be raised on to the stage by a lift.

Among the playwrights of the eighteenth century were Richard Sheridan and Oliver Goldsmith in England and Johann Schiller in Germany. Some actors became very famous, especially the Englishman David Garrick. The idea of 'star' actors grew in the nineteenth century, with Edmund Kean, Henry Irving and Sarah Bernhardt. The leading playwrights were Henrik Ibsen, a Norwegian, and Anton Chekhov in Russia.

The modern theatre 'revolution' began in the 1950s, with John Osborne's play *Look Back in Anger*, and was carried on by Harold Pinter in the 1960s.

Today, there are many types of theatre, from large national companies performing well-known works, to smaller 'fringe' or 'off-Broadway' groups putting on new, unusual and sometimes controversial plays that might otherwise never be staged.

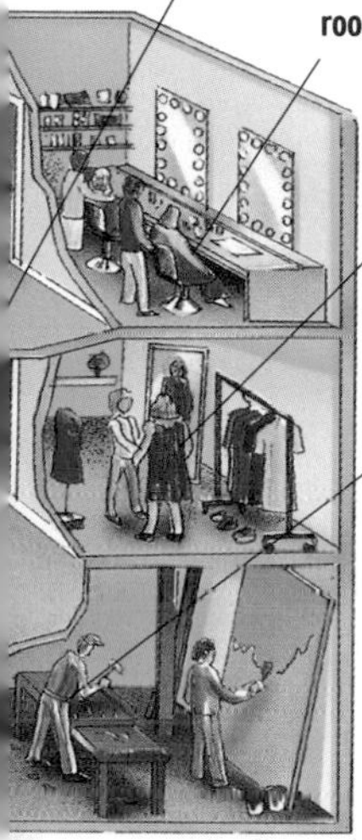

Lighting control console. Operators can brighten or dim any of the stage lights.
Wardrobe department where costumes are made and stored
Actors' dressing rooms
Carpentry department where stage sets are built

Movie facts and feats

Sherlock Holmes

- The character portrayed most often on the screen is Sherlock Holmes, the great detective created by Sir Arthur Conan Doyle. Since 1900, he has been played by 75 actors in 211 films.
- Hollywood, home of the American film industry, was founded in 1907.
- Mickey Mouse is over 70 years old; he first appeared in 1928.
- The highest price paid at auction for a film prop was US$275 000, for James Bond's Aston Martin car in 1986.
- The only actor to have won four Oscars is Katharine Hepburn. John Ford has won four as a director.

Katharine Hepburn

Cinema

The first motion picture was made in 1895 by two French brothers, Louis and Auguste Lumière. Early films were all silent, and had titles on the screen to explain the plot. The cinema rapidly became popular, and some film actors, such as Charlie Chaplin and Rudolph Valentino, became famous all over the world. The first full-length film with sound was *The Jazz Singer*, made in the USA in 1927.

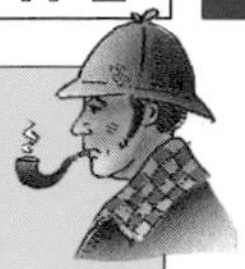

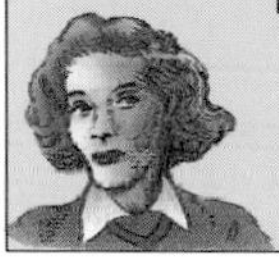

At first, films were in black and white. The earliest full-length film made in Technicolor was *Becky Sharp*, which appeared in 1935.

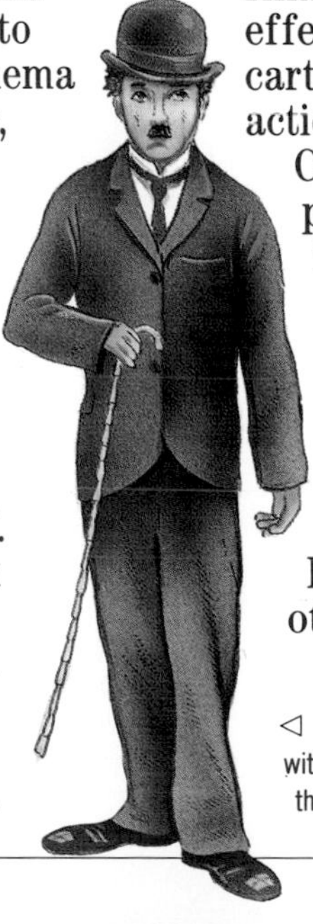

Since then, there have been many innovations, including 3-D films, wide-screen cinemas, special effects and the superimposition of cartoon characters on to live action films.

Cartoon films were pioneered in the USA in the 1900s by the Fleischer brothers. The most famous cartoon-maker of all time was Walt Disney, who created Mickey Mouse, Donald Duck and many other popular characters.

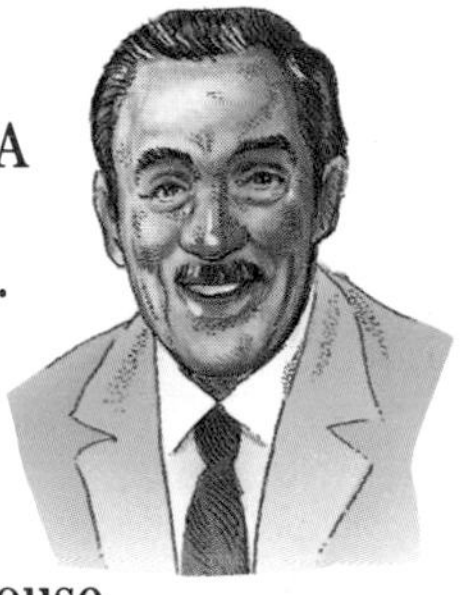

Walt Disney

◁ Charlie Chaplin's silent movie character of a tramp with a funny walk was loved by millions of people all over the world.

Music

People have been making music ever since prehistoric times. The earliest music was probably made by chanting voices. The oldest known musical instruments are mammoth bones found in Russia. They may have been knocked together or blown through to make sounds, some 35 000 years ago.

In early civilizations, such as those in Sumeria, Egypt and the Indus Valley, music was made both for pleasure and for use in religious ceremonies. The ancient Greeks also used music in their plays, but very few pieces of music have survived from that time, and none at all from the later Roman period.

From early Christian times up to the Middle Ages and beyond, almost all music was religious. In Europe, it consisted mainly of chants, including the Gregorian chants that are still used today. Further east, in the Byzantine Empire, music was often in the form of hymns.

Some of the first secular, or non-religious, music developed in the Middle Ages, when bands of minstrels roved from place to place and performed music in exchange for food and shelter.

Famous composers

Bach, Johann Sebastian (1685–1750) Composed over 190 works, including a 'Mass in B minor' and six 'Brandenburg Concertos'.

Beethoven, Ludwig van (1770–1827) One of the greatest classical composers, whose works include nine symphonies and 33 piano sonatas.

Haydn, Joseph (1732–1809) Wrote many pieces, including 104 symphonies.

Monteverdi, Claudio (1567–1643) Italian composer of church music, including masses and vespers, and operas such as 'Orfeo'.

Mozart, Wolfgang Amadeus (1756–1791) Perhaps the greatest composer of all time. Began composing at the age of 5 and wrote at least 626 works before his death at 35.

Mozart

Schubert, Franz Peter (1797–1828) Austrian composer of many songs, symphonies, piano sonatas and string quartets.

Stravinsky, Igor (1882–1971) One of the main composers of the twentieth century, whose works include ballet music such as 'The Firebird' and 'The Rite of Spring'.

Tchaikovsky, Peter Ilyich (1840–1893) Russian composer of symphonies and music for operas and ballets, including the '1812 Overture', the 'Nutcracker Suite' and 'Swan Lake'.

Tchaikovsky

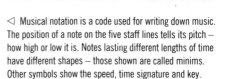

◁ Musical notation is a code used for writing down music. The position of a note on the five staff lines tells its pitch – how high or low it is. Notes lasting different lengths of time have different shapes – those shown are called minims. Other symbols show the speed, time signature and key.

122

◁ Stringed instruments work on the principle that a tightly stretched cord or string will make a sound if it is vibrated. In the case of a cello (left), a violin or a viola, the strings are vibrated by a bow being drawn across them.

Opera, which is a combination of music, singing and acting, began in sixteenth - century Italy. Some poets there had the idea of setting Greek stories to music and acting them out on stage. At first, the drama was more important than the singing, but by the early seventeenth century, the Italian composer Claudio Monteverdi was writing the first true operas. Monteverdi was also one of the first composers to use an orchestra.

The person who did most to establish the shape of the modern orchestra was Joseph Haydn, who lived in Vienna in the early eighteenth century. At that time, Vienna was the centre of the musical world, where Wolfgang Amadeus Mozart, Ludwig van Beethoven and Franz Schubert composed some of the greatest classical music ever written.

Conducting

The conductor of an orchestra uses his hands or a baton to tell the musicians what rhythm to play and how loudly. More important, a conductor has to interpret the composer's music in his own way and then tell the orchestra how to play it. So, if two conductors direct performances of the same piece of music, the results will be different in many ways, even though the musicians are playing the same notes on the same instruments.

▽ A modern orchestra may have more than 100 musicians playing instruments divided into four categories – strings, brass, woodwind and percussion. The piano uses the principles of both percussion and strings.

Percussion

Piano

Brass

Woodwind

Strings   Conductor   Strings

Ballet

Ballet combines music, mime and dance. It began over 300 years ago, as entertainment for the royal families of Europe. The style known as classical ballet has developed over the years since that time. The steps and jumps in classical ballet are still known by their original French names, such as jeté, entrechat and pirouette.

As in music, there was a romantic movement in ballet in the nineteenth century. In works such as Filippo Taglione's 'La Sylphide' and Adolphe Adam's 'Giselle', dancers wore costumes and used movements that made them appear to float across the stage.

Early in the twentieth century, Isadora Duncan and some other dancers moved away from classical ballet to perform a freer type of dance. Their work greatly influenced the Ballets Russes, the company established by the Russian Sergei Diaghilev, which was then regarded as the best in the world.

After Diaghilev died in 1929, national ballet companies grew up to carry on and develop his work, including the Kirov and Bolshoi companies in Russia and the Sadler's Wells in Britain. Later, the American choreographer Martha Graham pioneered a new, modern, style of ballet. Many dancers now train in classical ballet before changing to modern, or contemporary, dance, although both styles are still extremely popular.

▽ The five positions. Every ballet movement begins and ends with one of these positions.

First   Second   Third   Fourth   Fifth

In the nineteenth century, so-called romantic music was popular, especially the orchestral works of composers such as Johannes Brahms, Peter Tchaikovsky and Frédéric Chopin, and the operas of Richard Wagner and Giuseppe Verdi.

Romanticism died out in the early twentieth century, giving way to new musical sounds. Among the best-known twentieth-century composers are Ralph Vaughan Williams, Benjamin Britten, Aaron Copland and Igor Stravinsky.

Musical instruments

Most instruments fall into one of three classes – percussion, wind or stringed. Percussion instruments, such as drums, are played by being struck. Wind instruments include brass, such as trumpets and French horns, and woodwind, like oboes and flutes; they are basically hollow tubes that are blown through. Stringed instruments include violins, cellos and double basses, and are played by being plucked or bowed.

124

Popular music

Each era has its own styles of popular music; in the nineteenth century it was the waltz, while in the 1930s and 40s the music of large dance bands had great appeal. Nowadays, popular music comes in a wide range of styles, including jazz, disco, country, blues and rock, most of which have their origins in the USA. The basic appeal of most popular music is that it is light, has a strong rhythm and is easy to listen to.

The modern age of popular music began with rock and roll in the mid-1950s. It developed from earlier styles, especially the blues, jazz and country music, but it had a much greater appeal. Performers such Bill Haley, Buddy Holly, Little Richard and Elvis Presley drove millions of young fans wild with excitement.

The 1960s saw the rise of the Beatles, four likeable lads from Liverpool who shot to fame and fortune all over the world – even in the USA, which had, until then, been dominated by American artists.

◁ Elvis Presley – often known as 'the King' – had his first hit with 'Heartbreak Hotel' in 1956. He went on to sell millions of records and starred in over 30 films.

Other British successes in the 60s were the Rolling Stones and The Who. Americans Bob Dylan and Stevie Wonder also won fame in the 60s.

The 70s was the decade of glam rock by David Bowie, Elton John, Gary Glitter and others and punk rock, led by the Sex Pistols and the Clash.

In the 80s, new electronic instruments often linked to computers were used by groups like Ultravox and the Eurythmics to produce new sounds. The most poular solo artists were Michael Jackson and Madonna.

Late in the decade, fast, electronic dance music and hip-hop, or rap, came to the fore, and these styles continued into the early 90s.

In the mid-90s, 'boy bands' such as Take That and Boyzone became very popular. They were followed by the hugely successful all-girl group, the Spice Girls.

The Beatles

Madonna

125

Painting

△ 'The Last Supper', painted between 1498 by Leonardo da Vinci, one of the most famous artists of the Italian Renaissance. It shows Jesus Christ and his disciples eating their last meal together before Jesus was crucified.

The oldest paintings that can still be seen are images of animals painted on the walls of caves in France and Spain, around 15 000 years ago. Since then, almost all civilizations have produced some fine paintings – including the ancient Egyptians, the Minoans of Crete and the Guptas of India – although almost nothing remains of Sumerian and Greek painting.

Until a few centuries ago, most paintings in western civilizations were of religious subjects.

◁ A page from an illuminated manuscript. Between the third and the thirteenth centuries, illustrations like this on the pages of religious books were the main types of painting done in western Europe.

Early Christian paintings were often in the form of illuminated letters in manuscripts or images of Jesus Christ and other religious figures painted on wooden panels for church altars.

One of the finest periods in European painting was the Renaissance, which began in Italy during the fourteenth century. Artists such as Giotto, Leonardo da Vinci, Michelangelo and Titian developed more realistic styles of painting than before, of both landscapes and portraits.

The world's most expensive paintings

1 'Portrait of Dr Gachet' by Vincent Van Gogh – $82 500 000
2 'Au Moulin de la Galette' by Pierre Auguste Renoir – $78 100 000
3 'Self Portrait' by Vincent Van Gogh – $71 500 000
4 'Still Life With Curtain, Pitcher and Bowl of Fruit' by Paul Cezanne - $60 500 000

◁ The Dutch artist Vincent Van Gogh sold only one painting during his life, and that was to his brother, Theo. He led a very disturbed life and eventually killed himself in 1890, at the age of 47. Almost a hundred years later, his painting called 'Sunflowers' was sold for £22 500 000 (about $38 000 000), and since then three other Van Gogh pictures have reached even higher prices.

Paintings continued to look realistic until the 1870s, when a group of young French artists began looking at their subjects in a different way. They were called the Impressionists, because they used dabs of colour to capture the effect of light and shade. They were also among the first artists to go outside to paint landscapes. Early painters dreamt up imaginary landscapes in their studios.

△ 'Senecio' by the Swiss painter Paul Klee, who lived from 1879 to 1940. Klee was a major figure in twentieth-century art. He produced over 9000 works, mostly in abstract styles.

△ 'White Waterlilies and Bridge', painted by Claude Monet. He was perhaps the greatest of the Impressionist painters. Others include Camille Pissarro, Pierre Auguste Renoir and Georges Seurat.

In the twentieth century, painters have experimented with many new styles, including Cubism, developed by Pablo Picasso, abstract art, Surrealism, Abstract Expressionism, Pop Art, which was invented by Richard Hamilton, and Photorealism.

Sculpture

People have been making sculptures out of solid materials for thousands of years. Sculptors have used all types of stone, concrete, metals such as bronze, wood and plastic.

◁ In ancient Greece and Rome, sculptures were sometimes 'cast' in copper or bronze. The metal was heated until it became molten and was then poured into a specially made mould.

▽ Many sculptures are of people but, as in painting, they do not always look exactly like humans. The famous twentieth-century sculptor Henry Moore created works that were based on human shapes but were influenced by other shapes in nature.

127

Millennium Dome

To commemorate the New Millennium, the British government commissioned the architect Richard Rogers to design a vast exhibition building which would house attractions to both thrill and educate the public in the year leading up to the start of the New Millennium on 1 January 2001. The result was London's Millennium Dome, the largest domed structure in the world and twice the size of its nearest rival, the USA's Georgia Dome.

The translucent plastic roof is suspended from twelve 100-m-tall steel masts and held in place by over 70 km of high-strength cables.

The roof stands 50 m high at the centre and measures 320 m across. It is more than one kilometre in circumference, with a floor-space of more than 80,000 sq metres. It is designed to hold around 35,000 visitors at any one time.

Inside the Dome

Fourteen vast, themed attractions are arranged in a circle around a central performance arena. Each attraction or 'zone' celebrates a different aspect of life, and looks at exciting possibilities for the New Millennium.

Dome data

- The Dome cost more than £750 million to build.
- The roof is as tall as Nelson's column and strong enough to support the weight of a jumbo jet.
- The air beneath the Dome will weigh more than the materials it is made of.
- The Dome is big enough to hold 18,000 double-decker buses, 117 tennis courts, or 12 soccer pitches.
- Around 12 million people were expected to visit the Dome during the year 2000.

▷ The zones inside the Dome: **1** Body, **2** Learn, **3** Work,
4 Transaction, **5** Rest, **6** Mind, **7** Spirit, **8** Communicate,
9 National Identity, **10** Global, **11** Living Island, **12** Mobility,
13 Local, **14** Play.

There are zones on learning, the mind, the body, skills, transport, communication, money, spirituality, the environment, and many more.

The New Millennium

A millennium is a period of 1,000 years. In the globally recognized Gregorian calendar, the date 1 January 2001 marks the end of the second millennium and the beginning of the third since the calendar began. The Gregorian calendar was devised by the 6th-century scholar Dionysius Exiguus, who took the birth of Jesus as the starting point. Rather than starting with the year zero, this calendar began with the year AD 1.

Dionysius did not accurately establish the date of Jesus' birth, and modern scholars now think he actually was born sometime earlier, between 4 and 6 BC.

∨ The massive roof of the Dome is supported by 12 steel masts. There is enough space inside to contain 13 Albert Halls, or two Wembley Stadiums, the Eiffel Tower on its side, or even Egypt's Great Pyramid at Giza.

Historical dates

BC (c. = circa)

c.10 000	Farmers grow first cereal crops in Fertile Crescent
c.7500	First settlements built
c.4000	Metal (bronze) first made
c.3500	Plough and wheel invented
c.3100	Egypt becomes united under King Menes
c.3000	First cities built in Sumer, Mesopotamia
c.2600	Rise of Indus Valley civilization in India
c.2500	Rise of Minoan civilization on island of Crete
c.2450	Great Pyramid of Khufu built at Giza, Egypt
c.2100	Start of Babylonian civilization in Mesopotamia
c.2000	First Phoenician cities built in eastern Mediterranean
c.1650	Foundation of Hittite empire in Anatolia
c.1600	Mycenaean civilization in Greece
c.1200	Start of Olmec and Chavín civilizations in South and Central America
c.900	Kingdom of Kush emerges in north-east Africa
c.800	Rise of city-states in Greece; beginning of Etruscan civilization in Italy; rise of Celts in Europe
776	First Olympic Games held in Greece
c.720	Assyrian empire at height of its power in Mesopotamia
559	Beginning of Achaemenid empire in Persia
509	Founding of the city of Rome
490	Athenians defeat Persians at Battle of Marathon
323	Death of Alexander the Great
55	First Roman invasion of Britain led by Julius Caesar

◁ Minoans in the main courtyard of their palace at Knossos, Crete. The first palace on that site was built in 2000 BC.

AD

29	Crucifixion of Jesus
43	Romans invade Britain
79	Mt Vesuvius erupts destroying Roman cities of Pompeii and Herculaneum
122	Building of Hadrian's Wall
c.117	Roman empire at its largest extent under Emperor Trajan
146	Rome destroys city of Carthage in North Africa
285	Roman empire divided into eastern and western parts
c.300	Rise of Mayan cities in Central America
320	Start of Gupta empire in India
330	Emergence of Byzantine empire
370	Huns invade Europe
410	Visigoths sack Rome
476	Fall of the Roman empire in the West
638	Arabs conquer Jerusalem
711	Muslims from North Africa invade Spain
793	First Viking raids in Europe
c.1000	Vikings reach coast of Labrador, North America
1066	Normans invade and conquer Britain
1095	Start of Crusades to recapture Palestine from Muslims
1215	Magna Carta sealed by King John in England
c.1300	Rise of the Ottoman Turks
1305	Pope moves to Avignon
1325	Aztecs build capital at Tenochtitlán, Mexico
1337	Start of Hundred Years' War between England and France (ends 1453)
1341	Black Death begins in Asia
1348	Black Death reaches Europe
1381	Peasants' revolt in England
1421	Peking becomes capital of China
c.1450	Start of Inca empire in Peru

△ A Roman soldier of about AD 100

◁ In 1588, English ships fought off a much larger Spanish fleet – or armada – that was intended to carry an army from mainland Europe to invade England.

1453	Ottoman Turks capture Constantinople; first book printed using moveable type
1494	Treaty of Tordesillas divides the unexplored world between Spain and Portugal
1517	Martin Luther attacks practices of Catholic Church
1521	Spaniards under Hernán Cortés conquer Aztecs
1526	Start of Mughal dynasty in India
1534	Spaniards under Francisco Pizarro conquer Incas; Reformation in England
1536	Dissolution of monasteries in England
1571	Ottomans defeated at Battle of Lepanto
1588	English fleet defeats Spanish Armada
1605	Gunpowder Plot fails to blow up English Parliament
1607	First British colony in North America
1618	Thirty Years' War starts in Bohemia (ends 1648)
1642	English Civil War begins (ends 1645)
1652	Cape Colony founded in southern Africa; start of Anglo-Dutch Wars (end 1674)
1665	Great Plague strikes London
1666	Great Fire of London
1688	Glorious Revolution in England; William of Orange becomes king
1775	Start of American War of Independence (ends 1783)
1788	First British colony in Australia
1789	Start of French Revolution
1804	Napoleon becomes Emperor of France
1815	Napoleon defeated at Battle of Waterloo
1833	Britain abolishes slavery
1857	Indian Mutiny
1861	Start of American Civil War (ends 1865)

▽ A soldier in Oliver Cromwell's New Model Army during the English Civil War of 1642-45.

△ A locomotive and coach of the Liverpool and Manchester Railway in the 1840s.

1863	Slavery abolished in USA
1869	Suez Canal opened
1914	Start of First World War (ends 1918)
1917	Russian Revolution
1929	Wall Street Crash; start of the Great Depression
1933	Adolf Hitler comes to power in Germany
1936	Start of Spanish Civil War (ends 1939)
1939	Start of Second World War (ends 1945)
1945	First atomic bomb dropped on Hiroshima, Japan; establishment of United Nations
1965	USA enters Vietnam War (withdraws 1973)
1969	British troops sent to Northern Ireland
1973	Britain, Ireland (Eire) and Denmark join European Economic Community (EEC)
1976	Death of Chinese leader Mao Tse-tung
1979	USSR invades Afghanistan (withdraws 1989)
1980	Start of Iran-Iraq War (ends 1988)
1982	Falklands War between Britain and Argentina
1986	Nuclear disaster at Chernobyl, USSR
1989	Communist governments in Eastern Europe brought down by popular revolutions; democracy demonstrators in Beijing attacked by Chinese government troops
1990	East and West Germany reunited; Iraq invades Kuwait; Nelson Mandela released from prison in South Africa
1991	Gulf War in Iraq and Kuwait; break-up of USSR
1992	Break-up of Yugoslavia; plans to end apartheid approved by voters in South Africa
1993	Czechoslovakia splits into Slovakia and Czech Republic
1999	War between NATO forces and Yugoslavia

△ British and German fighter aircraft of the Second World War. The badge bears the swastika emblem of Nazi Germany.

Exploration and discovery

Marco Polo and his uncles meet Emperor Kublai Khan of China in 1275.

AD

c.1000 Viking Leif Ericsson sails to Newfoundland

1271 Beginning of travels of Marco Polo

1352 Ibn Battuta is first Western traveller to visit kingdom of Mali, West Africa

1487 Bartolomeu Diaz sails round southern tip of Africa

1492 Christopher Columbus discovers Caribbean islands

1498 Vasco da Gama enters Indian Ocean and sails to India; Columbus discovers mainland of South America

1500 Pedro Cabral claims Brazil for Portugal

1513 Vasco Nuñez de Balboa crosses isthmus of Darien from the Atlantic to the Pacific Ocean

1519 Ferdinand Magellan discovers strait between Atlantic and Pacific oceans

1522 One of Magellan's ships completes first voyage around the world

1534 Jacques Cartier explores St Lawrence River, Canada

1542 Franciso de Orellana sails down River Amazon in South America to Atlantic Ocean

1606 Willem Jansz becomes first European to land in Australia

1610 Henry Hudson finds Hudson Bay, Canada

1616 William Baffin discovers Baffin Bay, Canada

1618 Pedro Paez discovers source of the Blue Nile in Africa

◁ In about 1300 BC, Melanesian settlers first sailed to the island of Fiji in double-hulled canoes. They later travelled to Tonga and Samoa before spreading out to colonize many other islands. By AD 1000 they had visited almost every island in Polynesia.

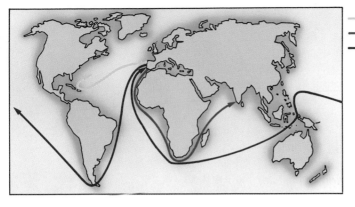

Columbus
da Gama
Magellan

◁ The routes followed by Christopher Columbus to the New World in 1492, Vasco da Gama to East Africa and India in 1498, and Ferdinand Magellan's voyage around the world from 1519 to 1522.

1642	Abel Tasman discovers New Zealand and Tasmania
1652	Founding of the Cape Colony by Dutch settlers in southern Africa
1688	William Dampier visits north-west coast of Australia
1728	Vitus Bering discovers Bering Strait between North America and Asia
1768	James Cook begins charting coasts of New Zealand and Australia
1778	Cook discovers Hawaiian Islands
1783	First flight in hot-air balloon, in Paris
1796	Mungo Park reaches River Niger in Africa
1804	Meriwether Lewis and William Clark begin journey across USA from St Louis to Pacific coast
1835	Boers in southern Africa begin 'Great Trek' from the Cape
1846	Evarist Huc and Joseph Gabet are first Westerners to visit forbidden city of Lhasa, Tibet
1855	David Livingstone discovers Victoria Falls, Africa
1858	Source of the Nile found by John Hanning Speke
1865	Matterhorn climbed by Edward Whymper
1869	Completion of first trans-continental railway in USA

▷ The first manned flight took place on 21 November 1783, when two people took to the air in a hot-air balloon designed by the Montgolfier brothers. The flight lasted just 25 minutes.

1877	Henry Morton Stanley sails down Congo river in Africa and reaches Atlantic Ocean
1888	Fridtjof Nansen makes first crossing of Greenland
1909	Robert Peary becomes first to reach North Pole
1911	South Pole first reached by Roald Amundsen
1929	Admiral R. Byrd is first person to fly over South Pole
1957	USSR launches first space satellite, *Sputnik*
1959	First photographs taken of far side of the Moon by USSR craft *Luna 3*
1960	Bathyscape *Trieste* reaches deepest ocean bed in Marianas Trench, Pacific Ocean
1961	Yuri Gagarin of USSR becomes first man in space
1965	Alexei Leonov of USSR is first man to walk in space; US Mariner space probe sends back data from Mars
1969	Americans Neil Armstrong and Edwin Aldrin become first men to land on the Moon
1972	USA launches *Skylab* experimental space station
1976	US spacecraft V*iking I* and *II* land on Mars
1979	US *Voyager* probes reach Jupiter
1980	*Voyager I* flies past Saturn
1981	Launch of US Space Shuttle, first re-usable space vehicle
1986	USSR launches first permanently manned space station, *Mir*
1990	USA launches Hubble optical space telescope
1993	Shuttle astronauts repair Hubble space telescope

△ In 1970, the Norwegian explorer Thor Heyerdahl sailed across the Atlantic in a reed boat, Ra.

◁ The Vostok rocket that launched Yuri Gagarin into space on 12 April 1961.

▷ In 1984, Bruce McCandless became a human space satellite when he flew 100 m from the Space Shuttle using a manned manoeuvring unit powered by gas thrusters.

SCIENCE

Science is the study of the Universe and the things in it, what they are like and how they behave. It is based on making observations, carrying out experiments and taking measurements, and then working out laws to describe the results that are obtained.

Science has many areas of study. For example, physics examines matter and energy, chemistry is about the elements that form all substances in the Universe, and biology is the study of living things. Astronomy deals with the galaxies, stars and planets, and geology is the study of the history and structure of the Earth. All sciences are linked by mathematics, the study of number, quantity, shape and space.

Famous scientists
Archimedes (287-212 BC) A Greek who studied many things, including physics, astronomy and mathematics.
Galileo Galilei (1546-1642) Experimented with forces and motion, but is best known for the discoveries he made about the Universe using a telescope.
Isaac Newton (1642-1727) Studied light, forces and motion, and formulated the idea of gravitation which attracts each object in the Universe to all others.
Thomas Alva Edison (1847-1931) Patented almost 1300 inventions, including the gramophone and the electric light bulb.

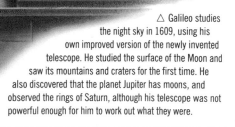

△ Galileo studies the night sky in 1609, using his own improved version of the newly invented telescope. He studied the surface of the Moon and saw its mountains and craters for the first time. He also discovered that the planet Jupiter has moons, and observed the rings of Saturn, although his telescope was not powerful enough for him to work out what they were.

137

Science topics

Atoms

Ever since the time of the ancient Greeks, 2500 years ago, people have believed that everything in the Universe is made up of atoms. Yet, real evidence that atoms exist was first found only 200 years ago.

Atoms are too tiny for us to see. Yet they are made up of even tinier pieces. We now know that each atom has a central part, called the nucleus. Inside the nucleus are particles called neutrons and protons. Flying around the nucleus are other particles called electrons.

Atoms of different substances all consist of these particles. What makes an atom of, say, oxygen different from one of iron is the number of particles. An oxygen atom has 8 protons, 8 neutrons and 8 electrons; an iron atom has 26 protons, 30 neutrons and 26 electrons.

Molecules

Some substances exist in the form of single atoms. Others only exist naturally if two or more atoms are joined together to form a molecule. Oxygen, for example, exists as a molecule made of two oxygen atoms.

Elements and compounds

Although there are thousands of different substances in the Universe, there are only just over 100 different atoms. Some substances, such as oxygen, iron and gold, are made from just one type of atom.

◁ An atom of carbon, with 6 protons and 6 neutrons in its nucleus, and 6 electrons orbiting around.

These substances are called elements. Others, called compounds, consist of combinations of two or more atoms. Common salt, for example, is a compound known as sodium chloride, and is made up of sodium atoms joined to chlorine atoms.

Sub-atomic particles

When electrons or neutrons are fired at a nucleus of another atom, the nucleus may break up and other particles are produced. Most of these so-called 'elementary' particles last only for a short time.
- **Leptons** come in several types: muons, neutrinos, taus and electrons
- **Photons** hold leptons together
- **Hadrons** include pions, kaons, neutrons and protons
- **Quarks** are the minute building blocks from which neutrons, protons and other hadrons are made
- **Gluons** 'glue' quarks together

Matter

Everything in the Universe around us consists of matter. Matter comes in three states – solid, liquid and gas. Water, for example, is normally liquid. If it is heated to 100°C it turns to a gas – steam – and if it is cooled down to 0°C it becomes solid – ice.

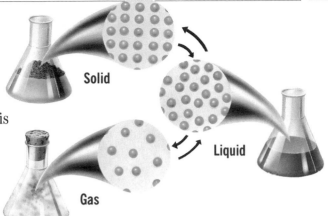

Solid

Liquid

Gas

Matter is made from atoms and molecules. If you rest your elbow on a wooden table, it does not sink in. This is because the atoms and molecules that make up the wood are all held together by what are called electromagnetic forces.

Even so, atoms and molecules are always moving, vibrating backwards and forwards in all

△ Whether or not a substance is solid, liquid or gaseous depends upon how fast its atoms or molecules are moving. Heating a substance makes its atoms and molecules vibrate faster; cooling makes them vibrate more slowly.

directions. In a solid they are vibrating relatively slowly; in a liquid they are moving faster; and in a gas they are whizzing about so fast that the electromagnetic forces can't hold them together.

Gases

The atoms or molecules of a gas are spread far apart. Because of this, many gases, like air, are impossible to see. It also means that gases are easy to compress, or squeeze.

When a gas is squeezed, it takes up less space, or volume. If it is heated, its atoms or molecules spread out and take up more space. If they are in a sealed container and can't spread out, they exert more pressure.

◁ If all the gas inside a container were sucked out, the empty space left would be called a vacuum. A vacuum exerts no pressure at all. In 1654 Otto von Guericke tried to create a vacuum inside a metal sphere consisting of two halves. It took 16 horses to pull the sphere apart because the pressure of the air outside pushed the halves together tightly.

139

Forces and motion

A force is something that affects the shape or motion of an object. There are four main types of force: electric, magnetic, nuclear and gravitational.

The scientist Isaac Newton first discovered what forces are in 1687. He set out three laws of motion explaining how forces make things move. He also showed that one special force, gravitation, acts throughout the whole Universe.

◁ If a sphere is placed on a slope, it rolls down because there is a force acting upon it. That force is the sphere's own weight. The weight of an object is a measure of how strongly it is being pulled towards the Earth by gravity.

Newton's laws of motion

• An object will stay still or keep moving at the same speed in a straight line unless a force acts upon it. This idea is called inertia.
• A moving object moves faster, or accelerates, when acted on by a force.
• Forces act in pairs; for every action there is an equal, opposite reaction. When you push on an object it pushes back with an equal force.

▷ Newton found that gravitation attracts every object in the Universe to all others. The size of the force of gravitation between two objects depends on their masses (how much matter they contain) and the distance between them.

Flight

Birds and aeroplanes can fly because of the way in which air passes over and under their wings. The top of a wing is curved, and so air passing over it has to travel further than air flowing along a straight path underneath the wing. This causes the air pressure above the wing to fall. The pressure below the wing is greater, and this lifts the wing – and the plane or bird – upwards. The faster a wing moves through the air, the greater the lift. That is why a plane has to build up speed on a runway before it can take off.

Elasticity

When you pull on a rubber band, it stretches and then returns to normal when you let it go. But if you pull too hard, the band will stretch and then break. The same thing happens when a weight is hung from one end of a length of wire. If the weight is not too heavy, the wire stretches and

▷ The more weight that is applied to this balance, the more the spring inside it stretches.

⊲ A suspension bridge is held up by wires hung from curved metal rods that are attached to tall towers. The wires must not be able to stretch so much that they break.

returns to normal when the weight is removed. This is called elastic stretching. If a heavier weight is used, the wire will stretch but will not return to its normal length. It is said to have been stretched beyond its elastic limit. If the weight is increased further, the wire becomes what is called plastic, and stretches very rapidly and then breaks.

The force that is put on an object to make it stretch is called the stress, and the amount by which it stretches is the strain.

Machines

A machine is any device that is used to overcome a force called the load. When this force is applied at one point, the machine works by applying another force, the effort, at a different point. Levers, pulleys, wheels and axles, screws and inclined planes are all types of machine.

A lever is one of the simplest machines. It consists of a rigid object that pivots about a turning point, or fulcrum. Levers are called first-, second- or third-class according to the position of the fulcrum, load and effort.

A doorknob is an example of a wheel and axle, and a ramp is a type of inclined plane.

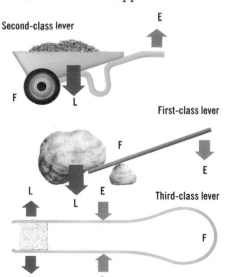

Second-class lever

E

F   L

First-class lever

F

E

L   E

L

Third-class lever

F

L   E

△ The three classes of levers. E is the effort, L is the load and F is the fulcrum about which the lever pivots.

▷ A pulley is a type of machine often used for lifting loads. A string is wound over one or more pulley wheels and when it is pulled the load is lifted. Usually, the more pulley wheels there are, the greater the load that can be lifted with the same effort.

◁ When a pendulum swings, energy is changed from one form to another. At the top of the swing, it is all gravitational potential energy, and at the bottom it is all kinetic.

Energy and power

When a force moves an object we say that work is done. The capacity to do work is called energy. Energy comes in many different forms and can be changed from one to another, but it can't be destroyed.

The different forms of energy are divided into two groups. Potential energy is energy stored in an object or system because of its position, shape or state. This group includes gravitational, electromagnetic and nuclear potential energy. The other group, kinetic energy, is to do with the movement of objects.

Power is a measure of the rate at which energy is changed from one form to another, or the rate at which work is done.

▷ The energy stored in fuel – called chemical energy – is a type of electromagnetic potential energy. When fuel burns, this energy is converted to kinetic energy and gravitational potential energy.

Power and pollution

Most electricity is made in power stations by burning oil, gas or coal. However, these fuels all produce pollution. Non-polluting power can be made in other ways, as in these examples.

◁ **Hydroelectric power** can be made by damming a lake or river and releasing the water through turbines which generate electricity.

▷ **Wave power** can be generated by small turbines on the surface of the sea that are moved up and down by the waves.

◁ **Tidal power** can be made by damming a river estuary and allowing water to flow through turbines when the tide rises and falls.

▷ **Solar power** is made by converting the Sun's heat and light into electricity.

◁ **Wind power** is generated by giant windmills which are often built in large numbers at so-called wind farms.

▷ **Geothermal power** uses the heat inside the Earth to boil water and make steam to drive turbines.

▷ Thermometers measure the temperature of things – how hot they are. The one on the left was invented by the scientist Galileo in about 1600. The other is a modern clinical thermometer for taking people's temperatures.

Heat

Heat is a form of energy. When an object is heated its molecules absorb the energy and convert it into kinetic energy, which means they vibrate more quickly. Most objects expand when they are heated, which partially explains how most thermometers work. For example, when the mercury inside a clinical thermometer is heated, it expands and rises up the tube. We can then read the temperature on the scale. The glass from which the tube is made hardly expands at all.

Heat flows from place to place when there is a difference in temperature between them. It keeps flowing until the temperatures are equal. The ways in which heat flows are called conduction, convection and radiation.

Conduction occurs when a solid object is heated. The electrons and molecules nearest the heat vibrate more rapidly and bump into those near them, passing on some of their energy. In this way, heat spreads through the object.

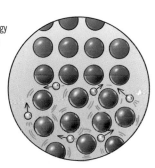

▷ In conduction, energy is spread by molecules and electrons colliding. Most metals are good conductors. Bad conductors, such as wood, glass and rubber are called insulators.

Heat travels through most liquids and gases by convection. When they are heated, liquids and gases expand, become less dense and rise. They are replaced by cold liquid or gas which is then heated, and so on. A great deal of radiated heat comes to us from the Sun in the form of infrared rays. They are similar to light rays.

◁ When cold water is heated in a saucepan, the water nearest the heat is warmed. It expands, becomes less dense and rises. Then it cools, becomes more dense and sinks down again. The movement of water sets up currents, called convection currents, which transfer heat from the bottom of the liquid to the top.

Light

Light travels in straight lines. It can be reflected, or bounced off shiny surfaces, and refracted, or bent, as it passes from one transparent material to another.

▽ In 1666, Isaac Newton found that sunlight – or white light – is made up of rays of light of all the colours of the rainbow.

Light rays are refracted when they pass from one material into another that is more dense or less dense. For example, light rays bend when they pass from water into air, or from air into glass. We have natural lenses at the front of our eyes which refract light and focus it on the retina at the back of the eye. However, the eyes of people who are short- or long-sighted do not focus light at the right place, and their vision is blurred. Glass or plastic spectacle lenses can be made to refract the light just enough to correct this blurring.

When sunlight passes through a glass prism, it emerges as a rainbow-coloured series of bands. The scientist Isaac Newton showed that light is actually made up of these colours, and that the prism separated the rays by refracting each colour a different amount. He passed the coloured rays through a second prism and saw that they came together again as white light.

Lenses

A convex lens focuses light rays to a point. A concave lens spreads out the rays.

Convex lens

Light rays

Focus

Concave lens

Light rays

We make use of reflection when we use mirrors. When a ray of light hits a flat mirror, the angle at which it reaches the mirror – the angle of incidence – is the same as the angle at which it bounces off – the angle of reflection. The image of something in a mirror is reversed left to right.

▽ Fibre optic cables are made of thousands of long glass fibres. When a light is shone in one end of the fibres, it passes along them rather than escaping through the sides. This happens because the light rays are reflected off the sides and 'bounce' their way along the length of the fibres.

Electromagnetic waves

Light travels in waves, rather like ripples in water. The light we see is called the visible spectrum. There are other waves that we cannot see. On the far side of the red end of the visible spectrum are infrared waves, microwaves and radio waves. At the other end of the visible spectrum are ultra-violet rays, X-rays and gamma rays. The distance between one wave and the next is called the wavelength. Different types of electromagnetic waves have different wavelengths. Light and other electromagnetic waves travel at 300,000 km per second.

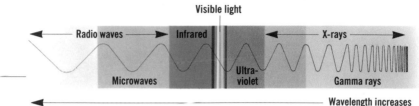

Visible light

Radio waves → Infrared ← X-rays →

Microwaves

Ultra-violet

Gamma rays

Wavelength increases

Sound

Sound is made when an object vibrates. The object pushes the air molecules in front of it, squashing them up in an area of high pressure. When the object moves back, it leaves an area of low pressure. The areas of high and low pressure move outwards from the object as sound waves.

Electromagnetic waves, like light waves, do not need anything to travel through; they can pass through a vacuum. But sound needs a 'medium' with molecules that can be bunched together and spread out. The speed of sound varies with the medium. In air it is 332 metres per second; in seawater it is about 1500 metres per second.

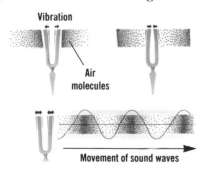

Vibration

Air molecules

Movement of sound waves

△ By pushing on the air molecules, a vibrating tuning fork makes sound waves that travel through the air. The distance between two waves is the wavelength of the sound. The height of the wave from the mid-point to the top is its amplitude. The greater the amplitude, the louder the sound. The number of complete sound waves that pass in 1 second is called the frequency. The higher the frequency, the higher the pitch of the sound.

▷ Sound waves can be reflected, refracted and diffracted (bent around corners). By sending out sound waves and measuring the time it takes for them to be reflected back from the sea-bed, the depth of the ocean can be calculated.

Electricity

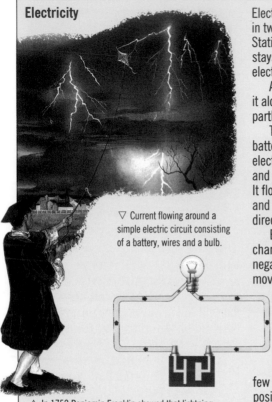

▽ Current flowing around a simple electric circuit consisting of a battery, wires and a bulb.

△ In 1752 Benjamin Franklin showed that lightning flashes are actually huge electric sparks.

Electricity comes in two main forms. Static electricity stays in one place, while electric currents flow from place to place.

▷ A battery stores electrical charge.

An electric current needs a force to push it along a wire. The size of a current depends partly on the size of the electrical force.

The type of electric current produced by a battery is called direct current, or DC. The electricity we use in our homes for lights, TVs and so on is called alternating current, or AC. It flows around a circuit first in one direction and then the other. The current changes direction many times each second.

Electricity is caused by electrically charged particles, which can have positive or negative charges. An electric current is the movement of electrons, which are negatively charged. Electricity flows easily through some materials, called conductors, but not through others, which are said to be insulators. Conductors have many electrons that are free to move; insulators have very few or none. Some objects can become positively charged by losing electrons, or negatively charged by gaining electrons.

Magnetism

Magnets attract objects made of iron, steel and certain other metals. Most metals, cloth, paper, plastic and glass are not magnetic.

Not all parts of a magnet are equally magnetic. The most magnetic parts, called the north pole and the south pole, are usually at or near the ends of a magnet. The north pole of one magnet attracts the south pole of another, but two north poles or two south poles repel each other.

Around a magnet there is an area in which magnetism can be detected. This area is called the magnetic field.

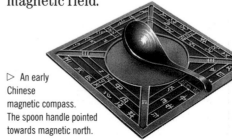

▷ An early Chinese magnetic compass. The spoon handle pointed towards magnetic north.

146

The field is strongest near the poles and gets weaker further away from them.

The Earth is a huge magnet, with north and south magnetic poles (not the same as the geographic North and South poles). A compass is a magnetic needle that can move freely. It lines itself up with the Earth's magnetic field and points to magnetic north.

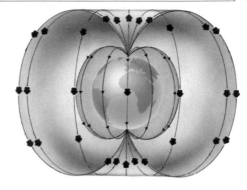

△ The Earth's magnetic field acts as if there were a huge bar magnet at the centre. The field can be detected 80 000 km out in space.

◁ A simple bar magnet

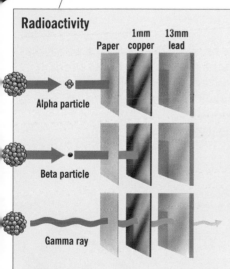

Radioactivity

Paper | 1mm copper | 13mm lead

Alpha particle

Beta particle

Gamma ray

△ There are three types of radiation. Gamma rays are the most powerful and alpha particles the weakest.

Radiation is energy given off by some substances in the form of small particles – called alpha and beta particles – and gamma rays. It is caused by the fact that the nuclei of some atoms are not stable and, as a result, they break up, producing a slightly smaller nucleus and some energy.

The atoms of a particular element all have the same number of protons in their nuclei, but some may have more neutrons than others. Atoms of one element that have different numbers of neutrons are called isotopes. Many isotopes are stable but some are not and these are said to be radioactive.

The nucleus at the centre of an atom contains a huge amount of energy, which can be released in what are called nuclear reactions. Fission is a type of reaction in which a heavy, unstable nucleus is split into two or more smaller nuclei, some neutrons and energy. Fusion is a different type of nuclear reaction in which two small nuclei are made to combine into a single heavy one, giving off large amounts of energy.

▷ Fission can occur naturally, but the most common way of making it happen is to fire a particle, such as a neutron, at a heavy nucleus. The nucleus absorbs the neutron, becomes unstable and breaks down.

Astronomy

Astronomy is the study of the Universe and the galaxies, stars, planets and other bodies it contains. This study began thousands of years ago, when ancient peoples watched and recorded the movement of the stars across the night sky, and the rising and setting of the Sun and Moon.

Until about 450 years ago, almost everyone thought that the Earth was at the centre of the Universe. In 1543 the astronomer Nicolaus Copernicus claimed that the Sun, and not the Earth, was at the centre. Few people believed him until, in 1609, Galileo Galilei first looked at the heavens through a remarkable new invention – the telescope. His observations of the Moon, Venus and other bodies eventually convinced people that the Sun is at the centre.

We now know that the Universe is far, far bigger than Galileo could have imagined. The Sun is merely the centre of our Solar System and is just one star among many billions of others.

Most of the knowledge that we have about the Universe has been collected using telescopes. Some are ordinary optical telescopes, like that used by Galileo. Others pick up radio waves, X-rays, gamma rays, ultraviolet or infrared rays given off by distant stars. The signals they collect are then analysed by computers.

Space exploration has also added to our knowledge. Astronauts have landed on the Moon and brought back pieces of rock. Unmanned space probes have been sent far out into the Solar System to send back pictures and scientific information on the outer planets.

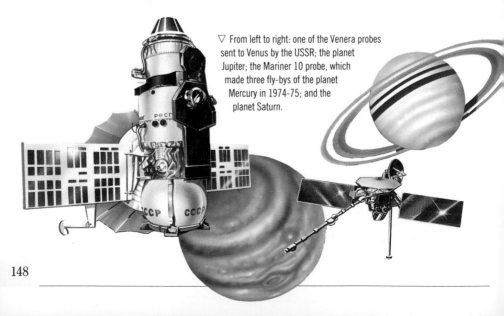

▽ From left to right: one of the Venera probes sent to Venus by the USSR; the planet Jupiter; the Mariner 10 probe, which made three fly-bys of the planet Mercury in 1974-75; and the planet Saturn.

Medicine

Medicine is as old as human civilization, but people only began to find out about the detailed workings of the human body in the seventeenth century. In 1628, William Harvey discovered that blood is pumped around the body by the heart. Cells, from which all living things are made, were first seen through a microscope in 1665.

◁ Hypodermic syringes are used to inject medicines into the body.

In 1857, Louis Pasteur discovered that air contains tiny living organisms, or microbes. Since then scientists have shown that many diseases are caused by microbes which we call germs or bacteria.

▷ Penicillin and other antibiotic drugs can destroy infectious organisms that cause diseases.

Medicine has advanced rapidly in the last 150 years, with developments such as aspirin, antibiotics, antiseptic techniques, the heart pacemaker, organ transplant operations and laser surgery. Even so, we still do not know how to cure many illnesses and diseases, including the common cold.

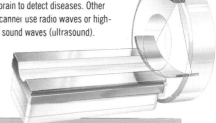

▷ This modern X-ray machine scans a patient's brain to detect diseases. Other types of scanner use radio waves or high-frequency sound waves (ultrasound).

Genetics

You may have noticed that children often look like one or other of their parents – with the same colour eyes or hair, similar facial features, and so on. This is because some characteristics are passed from parents to their children in a process known as heredity. Genetics is the study of heredity.

Characteristics are passed on by genes – tiny sets of 'coded' instructions contained in thread-like structures called chromosomes, found in the centre of every living cell. Every species has its own number of chromosomes; humans have 46 in every cell. One chromosome consists of a single molecule of DNA (deoxyribonucleic acid), which is a chain of about 1000 genes joined together. The DNA of every single plant and animal is different from all others.

Some genes – called 'dominant' genes – mask out the instructions given by other, 'recessive', genes. For example, if a child is born to a father whose recessive gene orders fair hair and a mother whose dominant gene orders dark hair, the child will usually have dark hair.

▷ The DNA molecule consists of two chains of units called nucleotides coiled around each other in a double helix (which looks like a twisted ladder). Each gene is about 250 'rungs' of the DNA ladder. In order to multiply, cells divide in two. When this occurs, the DNA in a cell breaks down to form two matched pairs of chromosomes.

149

Inventions

BC (dates are approximate)

△ People first learned to make fire over a million years ago.

5 million	Tools made from pebbles in Africa
1 million	Fire; wooden spears with charred tips
200 000	Stone hand axes
30 000	Carved bone weapons and tools
13 000	Cave paintings; weaving and leather-making; oil lamps
10 000	Sickles and digging sticks; wooden and mud huts
8000	Plough and flail; pictographic writing; granaries built from mud-bricks
6000	Weaving looms; scales and weights; coiled clay pots
5000	Ox-drawn plough in Mesopotamia
4000	Saw in Egypt

◁ An early flint sickle used for reaping grasses and cereals

3000	Wheels and carts; copper, bronze and gold articles; calendars; hieroglyphic writing; pottery made using potter's wheel and kiln; reed and wooden river boats and rafts
2600	Glassware; soap in Babylonia
2250	Maps in Mesopotamia
2000	Abacus in China; city water supply in Indus River valley
1320	Iron-working in Anatolia
1200	Iron and steel tools and weapons; ocean-going sailing ships
1000	First alphabets; metal coins
600	Iron welding; cast iron
530	Aqueduct (by Romans)

▷ An open-air school in Egypt in about 2000 BC. The scroll held by the teacher is papyrus made from reeds that grow beside the River Nile.

△ In about 1320 BC, the Hittites of Anatolia (modern-day Turkey) began beating wrought-iron weapons from iron ore.

▽ The first metal coins were made between 1000 and 800 BC.

500	Greek map of the world
400	Kites in China
250	Archimedes screw; gun in Greece
150	Parachute; parchment
100	Central heating; brass; waterwheel
59	Newspapers in Rome
47	Encyclopedia of Marcus Terentius Varro
25	Suspension bridge in China

AD (earliest dates are approximate)

▽ An armillary sphere. This device was invented by the Chinese to show the positions of the Sun, the Earth and the other planets.

105	Chinese paper-making
150	Water clocks; surgical instruments
200	Acupuncture; wheelbarrow; veterinary medicine
400	metal stirrups; numeral zero for decimal counting
500	Armillary spheres in China
600	Windmills in Syria
700	Horse collar and harness
725	Mechanical clocks in China
800	Wood-block printing; gunpowder

900	Optical lenses
1000	First use of gunpowder in warfare in China
1100	Gothic cathedrals in Europe
1202	Modern method of counting; accountancy
1250	Glass spectacles by Spina and Armati in Italy
1300	Spinning wheel; linen underwear; canal locks and weirs; cross-staff for navigation
1350	Printing with metal type in Korea; weight-driven clocks
1500	Banknotes in Europe
1550	Quadrant for navigation
1590	Microscope by Janssen in Netherlands
1600	Thermometer; sheet glass for windows and mirrors
1608	Telescope in Netherlands, possibly by Lippershey
1712	First practical steam-engine in UK; glass fibre
1733	Flying shuttle for weaving looms
1745	Chemical battery (Leyden jar)
1764	Spinning jenny by James Hargreaves in UK
1769	Steam-powered car (Cugnot's road carriage) in France
1779	Spinning-mule by Samuel Crompton in UK
1782	James Watt's improved steam-engine in UK
1783	Hot-air balloon by Montgolfiers in France
1792	Volta's first electric battery; gas lighting
1795	Pencil by Conté in France
1796	Vaccination (smallpox) by Jenner in UK

◁ The spinning jenny, invented in 1764 by James Hargreaves. This machine was able to spin several yarns at the same time, unlike the earlier spinning wheel which could spin only one at a time.

▷ In 1609, Galileo used these telescopes to make startling discoveries about the Universe. His telescopes were improved versions of the device invented in the previous year.

◁ Johannes Gutenberg was the first person to print books in Europe using moveable type. He is shown here at his printing press in about 1450, working on the edition of the Bible for which he is famous. Gutenberg did not invent printing. The ancient Chinese first printed books using wooden blocks in about 800 AD, and type (letters and numbers) made of metal was first used for printing in about 1350 in Korea.

1804	Steam locomotive running on rails by Trevithick in UK
1810	Canning process for foods by Appert in France
1815	Miner's safety lamp by Davy in UK
1816	First photographic image on metal plate in France
1820	Mechanical calculating machine by Babbage in UK
1828	Combine harvester by Lane in USA
1829	Typewriter by Burt in USA
1830	First public steam railway (Stockton and Darlington in UK); sewing machine; tarmacadam for road surfacing
1831	Electric generator and transformer by Faraday in UK
1836	Ship's propeller; hypodermic syringe by Pravaz in France
1837	Electric telegraph and code by Morse in USA
1838	Photography on paper by Fox Talbot in UK
1839	Bicycle by MacMillan in UK
1843	Underground railway by Pearson in UK
1844	Anaesthetics for surgery by Wells in USA
1845	Safety match by von Schrotter in Germany
1849	Safety pin; glider (first winged aircraft to carry a person)
1851	Mechanical lift (elevator) by Otis in USA; non-rigid airship
1853	Corrugated iron by Carpentier in France
1855	Refrigerator by Harrison in UK
1856	Synthetic dye; Bessemer Converter for making steel in UK
1859	First oil well; aspirin by Kolbe in Germany
1860	Pasteurization of milk; linoleum
1866	Dynamite; fire extinguisher

▷ The microscope was invented in 1590 by Zacharias Janssen. About 70 years later, Anton van Leeuwenhoek (right) made much more powerful versions and with them he was able to examine tiny animals and bacteria, which had never been seen before.

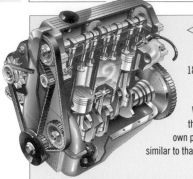

◁ A cutaway view of a modern petrol car engine. The first petrol engine was built by Gottlieb Daimler in 1885 and was used to power a bicycle. It was based on a gas-powered engine invented by Etienne Lenoir in 1862. The diesel engine was developed in 1892 by Rudolf Diesel.

▷ On 17 December 1903, the Wright brothers' Flyer I became the first aeroplane to fly under its own power. It had a petrol engine similar to that invented by Gottlieb Daimler.

1862	Etienne Lenoir's first gas-driven internal-combustion engine in Belgium
1868	Plastics; traffic lights; stapler; margarine in France
1870	Antiseptics for surgery; steam-powered motorcycle
1872	Electric typewriter; jeans by Levi-Strauss in USA
1876	Telephone; carburettor; microphone; carpet sweeper
1877	Edison's sound recording phonograph (gramophone)
1879	Electric light bulb by Edison in USA
1882	Skyscraper; electric power station; electric iron
1884	Fountain pen; large steam turbine; heat-resistant glass
1885	Petrol-driven internal-combustion engine
1887	Contact lenses by Fick in Germany; electric heater
1888	Gramophone record; pneumatic tyre; electric motor (AC)
1889	Photographic film; automatic telephone exchange; electric oven; automatic dishwasher
1892	Reinforced concrete; vacuum flask; diesel engine; escalator; cash register by Burroughs in USA
1893	Zip fastener by Judson in USA; toughened glass
1895	Radio broadcasting; cinema; electric drill; safety razor
1897	Cathode ray tube

▷ Guglielmo Marconi invented radio broadcasting in 1895. By 1901 he was able to send radio messages from one side of the Atlantic to the other.

1900	Rigid airship; loudspeaker; paperclip
1901	Wireless telegraphy; vacuum cleaner
1903	First powered aircraft flight
1905	X-ray machine
1907	Radio valve; fax machine; electric washing machine
1910	Synthetic rubber; neon lamp
1916	Detergents; battle tank
1920	Long-distance air travel
1925	Motorways; TV camera by Baird in UK
1926	Liquid-fuelled rocket; aerosol; Baird's mechanical TV
1928	Electric razor; tape recording; turbojet in UK
1931	Radio telescope; electric guitar; glass fibre
1932	Electron microscope in Germany
1935	Nylon by Carothers in USA
1937	Instant coffee; artificial heart
1938	Photocopier; ball-point pen
1945	Printed circuits; atomic bomb; microwave oven in USA
1946	Electronic computer in USA
1947	Transistor; polaroid instant camera
1950	Human kidney transplant; credit card
1954	Nuclear power station; non-stick pan
1956	Video recorder; optical fibres; heart pacemaker
1958	Microchip; non-stick plastics; epoxy resin adhesive
1960	Laser by Maiman in USA
1964	Word processor; acrylic paint; carbon fibres in UK
1966	Fibre optics; artificial blood by Clark and Gollan in USA
1967	First human heart transplant by Barnard in South Africa
1970	Factory robots; genetic engineering
1972	Pocket calculator in USA
1973	Colour photocopier; X-ray scanning in UK
1975	Desktop computer in USA
1979	Compact disc; ultrasound scanning
1988	Genetic fingerprinting in UK

△ A modern photocopier. The first such machine was invented in 1938.

△ Transistors enabled electronic equipment, including computers, to be made smaller than ever before.

◁ The first integrated circuits, or microchips, were made in 1958. Since then, they have become even smaller.

▷ A mechanical adding machine was invented in 1642. The pocket calculator (right) came 330 years later.

155

Exploring space

The first rockets, invented by the Chinese about 800 years ago, were powered by gunpowder. Most modern rocket engines use liquid fuel, such as kerosene or liquid hydrogen. The fuel is burned with liquid oxygen, producing gases that rush out of the nozzle at high speed and thrust the rocket forward.

▽ The inventor Robert Goddard is now regarded as the man who made space rockets possible. In the 1920s he developed the first liquid-fuelled rockets and eventually built one that travelled faster than the speed of sound. He patented over 200 rocket inventions, many of them well ahead of their time. Yet he was largely ignored during his own lifetime. In 1960, 15 years after his death, the US Government realized the importance of his work and paid $1 000 000 to use the inventions he had patented.

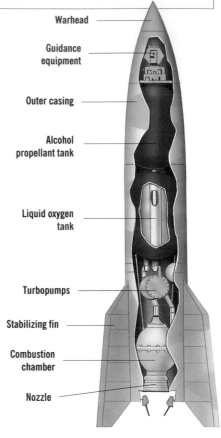

Warhead

Guidance equipment

Outer casing

Alcohol propellant tank

Liquid oxygen tank

Turbopumps

Stabilizing fin

Combustion chamber

Nozzle

△ The V2, developed in Germany in the early 1940s, was one of the first large rockets. It carried an explosive warhead in the nose and was used as a weapon during the Second World War. After the War its inventor, Werner von Braun, worked in the USA on America's space programme.

In order to escape from the pull of the Earth's gravity, a spacecraft must be travelling at over 40 000 km/h. To reach this speed, rocket engines have to be enormously powerful. What is more, the heavier the spacecraft, the more powerful the engines must be.

A single, huge rocket would be too heavy to get into space. Instead, several smaller rockets are stacked on top of each other in what are called stages. The stages ignite in turn to boost the speed of the craft, and they then separate and fall away as their fuel runs out. The craft becomes steadily lighter and travels faster.

Third stage fires to thrust craft into orbit, then separates

Second stage fires, boosts Apollo craft higher and faster, then separates

Stage separation skirt

First stage burns out and falls away

The first craft to enter space was a Soviet satellite, *Sputnik*, which went into orbit around the Earth in October 1957. Four years later, Yuri Gagarin of the USSR became the first astronaut. Since then, rocket technology has developed greatly. Between 1969 and 1972, the USA landed 23 people on the Moon. In 1981, the Space Shuttle began a new phase in the exploration of space.

△ The Saturn V rocket launched the American Apollo astronauts on their missions to the Moon. The rocket had three stages, the first of which provided a thrust of 3.5 million kg. Standing 111 m tall, the Saturn V was the world's tallest rocket, and it carried 3000 tonnes of fuel. The Apollo craft was thrust into Earth orbit just 11 minutes after blasting off from the Kennedy Space Center, Florida.

▽ Communications satellites like the one shown here are used to relay satellite TV programmes direct to homes, and to transmit telephone, telex, fax and computer data from one part of the world to another.

▽ Satellites are used for communications, for collecting weather data, for scientific research and for gathering military information. Below, from left to right, are a scientific satellite, an ocean survey satellite, a military reconnaissance satellite, the Hubble Space Telescope, a weather satellite and a communications satellite.

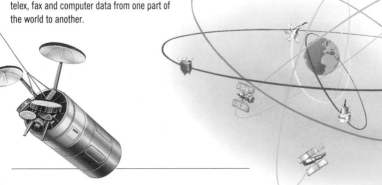

The Space Shuttle

Multi-stage rockets like the Saturn V could be used only once and then discarded. As each one cost millions of dollars to build, this was a huge waste of money.

Men on the Moon

On 21 July 1969, Neil Armstrong became the first person to walk on the Moon. He and Buzz Aldrin landed on the surface in a lunar module, and spent 2 hours there collecting rock and soil samples. They then blasted off again and rejoined the third crewman, Michael Collins, in the command module to return to Earth. That first Moon mission, Apollo 11, cost many millions of dollars. It was followed by six further landings, but no one has set foot on the Moon since 1972.

Shuttle turns around to fire retrorockets to slow down

Prepares to re-enter Earth's atmosphere

Re-enters atmosphere at 25 times the speed of sound. Heatshield reaches over 1800°C

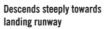

Descends steeply towards landing runway

In 1972 the USA decided to build a craft that could be used again and again. This idea led to the development of the Space Shuttle, which began its first mission on 12 April 1981.

▽ Skylab was a space station launched by the USA in 1973. Astronauts lived on board for up to 84 days. Russian astronauts have since spent up to 365 days aboard their Mir space station.

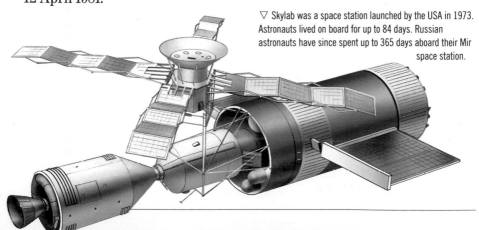

The Shuttle takes off vertically, using three engines of its own, two large booster rockets and a huge, 33-tonne fuel tank. The boosters fall away at a height of 47 km and are recovered and re-used. The fuel tank is released at 110 km and burns up.

The main part of the Shuttle is the orbiter. It is 37.2 m long and has a wingspan of 23.8 m. The forward compartment can carry up to eight people. The upper part is the flight deck, and below are the galley, or kitchen, the toilet and the crew's sleeping quarters.

Most of the orbiter's length is taken up by the payload bay, where the cargo is carried. At the rear are the three engines used during the launch. While in space, the craft manoeuvres using small rockets in the nose and tail.

▷ The Shuttle's huge payload bay can carry 29 tonnes of cargo into space and 14.5 tonnes back to Earth. The craft is often used to take satellites into space and place them in orbit around the Earth using a remote-controlled arm guided by the astronauts. It is even possible to repair faulty satellites in space, or bring them back to Earth.

Glides in to land at 400 km/h. After months of checking, it will be ready to fly again

There are five computers on board, four of which are used to fly the craft at any one time. They check each other's calculations constantly to prevent errors.

△ The orbiter lands rather like a jet airliner, although it descends much more steeply and about 20 times faster. On re-entering the Earth's atmosphere, friction causes the outside of the Shuttle to heat up. To prevent it from burning up, the craft is protected by a special heatshield and by strong carbon material on the nose and wing edges.

Deep space

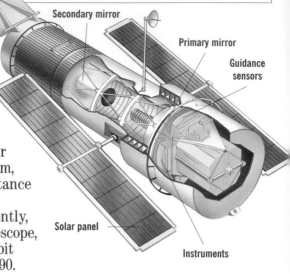

Secondary mirror

Aperture door

Primary mirror

Guidance sensors

Solar panel

Instruments

Because of the vast distances involved, it is not yet possible to send manned spacecraft to explore the far reaches of the Solar System. The outer planets, and stars beyond them, have to be studied from a distance by a variety of Earth-based telescopes and, more recently, by the Hubble Space Telescope, which was placed in orbit around the Earth in 1990. Spacecraft called probes can also be used to fly close to, or even land on, other planets and send information back to Earth as radio signals.

△ The Hubble Space Telescope was launched from the Space Shuttle in April 1990. Soon after, its main mirror was found to be faulty and had to be repaired by astronauts on another Shuttle mission in 1993. It is now sending back fascinating pictures of far-away stars.

△ The Galileo craft was launched in 1989. In 1995 it dropped a small probe into the clouds of Jupiter. This sent back information about the planet before being crushed by Jupiter's intense atmospheric pressure.

The first successful probe was *Luna 3*, which was launched by the USSR in 1959 and flew past the Moon. It sent back the first ever pictures of the Moon's far side. Since then, the American probe *Mariner 10* has flown past Mercury, several Russian *Venera* craft have landed on Venus, and *Viking* probes have visited Mars.

The outer planets have been studied by *Pioneers 10* and *11*, *Voyagers 1* and *2*, and *Galileo*. After flying past Jupiter, Saturn, Uranus and Neptune, in August 1989 *Voyager 2* headed for the edge of the Solar System and towards a neighbouring star, Sirius. If it survives, it will take 368 000 years to get there.

The human body

From the time we are born until we die, our bodies never stop working. Like all living things, the human body is made up of tiny building blocks, called cells. There are many different types of them. Each second, millions of our cells die and are replaced, but some last our whole lifetime.

◁ Bones form a skeleton which holds the body rigid, gives shape to the softer parts, and protects vital organs. It is also an anchor for the muscles, which move the different parts of the body. There are 206 bones in an adult skeleton. The largest bone is in the thigh and the smallest is in the ear.

Muscle

Muscles are made up of tissue containing thin, flexible fibres. Each fibre is connected to a nerve which stimulates the muscle to move. Muscle tissue also has many blood vessels which carry food matter to be broken down by the muscle for energy.

Fibre

Skeletal muscle

◁ Your body has about 650 muscles in three main types – skeletal, visceral and cardiac. Skeletal muscles move us around. They are attached to the skeleton by tendons. This type of muscle is also known as voluntary muscle because we are able to control them.
Visceral or smooth muscle is found in the walls of the stomach and intestines, where it helps to push food through the body, and in the blood vessels. Cardiac muscle is found only in the heart. Both visceral and cardiac muscles are known as involuntary muscles, because they work without us consciously controlling them.

Bones and joints

There are two types of bone – compact and spongy. Compact bone forms the outer layer of all bones. Spongy bone is found in short or fat bones, and at the ends of long bones, such as the femur (thigh bone). Spongy bone contains red bone marrow, which manufactures blood cells. Inside long bones are hollow spaces containing yellow bone marrow, a type of fat.

Bones are linked together by joints. Most are either hinge joints, like the knee and elbow, which allow movement in one direction, or ball-and-socket joints, such as in the hip and shoulder, which allow much more movement. Fixed joints, such as those between the bones in the skull, cannot move. Joints that move a lot are padded with gristle, or cartilage, and lubricated by a slippery liquid called synovial fluid.

Spongy bone

Compact bone

The nervous system

The brain is the body's control centre and, with the spinal cord, makes up the central nervous system. Nerves spread from the brain carrying messages (tiny electrical impuses) to and from these central areas.

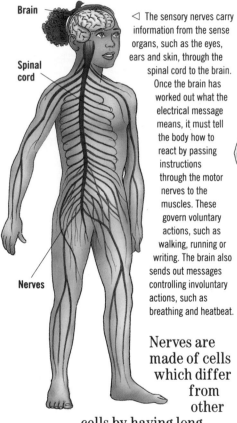

Brain

Spinal cord

Nerves

◁ The sensory nerves carry information from the sense organs, such as the eyes, ears and skin, through the spinal cord to the brain. Once the brain has worked out what the electrical message means, it must tell the body how to react by passing instructions through the motor nerves to the muscles. These govern voluntary actions, such as walking, running or writing. The brain also sends out messages controlling involuntary actions, such as breathing and heatbeat.

Nerves are made of cells which differ from other cells by having long extentions, like the branches of a tree, which link them together. Nerves can carry messages to and from the brain at up to 430 km/h. There are up to 10 000 000 000 nerve cells in the brain alone.

The digestive system

When you eat, food passes through the digestive system and is broken down into small chemicals that your body can use for growth, repair and energy.

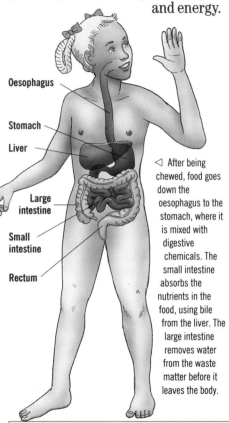

Oesophagus

Stomach

Liver

Large intestine

Small intestine

Rectum

◁ After being chewed, food goes down the oesophagus to the stomach, where it is mixed with digestive chemicals. The small intestine absorbs the nutrients in the food, using bile from the liver. The large intestine removes water from the waste matter before it leaves the body.

Reproduction

Every human starts life as a single, tiny cell – an egg that has been fertilized by a sperm. The cell divides and multiplies, and within

| Conception – egg fertilized by sperm | After 48 hours, embryo has four cells | After 3 days, embryo enters the mother's womb |

Heart and blood

The heart is a muscular organ that pumps blood around the body. It consists of four chambers. The lower two are called ventricles and the upper two, atria.

Main veins
Aorta
Pulmonary arteries

▷ When it beats, the heart goes through these actions: **1** blood enters the atria (red is oxygenated blood from the lungs via the pulmonary veins; blue is deoxygenated blood entering via the main veins, having passed around the body); **2** the atria contract and push blood into the ventricles; **3** the ventricles contract and push oxygenated blood into the aorta (main artery), and deoxygenated blood into the pulmonary arteries leading to the lungs; **4** all four chambers relax and the atria fill up with blood again.

1 2 3 4

Blood is a liquid containing millions of cells. There are three types of blood cells: red cells which contain a protein called haemoglobin that carries oxygen; white cells which fight off disease; and platelets which make the blood thicken and clot around a cut or scratch.

▷ Blood travels around the body in three types of blood vessels. Arteries (**1**) carry blood away from the heart. Veins (**2**) take blood back to the heart. Capillaries (**3**) are thin vessels through which oxygen and dissolved food pass outward to the body's cells, and carbon dioxide and waste pass inward. Capillaries lead off small arteries and finally join up again to form small veins.

Heart
Vein
Lung
Kidney
Ureter
Bladder
Artery

▷ The urinary system consists of the kidneys, bladder and ureters. The kidneys remove waste products from the blood and pass them through the ureters to the bladder, where they are stored in the form of a liquid called urine.

3 days it has grown to about 32 cells. By the time a baby is born, about 40 weeks after fertilization, it consists of billions of cells.

After 5 weeks, baby is about 10 mm long

By 8 weeks, major body parts are formed

By 12 weeks, baby is about 13 cm long

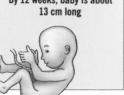

Respiratory system

Each time we breath in, or inhale, air enters our lungs. The lungs take oxygen from the air and pass it into the blood, which is pumped to all parts of the body by the heart. The body's cells need oxygen to keep them alive.

At the same time, the lungs remove carbon dioxide from stale, deoxygenated blood. The carbon dioxide then leaves the body when we breathe out, or exhale.

The senses

You have five senses: sight, hearing, taste, smell and touch. Your sense organs gather information about the world around you and pass it to the brain via the nerves. Your brain then interprets the information.

Sight

Light entering the eye is focused by the cornea, a transparent 'window' at the front, and by the lens behind it. They refract the light rays and make them converge. Between the cornea and the lens is a coloured disc, the iris, with a hole in the centre called the pupil. The size of the pupil can be adjusted to allow in more light or less. When you look at an object, the image of it is focused on to the retina at the back of the eye. The retina contains millions of light-sensitive cells, called rods and cones. They convert the image into nervous impulses which are sent along the optic nerve to the brain. Where the optic nerve joins the eye, there are no rods or cones; this point is called the blind spot. The fovea is an area densely packed with cone cells. When you look closely at an object, the fovea helps you to see it clearly.

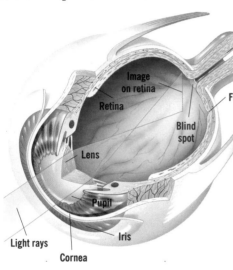

Optic nerve
Image on retina
Retina
Fovea
Blind spot
Lens
Pupil
Iris
Light rays
Cornea

△ The image of an object formed on the retina is upside-down. This is corrected by the brain, which interprets the information it receives from the retina as vision.

Hearing

The flaps of skin on the sides of your head help to funnel sound into a tube called the outer ear. At the end of this tube is the ear-drum, a thin, tightly stretched piece of skin which vibrates when sound waves reach it. Inside the middle ear, the vibrations push the tiny stapes bone against the wall of the cochlea – the main part of the inner ear. The cochlea is filled with a thick liquid and contains thousands of sensitive hairs. Vibrations in the liquid move the hairs, triggering nerve impulses which the brain interprets as sound.

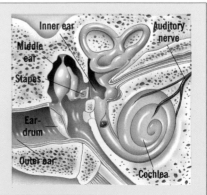

Inner ear
Auditory nerve
Middle ear
Stapes
Ear-drum
Outer ear
Cochlea

Taste and smell

The tongue and nose are closely linked – much of what you taste is actually the smell entering the nose. Hollows in your nose contain sensitive cells that detect chemical substances and, like the taste buds on the tongue, send impulses along nerves to the brain.

Bitter

Sour

Salty

Sweet

◁ The tongue is a highly flexible piece of muscle. On the tongue are taste buds, which are sensitive cells that recognize four basic flavours – sweet, sour, bitter and salty.

Touch

The skin contains many nerve endings. Some are touch receptors, which send impulses to the brain when the skin makes contact with something. Others are pain receptors which send impulses when any sensation, such as temperature or pressure is too great. Some parts of the body have more nerve endings than others. Your fingertips, for example, are more sensitive than the skin on your knees.

The skin
Skin is a flexible organ which covers the body, protecting it from harmful bacteria and ultra-violet rays. It is waterproof – keeping body fluids in and water out. Sweat glands in the skin produce sweat to cool down the body when it is too hot.

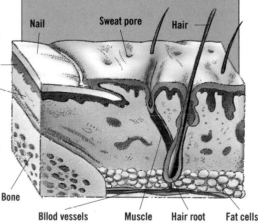

Nail   Sweat pore   Hair

Epidermis

Dermis

Bone

Bllod vessels   Muscle   Hair root   Fat cells

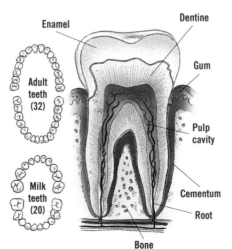

Enamel

Dentine

Adult teeth (32)

Gum

Pulp cavity

Milk teeth (20)

Cementum

Root

Bone

Teeth

During our life, we have two sets of teeth. Milk teeth appear at the age of 7 months and are all through by about 2 years. Adult teeth begin to appear at the age of 6 to 7 years and push out the milk teeth as they grow.

◁ The enamel of a tooth is the hardest substance in the body. The dentine beneath it is similar to enamel, only softer. Within the dentine is the pulp cavity. It is filled with tissue called pulp and contains blood vessels and nerve endings. The root is the part of the tooth that is fixed into the jaw. It is held firmly in place by a substance called cementum.

165

Facts and figures

- The acceleration due to gravity (the rate at which falling objects accelerate towards the Earth) is 9.81 m per second.

Light and sound
- The colours of the rainbow are red, orange, yellow, green, blue, indigo, violet.
- The speed of light in a vacuum is 299 792 458 m per second.
- The speed of sound in dry air at 0°C is 331 m per second. It increases if the air temperature increases.
- Humans can hear sound at frequencies between 20 and 20 000 Hertz.

Temperature scales
Thermometers measure temperature on two scales – Celsius (or Centigrade) and Fahrenheit.
- To change Celsius to Fahrenheit, multiply by 9, divide by 5 and then add 32.
- To change Fahrenheit to Celsius, subtract 32, multiply by 5 and divide by 9.
- Water freezes at 0°C or 32°F, and boils at 100°C, 212°F.
- Absolute zero is the lowest possible temperature, at which all atoms and molecules are thought to stop moving. It is calculated to be -273.15°C.

Periodic table of the elements

1 H — Atomic number
H — Chemical symbol

Metals
Metalloids
Non-metals

1 H																	2 He
3 Li	4 Be											5 B	6 C	7 N	8 O	9 F	10 Ne
11 Na	12 Mg											13 Al	14 Si	15 P	16 S	17 Cl	18 Ar
19 K	20 Ca	21 Sc	22 Ti	23 V	24 Cr	25 Mn	26 Fe	27 Co	28 Ni	29 Cu	30 Zn	31 Ga	32 Ge	33 As	34 Se	35 Br	36 Kr
37 Rb	38 Sr	39 Y	40 Zr	41 Nb	42 Mo	43 Tc	44 Ru	45 Rh	46 Pd	47 Ag	48 Cd	49 In	50 Sn	51 Sb	52 Te	53 I	54 Xe
55 Cs	56 Ba	57 La	72 Hf	73 Ta	74 W	75 Re	76 Os	77 Ir	78 Pt	79 Au	80 Hg	81 Tl	82 Pb	83 Bi	84 Po	85 At	86 Rn
87 Fr	88 Ra	89 Ac															

58 Ce	59 Pr	60 Nd	61 Pm	62 Sm	63 Eu	64 Gd	65 Tb	66 Dy	67 Ho	68 Er	69 Tm	70 Yb	71 Lu				
90 Th	91 Pa	92 U	93 Np	94 Pu	95 Am	96 Cm	97 Bk	98 Cf	99 Es	100 Fm	101 Md	102 No	103 Lw	104 Unq	105 Unp	106 Unh	107 Uns	108 Uno	109 Une

Temperatures

15 million °C centre of the Sun
5500 °C surface of the Sun

-39 °C mercury becomes solid
-88 °C coldest temperature recorded on Earth (Antarctica)

4500 °C centre of the Earth
1063 °C gold melts
660 °C aluminium melts
600 °C gas cooker flame
250 °C wood catches fire
100 °C water boils
58 °C hottest temperature recorded on Earth (Libyan desert)
37 °C normal body temperature
0 °C water freezes

-196 °C air becomes liquid
-230 °C surface of the planet Pluto
-273.15 °C absolute zero

Atomic no.	Chemical symbol	Element									
1	H	Hydrogen	27	Co	Cobalt	55	Cs	Caesium	83	Bi	Bismuth
2	He	Helium	28	Ni	Nickel	56	Ba	Barium	84	Po	Polonium
3	Li	Lithium	29	Cu	Copper	57	La	Lanthanum	85	At	Astatine
4	Be	Berylium	30	Zn	Zinc	58	Ce	Cerium	86	Rn	Radon
5	B	Boron	31	Ga	Gallium	59	Pr	Praseodymium	87	Fr	Francium
6	C	Carbon	32	Ge	Germanium	60	Nd	Neodymium	88	Ra	Radium
7	N	Nitrogen	33	As	Arsenic	61	Pm	Promethium	89	Ac	Actinium
8	O	Oxygen	34	Se	Selenium	62	Sm	Samarium	90	Th	Thorium
9	F	Fluorine	35	Br	Bromine	63	Eu	Europium	91	Pa	Protactinium
10	Ne	Neon	36	Kr	Krypton	64	Gd	Gadolinium	92	U	Uranium
11	Na	Sodium	37	Rb	Rubidium	65	Tb	Terbium	93	Np	Neptunium
12	Mg	Magnesium	38	Sr	Strontium	66	Dy	Dysprosium	94	Pu	Plutonium
13	Al	Aluminium	39	Y	Yttrium	67	Ho	Holmium	95	Am	Americium
14	Si	Silicon	40	Zr	Zirconium	68	Er	Erbium	96	Cm	Curium
15	P	Phosphorus	41	Nb	Niobium	69	Tm	Thulium	97	Bk	Berkelium
16	S	Sulphur	42	Mo	Molybdenum	70	Yb	Ytterbium	98	Cf	Californium
17	Cl	Chlorine	43	Tc	Technetium	71	Lu	Lutetium	99	Es	Einsteinium
18	Ar	Argon	44	Ru	Ruthenium	72	Hf	Hafnium	100	Fm	Fermium
19	K	Potassium	45	Rh	Rhodium	73	Ta	Tantalum	101	Md	Mendelevium
20	Ca	Calcium	46	Pd	Paladium	74	W	Tungsten	102	No	Nobelium
21	Sc	Scandium	47	Ag	Silver	75	Re	Rhenium	103	Lw	Lawrencium
22	Ti	Titanium	48	Cd	Cadmium	76	Os	Osmium	104	Unq	Unnilquadium
23	V	Vanadium	49	In	Indium	77	Ir	Iridium	105	Unp	Unnilpentium
24	Cr	Chromium	50	Sn	Tin	78	Pt	Platinum	106	Unh	Unnilhexium
25	Mn	Manganese	51	Sb	Antimony	79	Au	Gold	107	Uns	Unnilseptium
26	Fe	Iron	52	Te	Telurium	80	Hg	Mercury	108	Uno	Unniloctium
			53	I	Iodine	81	Tl	Thallium	109	Une	Unnilennium
			54	Xe	Xenon	82	Pb	Lead			

Area and volume ($\pi = 3.1416$)

Circle
Radius r
Diameter d = 2 x r

Circumference =
$2 \times \pi \times r$
Area = $\pi \times r^2$

Triangle
Sides a, b, c
Height h

Perimeter = a + b + c
Area = ½ x b x h

Rectangle
Sides a, b

a

b

Perimeter = 2 x (a + b)
Area = a x b

Cylinder
Radius r
Height h

h

r

Surface area (excluding ends)
= $2 \times \pi \times r \times h$
Volume = $\pi \times r^2 \times h$

Cone
Radius r
Height h
Side l

l

h

r

Surface area (excluding base)
= $\pi \times r \times l$
Volume = $\frac{1}{3} \times \pi \times r^2 \times l$

Rectangular block
Sides a, b, c

a

b

c

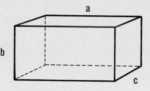

Surface area = 2 x (a x b) +
2 x (b x c) + 2 x (a x c)
Volume = a x b x c

Sphere
Radius r
Diameter d = 2 x r

d

r

Surface area = $4 \times \pi \times r^2$
Volume = $(4 \times \pi \times r^3) \div 3$

Computer terms

- **Binary** Computers use the binary system in which numbers are written as a combination of 0s and 1s (see page 234).
- **Bit** One single binary digit (a 0 or a 1), the smallest unit of computer storage.
- **Byte** A fixed number of bits – usually the number needed to define one character. For example, the byte 01000001 represents the letter A. One megabyte is 1 048 576 bytes.
- **CPU (central processing unit)** The 'brain' in a computer.
- **Disk** A device on which information is stored – especially a floppy disk or a hard disk.
- **RAM (random access memory)** Computer memory that keeps the information it holds only when the computer is switched on.
- **ROM (read-only memory)** Memory that keeps its information even when the computer is switched off.

CPU
(inside)

Keyboard

Disk drives

Mouse

NATURAL HISTORY

There are known to be about 1 400 000 species of plants, animals and other living things on Earth. Many biologists believe that there are countless other species that have not yet been discovered, and that the real total may be more than 10 000 000.

All life depends on plants, which recycle the gases in the atmosphere to produce the oxygen that is vital to life, and provide many animals with food.

In each habitat – forest, desert, sea or any other – the smallest organisms are eaten by larger ones, and they in turn are eaten by still larger creatures. Every species has its place and depends in some way on the others. So, if a single species becomes extinct, the whole balance of the habitat may be threatened.

▷ A food pyramid showing what eats what in the Arctic. The polar bear at the top depends on all the other organisms – the seals it eats, the haddock the seals eat, and the small fish, the animal plankton and the tiny plant-plankton right at the bottom.

▽ Tropical rainforests are the richest habitats on Earth and they contain more living species than any other.

Classification of living things

Classification is the grouping together of living things. Those with similar characteristics are placed in the same group. The largest groups are the five kingdoms. All of the organisms in a kingdom have some common features. Within a kingdom there are smaller groups containing organisms that have more features in common. These are called phyla (singular, phylum) in the case of

Monerans

The moneran kingdom contains about 4000 simple organisms, such as bacteria, that are neither plants nor animals.

- Bacteria
- Blue-green algae

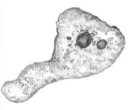

Protists

There are about 50 000 species of protists. They are simple organisms that have some characteristics of both plants and animals.

- Amoebas
- Diatoms
- Euglenas
- Golden algae
- Fire algae
- Yellow-green algae

Fungi

Fungi include mushrooms, toadstools and moulds, which are neither plants nor animals. There are over 100 000 species.

- True fungi
- Slime moulds

Key to classification charts

	Kingdom
	Division or phylum
	Class
	Sub-class
	Order

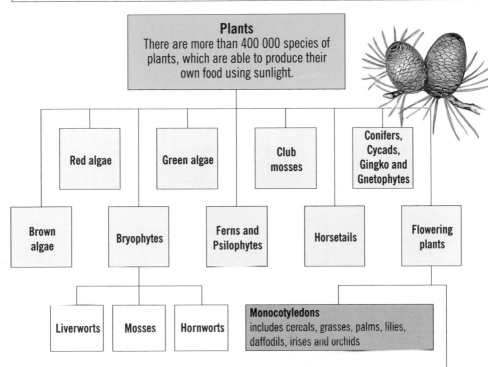

Plants
There are more than 400 000 species of plants, which are able to produce their own food using sunlight.

Red algae

Green algae

Club mosses

Conifers, Cycads, Gingko and Gnetophytes

Brown algae

Bryophytes

Ferns and Psilophytes

Horsetails

Flowering plants

Liverworts

Mosses

Hornworts

Monocotyledons
includes cereals, grasses, palms, lilies, daffodils, irises and orchids

animals, or divisions for other kingdoms. Next come classes, sub-classes, orders, families, genera and species – the smallest unit of classification. Only members of the same species are able to breed among themselves and produce offspring that can also breed.

Dicotyledons
includes deciduous trees (such as oak, beech, walnut and birch), fruit trees, food plants (such as potatoes, beans, cabbages and carrots), and a huge variety of bushes, shrubs and flowers (such as roses, tulips, ivies, nettles, honeysuckles, daisies, heathers, rhododendrons, poppies' and geraniums)

What are you?
As a human, you belong to the Animal kingdom, Chordate phylum and Mammal class. You are in the Primate order, together with apes and monkeys. Your family is the Hominids, your genus is *Homo* and your species is *sapiens.* For the sake of simplicity, you are known as *Homo sapiens.*

171

Animals

This is the largest kingdom; it may contain more than 10 million species. Unlike plants, animals are able to move around.

Sponges	Coelen-terates	Comb jellies	Flatworms	Ribbon worms	Round-worms

Coelenterates
Corals
Hydras
Jellyfishes
Sea
 anemones

Flatworms
Flukes
Free-living
 flatworms
Tapeworms

Insects	Arachnids	Crustaceans

Insects
Bees, wasps and ants
Beetles
Butterflies and moths
Cockroaches
Damselflies and
 dragonflies
Earwigs
Fleas
Flies, gnats and
 mosquitoes
Grasshoppers,
 crickets and locusts
Greenfly, pond skaters
 and other bugs
Lacewings and
 antlions
Lice
Mantids
Mayflies
Scorpionflies
Springtails
Stick insects
Stoneflies
Termites

Crustaceans
Barnacles
Branchiopods
Crabs and sea
 spiders
Flea shrimps
Lobsters, prawns
 and shrimps
Sea lice and wood
 lice
Water fleas

Arachnids
Harvestmen
King crabs
Mites
Pseudoscorpions
Scorpions
Spiders
Ticks

Albatrosses and
 petrels
Cranes and coots
Cuckoos and road-
 runners
Ducks, geese and
 swans
Eagles, hawks and
 vultures
Gulls, terns and
 waders

Herons, stalks and
 flamingoes
Kingfishers, bee-
 eaters and hornbills
Nightjars, swifts and
 hummingbirds
Ostriches, emus, kiwis
 and rheas
Owls
Parrots, woodpeckers
 and toucans

Pelicans, cormorants
 and gannets
Penguins
Pheasants, turkeys
 and jungle fowl
Perching birds
 (includes swallows,
 crows, robins, finches,
 warblers, thrushes,
 tits, starlings, wrens)
Pigeons and doves

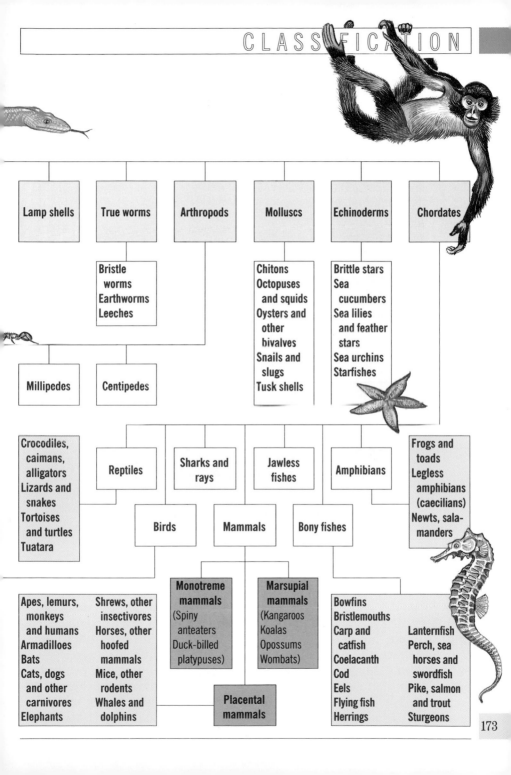

Lamp shells	True worms	Arthropods	Molluscs	Echinoderms	Chordates

Bristle
worms
Earthworms
Leeches

Chitons
Octopuses
and squids
Oysters and
other
bivalves
Snails and
slugs
Tusk shells

Brittle stars
Sea
cucumbers
Sea lilies
and feather
stars
Sea urchins
Starfishes

Millipedes	Centipedes

Crocodiles,
caimans,
alligators
Lizards and
snakes
Tortoises
and turtles
Tuatara

Reptiles	Sharks and rays	Jawless fishes	Amphibians

Frogs and
toads
Legless
amphibians
(caecilians)
Newts, sala-
manders

Birds	Mammals	Bony fishes

Monotreme mammals
(Spiny
anteaters
Duck-billed
platypuses)

Marsupial mammals
(Kangaroos
Koalas
Opossums
Wombats)

Apes, lemurs,
monkeys
and humans
Armadilloes
Bats
Cats, dogs
and other
carnivores
Elephants

Shrews, other
insectivores
Horses, other
hoofed
mammals
Mice, other
rodents
Whales and
dolphins

Bowfins
Bristlemouths
Carp and
catfish
Coelacanth
Cod
Eels
Flying fish
Herrings

Lanternfish
Perch, sea
horses and
swordfish
Pike, salmon
and trout
Sturgeons

Placental mammals

Evolution

The geological time scale
The Earth's history is divided into a number of periods. (mya = million years ago)

Pre-Cambrian	4600–570 mya
Cambrian	570–500 mya
Ordovician	500–435 mya
Silurian	435–395 mya
Devonian	395–345 mya
Carboniferous	345–280 mya
Permian	280–230 mya
Triassic	230–195 mya
Jurassic	195–141 mya
Cretaceous	141–65 mya
Tertiary	65–2 mya
Quaternary	2 mya–present

The plants and animals that lived on Earth millions of years ago were different from those of today. The process by which those early life forms developed and changed to become the plants and animals we see today is called evolution.

When the Earth was first made, about 4600 million years ago, it was covered with hot, molten rock and there were no living things at all.

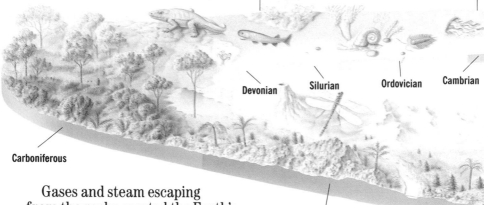

Devonian Silurian Ordovician Cambrian

Carboniferous

Permian

Gases and steam escaping from the rocks created the Earth's first atmosphere. After many millions of years, the planet's surface began to cool and a thin crust formed.

Water filled the hollows in the crust to make the first lakes and seas, and it was there that the earliest living things developed, over 3500 million years ago. They were probably tiny, simple organisms called bacteria.

When early plants grew in the seas about 1900 million years ago, they gradually produced enough oxygen to make the air breathable. Some 570 million years ago, animals with hard parts evolved. The remains of some of them have been preserved as fossils, which give us clues to the Earth's past.

The death of the dinosaurs

Dinosaurs were the dominant creatures on Earth during the Jurassic and Cretaceous periods. They were reptiles, and there were hundreds of different species of them in all shapes and sizes. Some fed only on plants, while others ate meat – including the flesh of the plant-eating dinosaurs and other animals that were living at the time.

Around 65 million years ago, at the end of the Cretaceous period, the dinosaurs and many other reptiles and plants died out.

No one knows why this happened. The most likely reason seems to be that a huge meteorite from space struck the Earth with immense force. This could have set off wildfires, giant tsunami, and a cloud of dust that rose up into the atmosphere causing the climate to change dramatically. All of these effects could have combined to wipe out the dinosaurs and other life forms.

After the death of the dinosaurs, more and more mammals appeared, and they have since come to dominate the Earth.

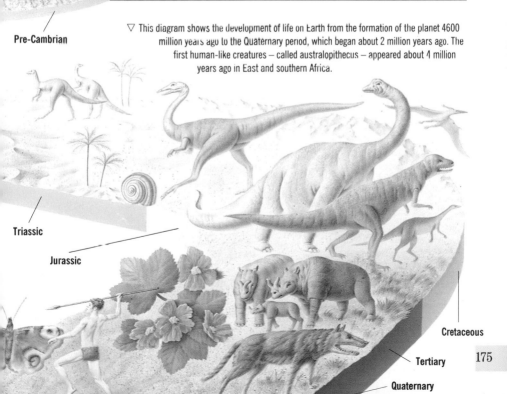

▽ This diagram shows the development of life on Earth from the formation of the planet 4600 million years ago to the Quaternary period, which began about 2 million years ago. The first human-like creatures – called australopithecus – appeared about 4 million years ago in East and southern Africa.

Pre-Cambrian

Triassic

Jurassic

Cretaceous

Tertiary

Quaternary

175

Darwin's theory

Iguana

Finches from different islands

Giant tortoise

◁ △ Darwin developed his theory of evolution after seeing many unusual plants and animals in the Galapagos Islands, off South America. Each island has its own species of finch, which has developed through adaptation to the habitat and the food available on that island.

In 1859, the English scientist Charles Darwin published a book called 'On the Origin of Species by Means of Natural Selection'. In the book, he put forward the idea of evolution – that the life we see on Earth now has developed over millions of years.

This was not a new idea: the Frenchman Jean-Baptiste de Lamarck first suggested it in 1806. What was new was Darwin's explanation of why living things evolve. He said that it was because of two things: adaptation and natural selection.

In a species with millions of individual plants or animals, there are always some individuals with slightly different characteristics from the rest. Usually, these differences have no use, but some may give an individual an advantage and help it to survive in a particular type of environment.

Over many generations, these useful differences – or adaptations – spread through the entire species living in that area. The effect of this is that a new species is created. It is different from the original species still living in other areas where the adaptations did not suit the environment and so were not useful.

According to Darwin, natural selection decides whether a species survives or becomes extinct. For example, if a number of different species of animals depend on a particular type of food, there may not always be enough to go round. If that food were in short supply for a long time, only the species best adapted to obtaining it would survive while other species would die out. Perhaps animals with a long neck would be able to reach food higher in the trees when all the food lower down has been eaten, and they would survive. Over many generations, the adaptation that produced a long neck would spread through the species, passing from parents to offspring.

▽ All the birds we see today may be descended from this creature, Archaeopteryx. It lived about 150 million years ago and was the first animal to have feathers.

Convergent evolution

Sometimes evolution makes different species look like each other. For example, dolphins and penguins are very different creatures, but they have developed the same streamlined shape because it is ideal for moving fast through water.

▽ This diagram is an evolutionary tree. It shows how all animals may have evolved from the first simple organisms.

The fossil record

Fossils are the remains of plants and animals that lived millions of years ago and have been preserved in rocks.

About 200 years ago, people began discovering the fossils of creatures that no longer existed, including the fossilized bones of dinosaurs. Since then, scientists have tried to piece together parts of the fossil record and show how living things have evolved.

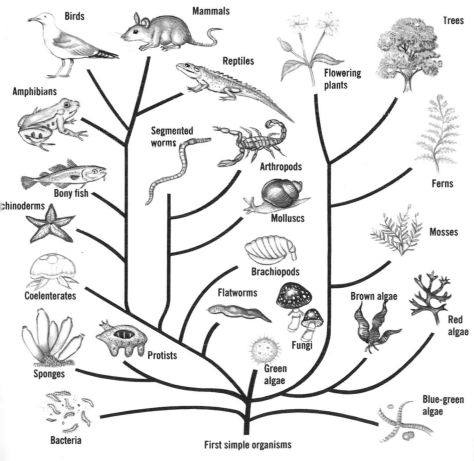

Birds

Mammals

Trees

Reptiles

Flowering plants

Amphibians

Segmented worms

Arthropods

Ferns

Bony fish

Echinoderms

Molluscs

Mosses

Coelenterates

Brachiopods

Flatworms

Brown algae

Red algae

Protists

Fungi

Sponges

Green algae

Blue-green algae

Bacteria

First simple organisms

Conservation

Many species of plants and animals on our planet are at risk, and in most cases they are threatened by human beings. The most common cause of extinction is loss of habitat – the places where wild animals and plants live are taken over or altered by people.

The most famous example of this is the Amazon rainforest in Brazil. Every day vast areas of rainforest are cleared to make room for farms, roads and towns. Many thousands of species could be wiped out and lost forever unless the destruction of the forest is halted.

There are many other examples: the giant panda has been pushed out of large areas of its natural habitat in northern China; the ploughing of the North American prairies has deprived the black-footed ferret of its home; and the Californian condor is being hunted to extinction by farmers.

Hunting has also been responsible for the extinction of many species in the past, and many others are threatened now.

◁ Many Californian condors have been hunted and killed, and there are now very few left. Unless they can be bred in captivity they may soon become extinct.

The Siamese crocodile has been hunted for its skin and is now extinct in the wild. It survives only on crocodile farms in Thailand. The North American red wolf has suffered a similar fate: there are now very few left except in zoos.

Not all the news is bad, though; there are some success stories in conservation. A few years ago, the numbers of both elephants and rhinos in Africa were falling fast as a result of poaching. Now, thanks to better protection for the animals and a ban on the trade in rhino horn and elephant ivory, there are many more of them.

◁ The Javan rhinoceros is almost extinct. It once lived in the dense forests of Indonesia, but hunters killed so many that in 1990 there were only about 50 left. They are protected now, but poachers still kill them for their horn.

In the 1970s, Project Tiger was begun in an attempt to prevent tigers being hunted to extinction in India, Nepal and Bangladesh. Eight large nature reserves were set up.

◁ Tigers are in danger because their jungle homes have been destroyed, they have been hunted for their skins and killed by farmers who accuse them of killing livestock.

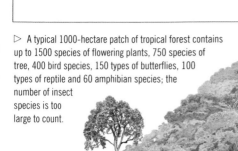

▷ A typical 1000-hectare patch of tropical forest contains up to 1500 species of flowering plants, 750 species of tree, 400 bird species, 150 types of butterflies, 100 types of reptile and 60 amphibian species; the number of insect species is too large to count.

The vital rainforests

The rainforests of South and Central America, South-east Asia and central Africa contain at least half of all the world's plant and animal species. Yet these forests are being destroyed or damaged at the rate of about 50 000 hectares each day. Almost half of the world's rainforests have disappeared in the last 50 years.

Most of the destruction is caused by poor people desperately trying to find land for farming. They clear and burn an area of forest and plant their crops. But after 2 or 3 years the soil loses its fertility and produces fewer crops, and the people move on to clear a new area of forest. In Central America, millions of hectares of forest have also been cleared to raise beef cattle for cheap hamburgers.

The tigers live there in safety, and the money paid by visitors to the reserves helps to pay for their running costs. Project Tiger has been a great success, although people are worried that tigers may once again be at risk from poachers.

One other animal that has been saved from extinction is Przwalski's horse – the only remaining wild horse. There were only a few of them left when Prague Zoo began breeding them. Now their future is much more certain.

△ Przwalski's horse

∇ An area of rainforest is cut and burned. When the vegetation has been removed, a single rainstorm can wash away 185 tonnes of topsoil from a single hectare.

179

Facts and figures

Animals

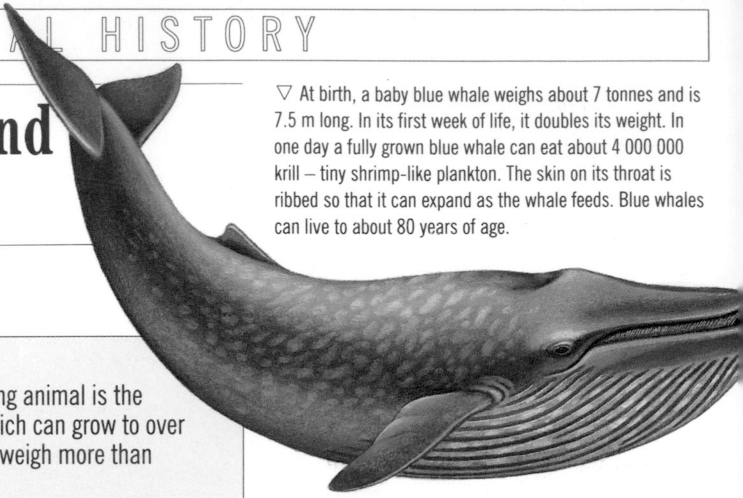

▽ At birth, a baby blue whale weighs about 7 tonnes and is 7.5 m long. In its first week of life, it doubles its weight. In one day a fully grown blue whale can eat about 4 000 000 krill – tiny shrimp-like plankton. The skin on its throat is ribbed so that it can expand as the whale feeds. Blue whales can live to about 80 years of age.

Largest
- The largest living animal is the blue whale, which can grow to over 33 m long and weigh more than 170 tonnes.
- The largest land animal is the African elephant. It can grow up to 4 m high and almost 11 tonnes in weight.
- The largest bird is the ostrich, at 130 kg. Among flying birds, the largest is the kori bustard which can weigh 18 kg.
- The biggest reptile is the saltwater crocodile. It grows to 5 m long and 1 tonne in weight.
- The largest insect is the goliath beetle at 110 mm long and weighing 100 g.
- The biggest fish – the whale shark – is up to 18 m long and weighs 40 tonnes.
- The largest mollusc is the giant squid, at 17.4 m long.

Smallest
- The bumblebee bat is the smallest mammal. Its wingspan is 150 mm and it weighs only 1.5 g.
- The smallest bird is the bee hummingbird, which is 57 mm long and weighs 1.6 g.

▷ Hummingbirds beat their wings at up to 80 times a second. They can hover on one spot while they suck nectar from flowers with their long tongues. They use up so much energy that they must eat half their own body weight in food every day.

▷ There are two species of elephants – the African elephant (shown here) and the smaller Indian elephant. An adult African elephant needs about 150 kg of food and 90 litres of water a day. Elephants are the only mammals that cannot jump – their leg muscles are not strong enough to lift their weight into the air. Elephants flap their ears to keep themselves cool.

- Among reptiles, the smallest creatures are geckos. Some are only 18 mm long.
- The smallest fish is the dwarf pygmy goby at 7.5 mm in length.
- The fairy fly is the smallest insect – an adult is only 0.02 mm long.

Tallest and longest

- The tallest land animal is the giraffe, which can measure 6 m from the ground to the tips of its horns.
- The longest mammal is the blue whale, at 33 m long.
- The reticulated python, at 10 m, is the longest land animal.

- The longest fish is the oarfish, at 14 m.
- The longest insect is the giant stick insect, which measures 380 mm.
- The Galapagos giant tortoise is the tallest reptile, standing 1.2 m high.

◁ Giant tortoises live on the Galapagos Islands in the Pacific Ocean. Each island has its own type of giant tortoise; each type has a different shell shape.

Most poisonous

- An Australian jellyfish called the sea wasp is the most poisonous creature. Its venom works so quickly that victims usually die a few minutes after being stung.
- The most poisonous land animal is the funnelweb spider of southern Australia. Its bite is deadly, and there is no effective treatment.
- The black-headed sea snake is the most poisonous reptile.
- Among fish, the stonefish horrida is the most venomous. It has spines that inject its victims with poison.

Fastest

- The fastest animal of all is the spine-tailed swift, which can fly at over 170 km/h.
- Peregrine falcons can reach speeds of 360 km/h when diving.
- The fastest land animal is the cheetah, which can run at 100 km/h over short distances.

▷ Cheetahs have long legs and a flexible spine. These help them to outrun gazelles and antelopes, which they hunt for food.

Strangest

- Perhaps the strangest creatures are the monotreme mammals, including the duck-billed platypus and echidna, or spiny anteater. Unlike other mammals, monotremes lay eggs. They also have spurs on their hind legs armed with poison for fighting off predators.

◁ Duck-billed platypuses live in south-eastern Australia and Tasmania.

181

Plants and fungi

Largest and tallest
- The largest plant is the 'General Sherman' tree, a giant redwood in the Sequoia National Park, USA. At one point it measures over 25.3 m around its trunk, and is thought to weigh over 2000 tonnes.
- The tallest living tree is a coast redwood in the western USA, which measures 111.25 m.
- The largest flowering plant is the stinking corpse lily, with blooms up to 0.91 m across.
- The largest ground-growing fungus is the giant puffball, which grows up to 1.94 m across.

▷ The giant redwood tree of California, USA.

Smallest
- The smallest plant is the water-living lemna aquatic duckweed, which grows to only 0.6 mm long.

Deepest roots
- The roots of a fig tree in South Africa are believed to have penetrated 120 m into the ground.

Oldest living
- The oldest living tree is a bristlecone pine in California, USA. It is about 4700 years old.
- Some botanists believe that giant redwood trees may live to be 6000 years old, and that the creosote bush might live for 11 700 years.

Strangest
- The oddest plants are carnivorous, insect-eating plants. The leaves of the Venus' flytrap, for example, spring shut, to trap flies that land on them. These plants live in areas where the soil lacks nutrients, which they obtain instead from the bodies of insects.

Stinking corpse lily

▷ The largest flower – the stinking corpse lily of South-east Asia.

▽ The leaves of the pitcher plant look like jugs and contain a sugar solution that attracts insects. The insects climb over the lip of the pitcher, slide down the slippery surface and can't then climb out again.

Pitcher plant

THE WORLD AROUND US

The Earth seems a huge place to us. Yet it is no more than a tiny speck in the Universe. Even the Sun is a small star

Some astronomers believe the Universe will expand for ever. Others think it will stop growing and then collapse back again, ending in a 'Big Crunch'.

◁ The Milky Way is a galaxy of average size, and yet it contains aproximately 100 000 000 000 stars. Our Solar System, which includes the Earth and the Sun, lies at the edge of the galaxy.

compared to many of the hundred billion others in our galaxy, the Milky Way. And there are millions of galaxies in the Universe.

Most scientists believe that the Universe began with the 'Big Bang', a huge explosion that occurred about 18 thousand million years ago. Since then, the Universe has been expanding outwards at an enormous speed.

Stars
Stars are glowing balls of gas that give out heat and light. They are formed from clouds of gas and dust which collapse under their own weight. As a cloud gets smaller, it starts to burn and release energy and becomes a star. When it starts to run out of fuel it expands into a red giant. The outer layers then drift off into space leaving only the dying centre – called a white dwarf.

The Solar System

The Solar System is a group of planets, moons, asteroids and comets in orbit around the Sun. It was formed about 4600 million years ago from a huge cloud of gas and dust. There are nine planets: Mercury, Venus, Earth, Mars, Jupiter, Saturn, Uranus, Neptune and Pluto.

Between the planets Mars and Jupiter there is a band of thousands of lumps of rock and metal, called asteroids. Most of them are only a few kilometres across.

The Sun

The star we call the Sun is at the centre of the Solar System. It is a huge ball of hot gas 1 392 000 km across, and is far larger than

The planets move around the Sun at different rates. Pluto, the furthest from the Sun, makes one complete orbit every 248 years, while Mercury, the closest, takes only 88 days. All the planets travel in the same direction around the Sun, in elliptical (oval-shaped) orbits, and spin as they move.

Some planets have satellites, or moons, orbiting around them. Astronomers believe there are about 60 such moons in the Solar System. The best-known is our own Moon, which moves around the Earth once every 27.33 days.

any of the planets. Even so, it is only of medium size compared to other stars in the Universe. It looks so bright to us because it is much closer than all the others.

Although it is made of gas, the Sun's mass is enormous – more than 333 000 times greater than the Earth. Because of this, the Sun has a very strong gravitational pull. It is the Sun's gravity that holds all the planets in orbit.

The temperature at the Sun's surface is 5500°C; at the centre it may be as hot as 15 million °C. On the surface there are dark,

Mercury

Asteroids

Earth

Venus

Jupiter

Moon

Sun

Mars

◁ The Sun and the planets are shown to scale in this picture. There are probably no other large planets to be discovered, although there may be other small, Pluto-sized planets in the outer reaches of the Solar System.

wind blows strongest when there are sunspots, which happens roughly every 11 years or so.

Eventually, the Sun will run out of hydrogen fuel. When this happens, it will expand to become a red giant and will swallow up the Earth and most of the other planets. The Sun will then become more dense and explode, destroying the rest of the Solar System. All that will remain will be a tiny white dwarf star. The good news is that scientists do not believe this will happen for another 5000 million years.

relatively cool patches, called sunspots. They are the sites of violent storms and eruptions. These storms also cause flames of hot gas, called solar flares or prominences, to leap thousands of kilometres into space.

The Sun is surrounded by the corona, a layer of gas that has boiled off from the surface. Gas streams away from the corona in the form of a solar wind that blows past the Earth and the other planets. The solar

▷ The Sun is 149.6 million km from Earth. It is so big that 1 300 000 Earth-sized planets could fit into it. Energy from the centre, or core, is spread outwards to the surface by radiation and by huge convection currents in the hydrogen and helium gases of which the Sun is made. The energy is then radiated into space, mainly as heat and light. The dark patches on the surface are sunspots.

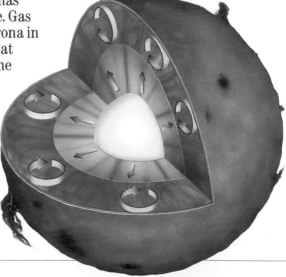

185

The planets

Mercury is the closest planet to the Sun. It has a large central core, probably made of nickel and iron. The surface is covered in craters, and the surface temperature ranges from -180ºC at night to 430ºC during the day. Mercury is both airless and waterless.

Venus has a dense atmosphere of mainly carbon dioxide which hides the surface under permanent cloud. This causes a greenhouse effect and traps in heat from the Sun. As a result, the surface temperature is about 480ºC. Above the surface, winds blow at up to 360 km/h. Space probes have detected a mountain 12 km high (taller than Mt Everest on Earth). There may also be active volcanoes on Venus.

Earth is the third planet from the Sun – just the right distance away for water to exist in liquid form. Oceans cover almost 75 per cent of the surface. See pages 190-232 for a closer look at Earth.

Earth

Moon

◁ When the Moon is directly between Earth and the Sun, it blocks out the Sun's light in what is called a total eclipse.

Sun

Mars was once thought to be capable of supporting life, but we now know that it has a very thin atmosphere which is 95 per cent carbon dioxide. The surface temperature varies from about -130ºC to -29ºC. There are a number of volcanoes; the largest, Olympus Mons, rises 23 km above the plains around it. Dust storms often hide the planet's surface, which has deep channnels cut into it that may have been made long ago by running water.

Asteroids are probably fragments of rock that were left orbiting the Sun when the Solar System was formed. There may be over 50 000 asteroids. About 2500 form a belt that orbits the Sun between Mars and Jupiter. The largest is about 936 km across.

Jupiter, the largest planet, is a ball of mainly hydrogen and helium gas. It spins very fast on its axis, and this causes the planet to be flattened at the poles. There is a very strong magnetic field. Jupiter's upper atmosphere is very turbulent, with bands of swirling red, brown, yellow and blue clouds, and the Great Red Spot – a huge system of storm clouds that is much larger than Earth.

Saturn is best known for the thousands of rings that surround it. They consist of pieces of rock and ice circling the planet at high speed and held in place by gravity. The ring system is 275 000 km across, but only about 100 m thick. The planet itself is a ball of mainly hydrogen gas and a rocky core.

Uranus is unusual in that its axis does not run top to bottom but side to side. Because of this it has 42 years of daylight followed by 42 years of night. The planet consists mainly of hydrogen with a thick cloud cover. There are 11 small rings made up of boulders.

Neptune consists of hydrogen and helium gases. The atmosphere is very violent, with winds of up to 2400 km/h. There are two rings around the planet, made up of tiny particles of dust.

Pluto, the smallest planet, is a tiny globe of frozen gases, probably consisting of ammonia, methane and water. Scientists think that Pluto may once have been a moon of Neptune that was thrown out of orbit and became a planet circling the Sun.

▷ In 1976, two Viking craft landed on Mars. Their cameras revealed high volcanoes and deep canyons on the Martian surface.

Planetary data

	Diameter (km)	Distance from Sun min (Mkm) max		Rotation period (days, hours, mins, secs)	Length of year (years, days)	Moons
Mercury	4878	46.8	69.4	58d 68h	88d	0
Venus	12 104	107.6	109	243d	224.7d	0
Earth	12 756	147.4	152.6	23h 56m 4s	365.26d	1
Mars	6794	207.3	249.2	24h 37m 23s	687d	2
Jupiter	142 800	741.6	817.4	9h 50m 30s	11y 314d	16
Saturn	120 000	1346	1512	10h 14m	29y 168d	17
Uranus	52 000	2740	3011	16-28h	84y 3d	15
Neptune	48 400	4466	4543	18-20h	164y 288d	8
Pluto	1145	4461	7364	6d 9h	247y 256d	1

The night sky

Many of the bright stars make patterns in the night sky. These groups of stars, or constellations, were first noted by Babylonian and ancient Greek astronomers, who imagined that some groups of stars looked like mythological characters. They gave the constellations names such as Pegasus the winged horse and Orion the hunter.

Comets

Comets sometimes appear in the night sky. They consist of lumps of rock and dust frozen together with ice and gas. They travel in highly elliptical orbits which take them far out into space and then back very close to the Sun. As they get near to the Sun, the frozen gases evaporate, releasing dust particles that form a bright head and a long, streaming tail which always points away from the Sun. The best-known comet is Halley's Comet, which appears every 76 years on average. It was first recorded as long ago as 240 BC.

▷ The stars in the northern sky.

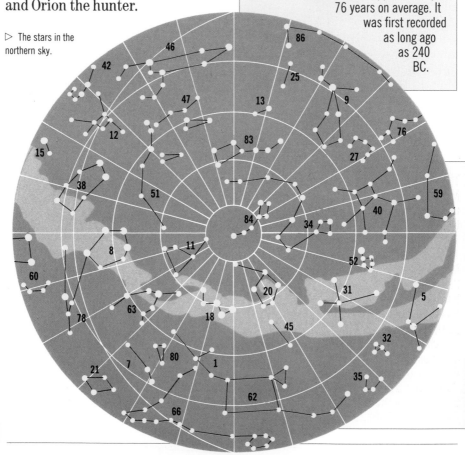

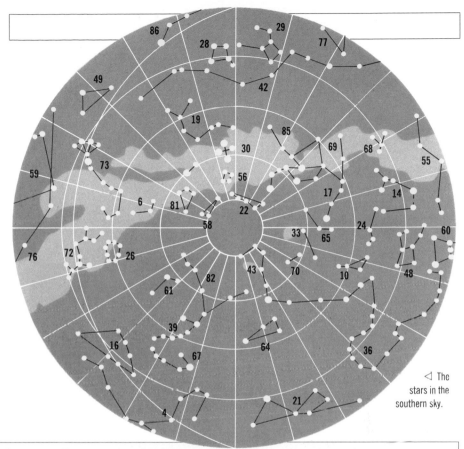

◁ The stars in the southern sky.

The constellations

Modern-day astronomers have grouped the stars into 88 constellations, which are listed here under their Latin names. The best-known are those in the Zodiac – the area of the sky crossed by the Sun. They are the 12 sun-signs of astrology, and are marked with a (Z).

1 Andromeda, 2 Antlia, 3 Apus, 4 Aquarius (Z), 5 Aquila, 6 Ara, 7 Aries (Z), 8 Auriga, 9 Boötes, 10 Caelum, 11 Camelopardalis, 12 Cancer (Z), 13 Canes Venatici, 14 Canis Major, 15 Canis Minor, 16 Capricornus (Z), 17 Carina, 18 Cassiopeia, 19 Centaurus, 20 Cepheus, 21 Cetus, 22 Chamaeleon, 23 Circinus, 24 Columba, 25 Coma Berenices, 26 Corona Australis, 27 Corona Borealis, 28 Corvus, 29 Crater, 30 Crux, 31 Cygnus, 32 Delphinus, 33 Dorado, 34 Draco, 35 Equuleus, 36 Eridanus, 37 Fornax, 38 Gemini (Z), 39 Grus, 40 Hercules, 41 Horologium, 42 Hydra, 43 Hydrus, 44 Indus, 45 Lacerta, 46 Leo (Z), 47 Leo Minor, 48 Lepus, 49 Libra (Z), 50 Lupus, 51 Lynx, 52 Lyra, 53 Mensa, 54 Microscopium, 55 Monoceros, 56 Musca, 57 Norma, 58 Octans, 59 Ophiuchus, 60 Orion, 61 Pavo, 62 Pegasus, 63 Perseus, 64 Phoenix, 65 Pictor, 66 Pisces (Z), 67 Piscis Austrinus, 68 Puppis, 69 Pyxis, 70 Reticulum, 71 Sagitta, 72 Sagittarius (Z), 73 Scorpius (Z), 74 Sculptor, 75 Scutum, 76 Serpens, 77 Sextans, 78 Taurus (Z), 79 Telescopium, 80 Triangulum, 81 Triangulum Australe, 82 Tucana, 83 Ursa Major, 84 Ursa Minor, 85 Vela, 86 Virgo (Z), 87 Volans, 88 Vulpecula.

The structure of the Earth

The Earth is made up of four layers. On the outside is the thinnest layer, called the crust. It varies from about 5 km thick under some parts of the oceans to 80 km in mountain areas. Beneath the crust is the mantle, which is about 2900 km thick. Near the top of the mantle, the rock is partly molten and it moves about very slowly, rather like thick treacle.

Scientists think that the core is made of a mixture of two metals – iron and nickel. The 2000-km thick outer core is molten, while the inner core is a solid ball measuring about 2700 km across.

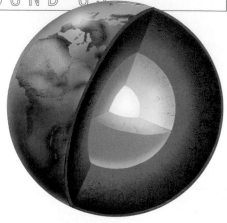

△ The layers of the Earth. The temperature of the inner core is thought to be about 4500°C but it is kept solid by the enormous pressure there.

The atmosphere

The Earth is surrounded by a thick blanket of air, called the atmosphere. It consists of a mixture of gases – 21 per cent oxygen, 78 per cent nitrogen and 1 per cent argon and other gases.

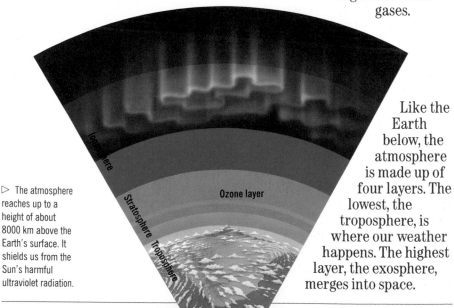

Ozone layer

Ionosphere

Stratosphere

Troposphere

▷ The atmosphere reaches up to a height of about 8000 km above the Earth's surface. It shields us from the Sun's harmful ultraviolet radiation.

Like the Earth below, the atmosphere is made up of four layers. The lowest, the troposphere, is where our weather happens. The highest layer, the exosphere, merges into space.

190

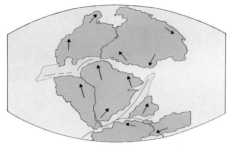

△ The super-continent of Pangaea was surrounded by a single ocean, called Panthalassa. Pangaea began to break apart 180 million years ago.

▷ By 135 million years ago North America was separating from Europe. Australia and Antarctica were moving away from Africa and a gap had opened between South America and Africa.

This process has continued right up to the present day. In fact, the plates are still moving, at a rate of between 1 and 10 cm a year. In some places beneath the oceans, plates are moving apart and new land is formed as molten rock rises up between them and cools. Where two plates collide, one dives down below the other and melts. Two plates may slide past each other. Usually they slide past smoothly but sometimes they stick. The pressure builds up until they finally pull free, causing earthquakes.

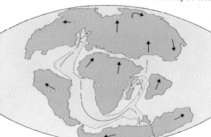

▽ About 65 million years ago, the continents looked more like they do today, although Australia and Antarctica were still joined together and Greenland was joined to Europe.

Moving continents

The Earth's crust is made up of a number of pieces, called plates. These plates float on the molten part of the mantle below and they have been moving slowly ever since the Earth was formed.

Around 275 million years ago, the Earth looked very different from today. All the land was joined together in one vast super-continent called Pangaea. About 180 million years ago, Pangaea began to break apart as the plates of the crust were pulled in different directions.

▽ The world today. The plate carrying India has collided with Asia, pushing up the Himalayas. There are now wide oceans between the continents.

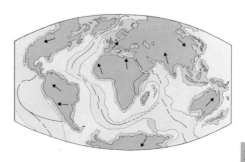

The Earth's surface

The surface of the Earth is changing constantly. Usually, this happens slowly: rocks are worn away by the sea, rivers or glaciers; new land is made at beaches and deltas; and rocks are pushed up to form mountains.

Mountains

The world's mountains have been pushed up above the surface in different ways. Some are called dome mountains and were pushed up by molten rock rising below the surface. Others formed when rocks were squeezed up into huge folds, often where the Earth's plates collided. Sometimes deep cracks, or faults, form in the Earth. If two faults run alongside each other, pressure may lift up the land between to form a block mountain. Mountain building takes millions of years. It is still happening today.

Violent changes

Sometimes the Earth's surface changes very suddenly. Some mountains are volcanoes, formed when hot, molten rock erupts through cracks in the Earth's crust. Earthquakes can also bring about rapid changes. They happen when vibrations, caused by forces beneath the ground, shake the rocks of the surface. Most earthquakes and volcanoes occur near the edges of the plates, often under the sea. Some volcanic islands, such as Hawaii, have formed above 'hot spots', sources of extreme heat in the Earth's mantle.

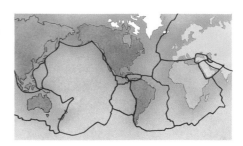

△ This map shows the Earth's plates. Some of the world's great mountain chains, including the Andes and the Himalayas, lie along plate boundaries.

▽ Mountains are often made when rocks are squeezed together sideways and folded (left). Block mountains and rift valleys are caused by cracks in the Earth's surface (right).

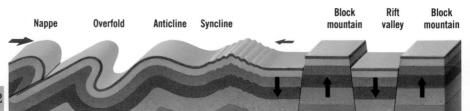

Nappe Overfold Anticline Syncline   Block mountain Rift valley Block mountain

Earthquake zone

▲ **Volcano**

◁ This map shows how the surface of the Earth would look if all the water were drained out of the oceans. The long mountain chains running through some ocean basins are where new rocks are being made. Also shown are the earthquake zones and volcanoes, most of which are on or near plate boundaries.

Volcanoes

Where there is a gap or hole in the crust, molten rock, or magma, is forced up to the surface. When it reaches the surface it is called lava. In a volcanic eruption, lava spills out. Sometimes the lava is very liquid and flows in red-hot streams. For example, the lava from the volcanoes of the Hawaiian Islands is runny. Other lava is thicker and may even be thrown out of a volcano in hard lumps. Some volcanoes blow out mainly ash and smoke. Others may become blocked and explode violently when they erupt.

When lava cools down it becomes solid rock. With each eruption, a new layer of rock is formed and the volcano becomes larger.

▽ Beneath volcanoes there are large amounts of magma. During an eruption, the magma forms lava, ash, gases and steam which burst out on to the Earth's surface. Some volcanoes have only a single vent, surrounded by a crater. Others have vents on their sides, too. Volcanoes that have not erupted for a long time are called dormant. Those that will never erupt again are said to be extinct.

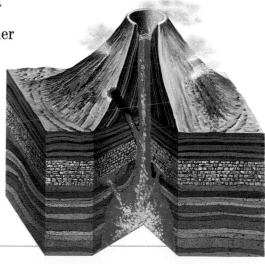

Rivers and glaciers

Rivers begin in areas of high ground and flow downhill to the sea. They might start from rainfall, underground springs or melting glaciers. In its upper course, a river runs downhill with a fast current, taking sand, gravel and rocks with it. In the middle course, the slope is gentler and the river flows more

△ As a river flows from high ground down to the sea, it gets wider and slower. If it is carrying lots of mud and silt, this may build up at the river mouth to form a flat area, or delta.

slowly. It can still wear away sand and rocks from its banks, though. In the lower course, the river slows down and its channel gets wider as it flows over an almost flat plain. It can only carry tiny pieces of material, called silt. The silt is dropped when the river flows into the sea.

◁ In an area of limestone rock, a river may disappear down a 'swallow hole' and flow below the surface. Underground streams may carve out deep caves and galleries in the rock before emerging lower down as springs.

A glacier is a river of ice that forms where snow builds up in a mountain hollow and turns to ice. When there is enough ice, it spills out of the hollow and slides downhill at a speed of about a metre per day. Rocks frozen into its base and sides scrape away the land and carve out a steep-sided valley. The ice melts as it moves downhill into warmer regions.

Deserts

Deserts are places where there is less than 25 cm of rain per year. They cover about 14 per cent of the land. Some deserts are sandy but most are rocky.

△ Streams may flow from the melting front, or 'snout', of a glacier. The brown bands in the ice are moraines – pieces of rock scraped from the sides of the valley as the glacier moves along.

▽ Most desert people live in oases – places where there is water. An oasis may occur where underground water seeps to the surface or where it can be reached by digging a well.

Sand dunes

In sandy deserts, the wind can blow sand into hills, or dunes. The crescent-shaped dunes (above left) are called barchans. They move across the desert as the wind rolls sand grains up the gentle slope and over the front edge. The long sand ridges (above right) are called seif dunes.

Currents, tides and waves

Surface currents
Scientists have found 38 main currents flowing through the surface waters of the oceans.

Warm current
Cold current

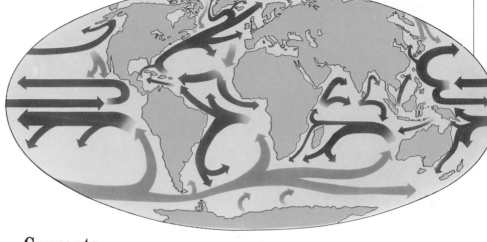

Currents

Water travels around the world's oceans in currents. They are like giant rivers flowing through the oceans. Some affect the surface water; others are deeper down.

Surface currents are caused by the world's winds, which blow warm water away from the Equator and cold water away from the poles. Currents must change direction when they meet land. The spin of the Earth also deflects them to the right in the Northern Hemisphere and to the left in the Southern Hemisphere.

Deep ocean currents begin in the polar regions, where cold water sinks and 'rolls' into the Atlantic, Pacific and Indian oceans. Warmer water flows in from the Tropics to take its place.

Tides

Along most coastlines, the level of the sea rises and falls twice every day. These changes are called tides.

Tides are caused by the Moon's gravity pulling on the water in the oceans. This causes it to bulge out on the side of the Earth facing the Moon, producing a high tide. A bulge also forms on the opposite side of the Earth because of the planet's rotation. These two bulges move around the Earth following the Moon, with troughs (low tides) between them. The Sun also affects the tides, but less than the Moon.

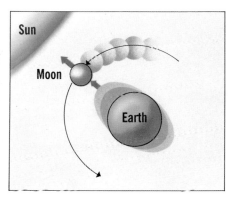

△ When the Sun and the Moon are pulling in the same direction, high tides are very high and low tides very low. These are known as spring tides.

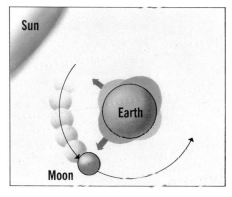

△ When the pull of the Sun is at right angles to that of the Moon, they partly cancel each other out and both high and low tides are small. These are called neap tides.

Waves

Waves are caused by wind blowing across the surface of the sea. The stronger the wind and the longer it blows in the same direction, the higher and faster the waves.

The most severe storms may produce waves up to about 20 m high, but some 'freak' waves are much taller. The highest recorded wave measured 34 m from the crest (top) to the trough (bottom).

Water does not move along when a wave passes. Each drop of water actually moves around in a circle and ends up roughly where it started.

◁ As a wave approaches the shore, it starts to build up. When the front edge of the wave becomes too steep, the top begins to move faster than the bottom and the wave topples over on to the shore.

Weather and climate

Our weather happens in the lowest layer of the Earth's atmosphere. The type of weather we have depends on whether the air is warm or cold, dry or moist. The air is kept moving by the heat of the Sun. As the air moves, the weather at a particular place changes.

The air cycle

Around the Equator, the Sun's heat warms the ground which heats the air above it. The warm air rises into the atmosphere where it cools and spreads out north and south. It sinks down to Earth and forms six bands of winds that blow across the Earth's surface. The winds don't blow directly from the north and south as they are deflected by the spin of the Earth.

◁ The world's six bands of 'prevailing' winds: trade winds (orange), westerlies (red) and polar easterlies (blue). Cold air (purple) blows around the poles.

The water cycle

The world's water is constantly on the move. The Sun's heat evaporates water in the oceans, rivers, vegetation and from the land, turning it into water vapour. This rises, cools and turns into tiny water droplets which form clouds. When the clouds are blown over the land they bring rain and snow. Rainwater and melted snow flow downhill, in rivers and under the ground, back towards the oceans. There the water starts its journey again.

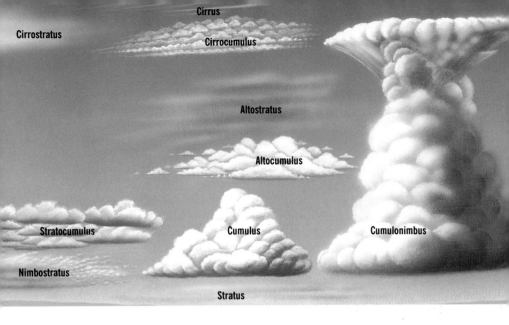

Cirrus

Cirrostratus

Cirrocumulus

Altostratus

Altocumulus

Stratocumulus

Cumulus

Cumulonimbus

Nimbostratus

Stratus

△ Different clouds form at different heights above the ground. The main types are stratus, cumulus and cirrus, but there are many variations. Stratus is a sheet of cloud; cumulus is a fluffy pile of cloud; and cirrus is a thin, streaky cloud. The prefix 'cirro' is added when a cloud is over 6000 m above the ground; 'alto' means between 2000 and 6000 m, 'strato' is below 2000 m and 'nimbo' means a rain cloud.

Clouds and rain

When water evaporates it turns into water vapour in the air. Warm air can hold more water vapour than cold air.

When warm, moist air rises, it cools down and the water vapour it contains turns to water droplets. Millions of these small droplets make a cloud.

Inside a cloud, some of the droplets bump into each other and join together to form heavier drops. If they become heavy enough, the drops of water will fall from the cloud as rain.

Cold air

Warm air

Warm air rising

Cold front

Rain

◁ Clouds can form when air rises and cools over mountains (top picture). Storm clouds form when moist air rises and cools rapidly on hot days (middle). Clouds also form when warm air rises above a layer of cold air (bottom). Warm air and cold air do not mix; warm air is lighter and it rises above cold air. The line along which two types of air meet is called a weather front. A warm front is followed by a mass of warm air, and a cold front comes before a mass of cold air.

△ Raindrops

△ Snowflakes

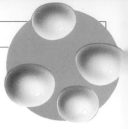

△ Hailstones

Rain, snow and hail

When rain falls from the clouds it is called precipitation. Snow and hail are also types of precipitation. Whether it rains, snows or hails depends on the temperature inside the clouds.

If the temperature is above 0°C, the point at which water freezes, rain will fall. If it is below freezing, the water vapour will turn to droplets that freeze as ice crystals. The crystals join together and fall as snow. If snowflakes fall through warm air they will melt and become raindrops, but if the air is cold they will stay frozen. Hail forms inside tall cumulonimbus storm clouds. Hailstones start as tiny ice crystals which are blown up and down by strong currents in a cloud. As they are blown about, water droplets freeze on to them making layers of ice. As more layers form, the hailstones grow larger and heavier. Eventually they become heavy enough to fall out of the cloud. Hailstones are normally between 5 and 50 mm across, but some are much larger.

▷ Thunderstorms happen when warm, moist air rises very quickly. Electricity builds up in the clouds and is released suddenly as flashes of lightning. Lightning heats up the air it travels through, making it expand and collide with the colder air around it. The expanding air makes the sound of thunder.

Climate and the seasons

The type of weather that a place normally has over a long period of time is called its climate. Climate depends mainly on how far away from the Equator a place is. Other factors also affect climate. For example, places close to the sea often have warmer climates than those far inland.

△ The hottest climates are in places close to the Equator. This is because the Sun's rays are strongest there.

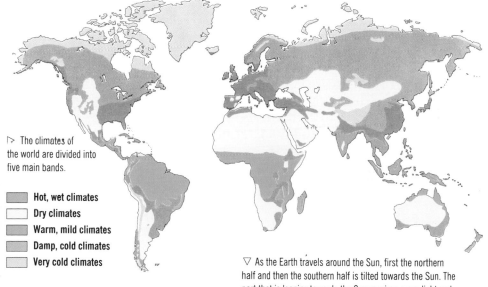

▷ The climates of the world are divided into five main bands.

- ▨ Hot, wet climates
- ☐ Dry climates
- ▨ Warm, mild climates
- ▨ Damp, cold climates
- ▨ Very cold climates

Seasons

In most places in the world, the climate includes several periods of different types of weather during each year. These periods are called the seasons. They occur because the Earth is tilted over to one side, and because it travels closer to the Sun at certain times of the year than at others.

▽ As the Earth travels around the Sun, first the northern half and then the southern half is tilted towards the Sun. The part that is leaning towards the Sun receives more light and heat. For example, when the northern half is tilted towards the Sun it is summer there and winter in the south. Six months later, the southern half is tilted towards the Sun and it is summer there and winter in the north.

Vegetation

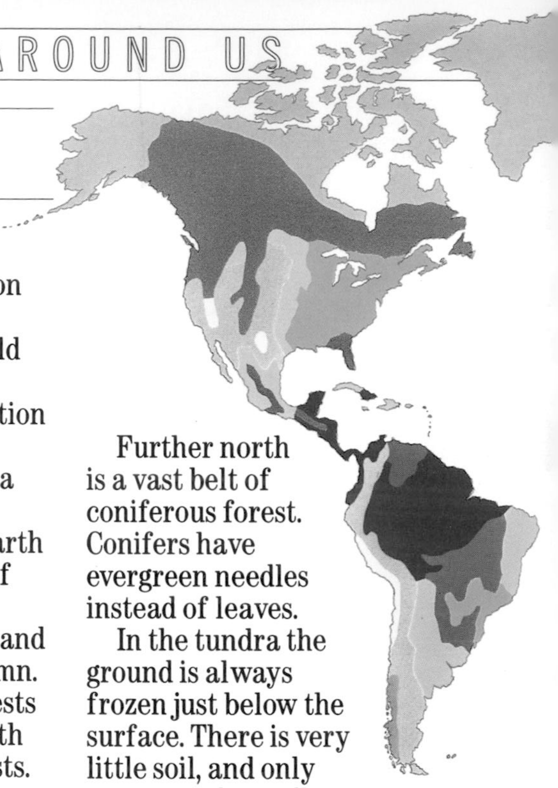

The types of plants that grow in a particular area depend upon the climate and the soils found there. Scientists divide the world into regions called biomes according to the type of vegetation that grows there.

Tropical rainforests grow in a belt around the Equator. They cover about 6 per cent of the Earth and contain a greater variety of plants than any other biome. Rainforest trees are evergreen and do not lose their leaves in autumn.

Temperate forests grow to the north of the rainforests. The main plants are broad-leaved deciduous trees.

Further north is a vast belt of coniferous forest. Conifers have evergreen needles instead of leaves.

In the tundra the ground is always frozen just below the surface. There is very little soil, and only mosses and tiny flowers can grow.

Grasslands grow where there is too little rain for forests but enough to stop the land being a desert. Mainly tough grasses grow there. Grasslands close to the Equator are called savanna.

Deserts cover about 20 per cent of the land. Plants growing there often have waterproof leaves and rubbery flesh for storing moisture.

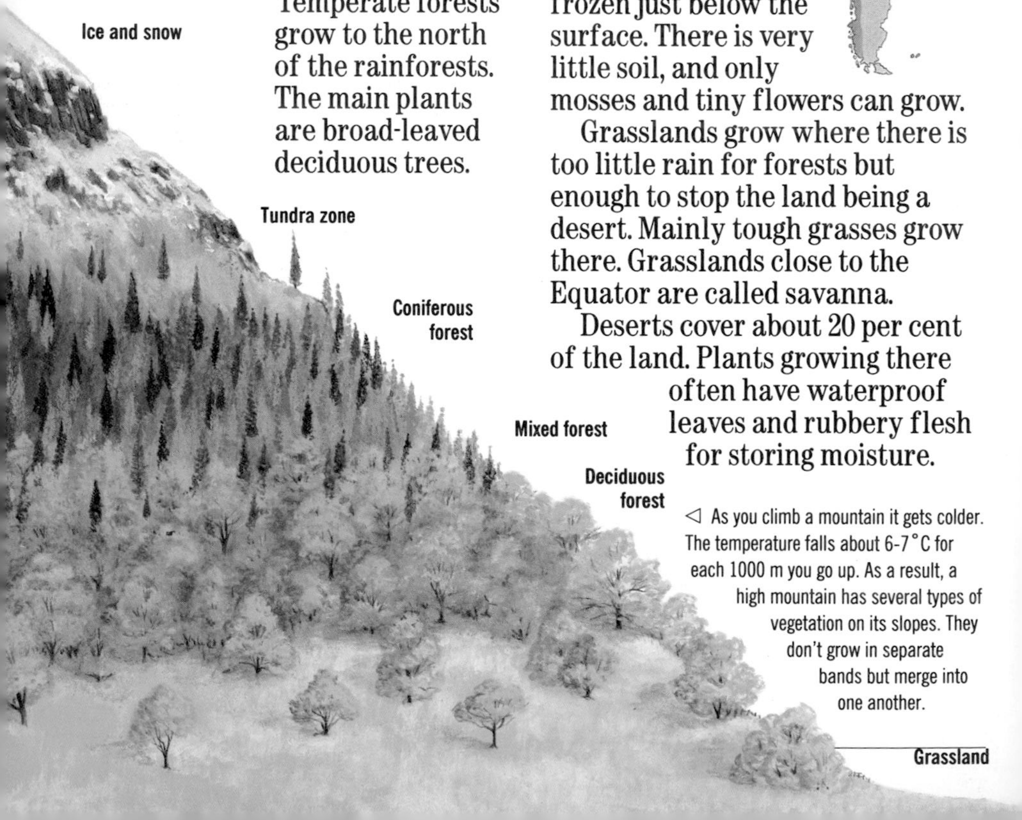

Ice and snow

Tundra zone

Coniferous forest

Mixed forest

Deciduous forest

◁ As you climb a mountain it gets colder. The temperature falls about 6-7 °C for each 1000 m you go up. As a result, a high mountain has several types of vegetation on its slopes. They don't grow in separate bands but merge into one another.

Grassland

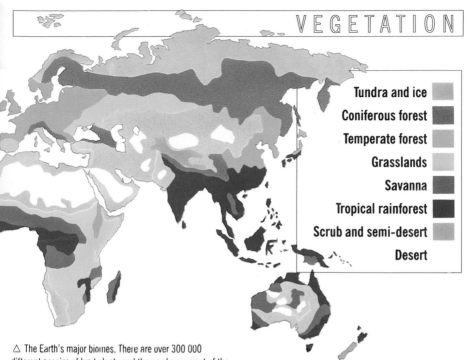

Tundra and ice
Coniferous forest
Temperate forest
Grasslands
Savanna
Tropical rainforest
Scrub and semi-desert
Desert

△ The Earth's major biomes. There are over 300 000 different species of land plants and they make up most of the living matter on our planet. They have managed to adapt to almost every environment: plants are found in the hottest deserts where it hardly ever rains, in icy Antarctic valleys where the temperature never rises above freezing, and on newly deposited volcanic lava.

▽ Plants that live in deserts have special ways of surviving long periods without rain. The cacti growing in the deserts of the south-western USA have very long roots to collect water from deep underground. They store the water in their thick, fleshy stems.

Earth in danger

Humans are damaging our planet in a number of ways – by using up precious resources too quickly, by destroying the habitats in which plants and animals live, and by pollution.

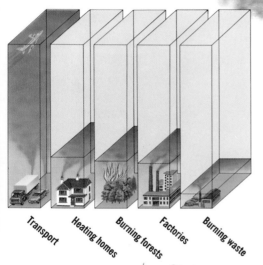

△ Transport is the single main source of air pollution. Cars are especially damaging to the environment because of the poisonous exhaust gases they produce, including carbon monoxide, nitrogen oxides and sulphur oxides.

◁ This diagram shows the major causes of air pollution. Transport, domestic heating and some factory pollution involve burning fossil fuels – oil, gas and coal.

Transport Heating homes Burning forests Factories Burning waste

Pollution

There are many forms of pollution. Factories and power stations pour dirty smoke and poisonous gases into the air. Water is polluted with toxic chemicals, oil and sewage. The soil is damaged by chemical fertilizers and pesticides, and by acid rain, which is caused by air pollution.

◁ Oil can pollute the sea when oil tankers run aground or collide and leak.

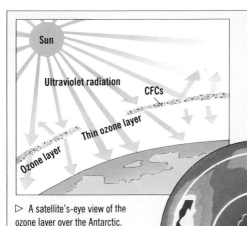

△ A satellite's-eye view of the ozone layer over the Antarctic.

The ozone layer

A layer of ozone gas in the Earth's atmosphere shields us from some of the Sun's harmful ultraviolet rays, which can cause skin cancer. Chemicals called CFCs (chlorofluorocarbons) – used for many years in aerosol cans and refrigerators – are destroying parts of the ozone layer. This is happening most over Antarctica, and also over North America, Asia, Europe and Australia.

Global warming

The atmosphere traps in some of the heat we get from the Sun. This is called the greenhouse effect. Many scientists think that too much heat is being trapped in because we are adding to the amounts of certain gases in the atmosphere. These 'greenhouse gases' – mainly carbon dioxide and methane – are produced by factories and by the burning of forests to make way for cities and farmland.

If the world's temperature does increase, even by a few degrees, the polar icecaps could begin to melt, raising the sea-level and flooding many coastal areas. In other places, food crops could be destroyed by hotter, drier climates, and wildlife could be threatened with extinction.

△ The atmosphere allows the Sun's heat to reach the Earth and keeps some of it in, rather like the glass in a greenhouse. The more greenhouse gases in the atmosphere, the more heat is trapped and the warmer the Earth becomes.

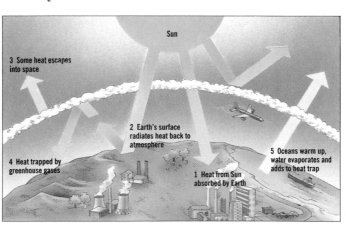

Countries of the world

In political terms, Russia is a European nation and on the maps in this chapter the whole country is included in Europe. However, geographically, part of it is in Asia.

The continents

There are seven continents – Australia and Oceania, Europe, Antarctica, South America, North America, Africa and Asia. Within the continents are more than 170 independent countries.

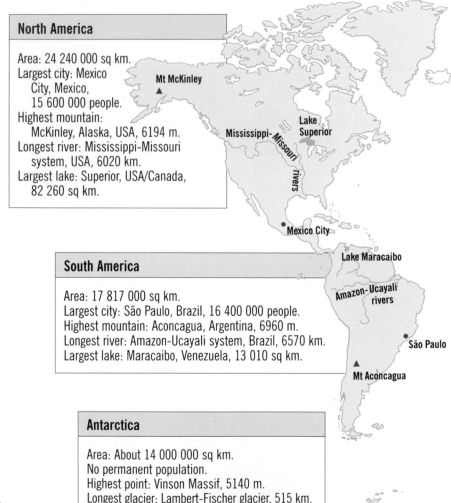

North America

Area: 24 240 000 sq km.
Largest city: Mexico City, Mexico, 15 600 000 people.
Highest mountain: McKinley, Alaska, USA, 6194 m.
Longest river: Mississippi-Missouri system, USA, 6020 km.
Largest lake: Superior, USA/Canada, 82 260 sq km.

Mt McKinley ▲

Mississippi-Missouri rivers

Lake Superior

Mexico City

Lake Maracaibo

South America

Area: 17 817 000 sq km.
Largest city: São Paulo, Brazil, 16 400 000 people.
Highest mountain: Aconcagua, Argentina, 6960 m.
Longest river: Amazon-Ucayali system, Brazil, 6570 km.
Largest lake: Maracaibo, Venezuela, 13 010 sq km.

Amazon-Ucayali rivers

São Paulo

▲ Mt Aconcagua

Antarctica

Area: About 14 000 000 sq km.
No permanent population.
Highest point: Vinson Massif, 5140 m.
Longest glacier: Lambert-Fischer glacier, 515 km.

COUNTRIES OF THE WORLD

Europe

Area: 24 265 000 sq km (incl. all of Russia).
Largest city: London, UK, 7 640 000 people.
Highest mountain: El'brus, Russia, 5633 m.
Longest river: Volga, Russia, 3531 km.
Largest lake: Caspian Sea, Russia/Iran/
   Turkmenistan/Kazakhstan/Azerbaijan
   371 000 sq km.

Asia

Area: 29 235 000 sq km.
Largest city: Tokyo-Yokohama, Japan,
   26 800 000 people.
Highest mountain: Everest, China/Nepal,
   8848 m.
Longest river: Chiang Jang (Yangtze),
   China, 6380 km.
   Largest lake: Caspian Sea,
      371 000 sq km.

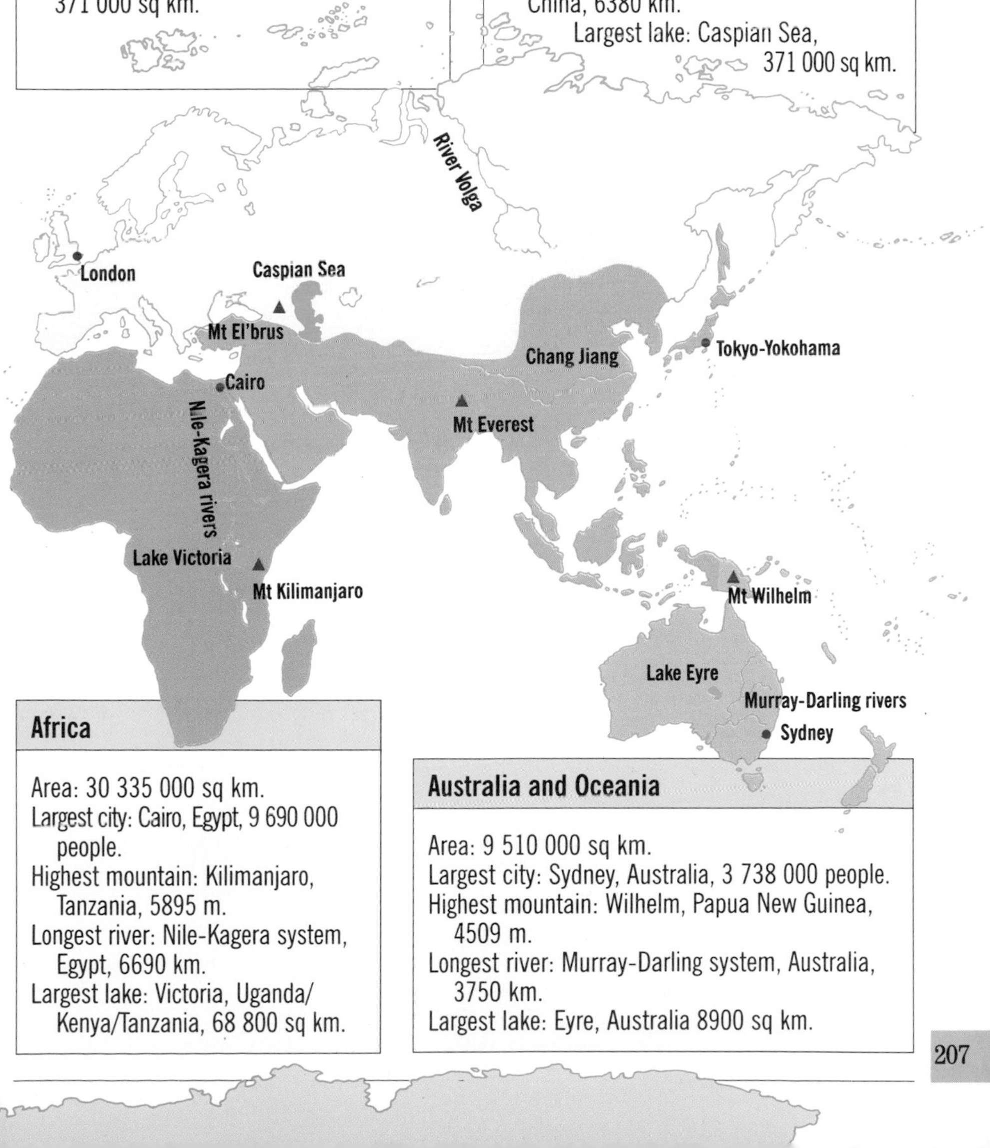

London
Caspian Sea
Mt El'brus
Cairo
Chang Jiang
Tokyo-Yokohama
Mt Everest
River Volga
Nile-Kagera rivers
Lake Victoria
Mt Kilimanjaro
Mt Wilhelm
Lake Eyre
Murray-Darling rivers
Sydney

Africa

Area: 30 335 000 sq km.
Largest city: Cairo, Egypt, 9 690 000
   people.
Highest mountain: Kilimanjaro,
   Tanzania, 5895 m.
Longest river: Nile-Kagera system,
   Egypt, 6690 km.
Largest lake: Victoria, Uganda/
   Kenya/Tanzania, 68 800 sq km.

Australia and Oceania

Area: 9 510 000 sq km.
Largest city: Sydney, Australia, 3 738 000 people.
Highest mountain: Wilhelm, Papua New Guinea,
   4509 m.
Longest river: Murray-Darling system, Australia,
   3750 km.
Largest lake: Eyre, Australia 8900 sq km.

North America

Cuba Area: 114 516 sq km. Population: 11 115 000. Capital: Havana. Language: Spanish. Main products: sugar, molasses, bananas, fish.

Antigua & Barbuda Area: 433 sq km. Population: 69 000. Capital: St John's. Language: English. Main product: tourism.

Bahamas Area: 13 933 sq km. Population: 293 000. Capital: Nassau. Language: English. Main products: tourism, rum, banking.

Barbados Area: 430 sq km. Population: 263 000. Capital: Bridgetown. Language: English. Main products: rum, molasses, tourism.

Belize Area: 22 964 sq km. Population: 230 000 Capital: Belmopan. Languages: English, Spanish. Main products: sugar, timber.

Canada Area: 9 970 610 sq km. Population: 30 194 000. Capital: Ottawa. Languages: English, French. Main products: minerals, timber, cereals, manufactured goods.

Costa Rica Area: 50 695 sq km. Population: 3 650 000. Capital: San José. Language: Spanish. Main product: coffee.

Dominica Area: 751 sq km. Population: 75 000. Capital: Roseau. Language: English. Main products: bananas, fruit, tourism.

Dominican Republic Area: 48 730 sq km. Population: 8 232 000. Capital: Santo Domingo. Language: Spanish. Main products: sugar, minerals.

Dependent territories and colonies

A number of small islands in the Caribbean Sea are not independent states but are governed by or associated with other countries.

- Anguilla, Bermuda, the Cayman Islands, the Turks & Caicos Islands, Montserrat and the British Virgin Islands are dependent territories or Crown colonies of the United Kingdom.
- Guadeloupe and Martinique are overseas departments of France.
- Puerto Rico and the American Virgin Islands are associated with the USA.
- Aruba, Bonaire and Curaçao (in the Lesser Antilles) are self-governing islands belonging to the Netherlands.

Greenland (Territory of Denmark) Area: 2 175 600 sq km. Population: 58 800. Capital: Godthåb. Languages: Danish, Inuit. Main products: fish.

Grenada Area: 344 sq km. Population: 85 000. Capital: St George's. Language: English. Main products: cocoa, nutmeg, bananas.

Guatemala Area: 108 880 sq km. Population: 11 562 000. Capital: Guatemala City. Languages: Spanish, Indian languages. Main products: coffee, minerals.

Haiti Area: 27 747 sq km. Population: 7 534 000. Capital: Port-au-Prince. Languages: French, Creole. Main products: coffee, sugar.

Honduras Area: 112 079 sq km. Population: 6 147 000. Capital: Tegucigalpa. Language: Spanish. Main products: bananas, coffee, timber.

Jamaica Area: 10 960 sq km. Population: 2 539 000. Capital: Kingston. Languages: English, Creole. Main products: bauxite, bananas, sugar, tourism.

BAHAMAS
CUBA
ZE
DOMINICAN REPUBLIC
BURAS   HAITI   ST KITTS   ANTIGUA & BARBUDA
ICARAGUA JAMAICA & NEVIS
PANAMA   ST LUCIA   DOMINICA
COSTA RICA   BARBADOS
                             ST VINCENT & GRENADINES
                             TRINIDAD & TOBAGO
          GRENADA

▽ These Eskimo hunters are drilling a hole in the Arctic ice. When they have drilled through to the sea below, they will wait to shoot any seals that come up to breathe. Their vehicle, a skidoo, is rather like a motorbike with skis for crossing the ice.

El Salvador Area: 21 392 sq km. Population: 6 059 000. Capital: San Salvador. Languages: Spanish, Nahuati. Main products: coffee, cotton.

GREENLAND
(Denmark)

Mexico Area: 1 972 545 sq km. Population: 95 831 000. Capital: Mexico City. Language: Spanish. Main products: oil, minerals, textiles, steel.

Nicaragua Area: 129 990 sq km. Population: 4 464 000. Capital: Managua. Languages: Spanish, English. Main products: coffee, cotton, meat.

Panama Area: 75 643 sq km. Population: 2 767 000. Capital: Panama City. Language: Spanish. Main products: canal traffic, banking, bananas.

St Kitts-Nevis Area: 269 sq km. Population: 42 000. Capital: Basseterre. Language: English. Main product: sugar.

St Lucia Area: 617 sq km. Population: 136 000. Capital: Castries. Language: English. Main products: bananas, cocoa, textiles.

St Vincent & Grenadines Area: 389 sq km. Population: 112 000. Capital: Kingstown. Language: English. Main products: bananas, arrowroot, tourism.

Trinidad & Tobago Area: 5128 sq km. Population: 1 138 000. Capital: Port of Spain. Language: English. Main products: oil, sugar, cocoa, coffee.

United States of America Area: 9 372 571 sq km. Population: 273 754 000. Capital: Washington, D.C. Language: English. Main products: foods, minerals, manufactured goods.

US states and their capitals

Alabama, Montgomery; **Alaska**, Juneau; **Arizona**, Phoenix; **Arkansas**, Little Rock; **California**, Sacramento; **Colorado**, Denver; **Connecticut**, Hartford; **Delaware**, Dover; **Florida**, Tallahassee; **Georgia**, Atlanta; **Hawaii**, Honolulu; **Idaho**, Boise; **Illinois**, Springfield; **Indiana**, Indianapolis; **Iowa**, Des Moines; **Kansas**, Topeka; **Kentucky**, Frankfort; **Louisiana**, Baton Rouge; **Maine**, Augusta; **Maryland**, Annapolis; **Massachusetts**, Boston; **Michigan**, Lansing; **Minnesota**, St Paul; **Mississippi**, Jackson; **Missouri**, Jefferson City; **Montana**, Helena; **Nebraska**, Lincoln; **Nevada**, Carson City; **New Hampshire**, Concord; **New Jersey**, Trenton; **New Mexico**, Santa Fé; **New York**, Albany; **North Carolina**, Raleigh; **North Dakota**, Bismarck; **Ohio**, Columbus; **Oklahoma**, Oklahoma City; **Oregon**, Salem; **Pennsylvania**, Harrisburg; **Rhode Island**, Providence; **South Carolina**, Columbia; **South Dakota**, Pierre; **Tennessee**, Nashville; **Texas**, Austin; **Utah**, Salt Lake City; **Vermont**, Montpelier; **Virginia**, Richmond; **Washington**, Olympia; **West Virginia**, Charleston; **Wisconsin**, Madison; **Wyoming**, Cheyenne.

The city of Washington, the capital of the USA, is in a special area called the District of Columbia (D.C.), which is not part of any of the fifty US states.

▷ The Statue of Liberty stands at the entrance to the harbour in New York, USA. It was given to the United States by France in 1886.

△ A fisherman on Lake Titicaca, Bolivia. His boat is made from totoras reeds which grow by the lake shore.

South America

Argentina Area: 2 766 889 sq km. Population: 36 123 000. Capital: Buenos Aires. Language: Spanish. Main products: cereals, wool, vegetable oils, meat.

Bolivia Area: 1 098 581 sq km. Population: 7 957 000. Capital: La Paz. Languages: Spanish, Aymara, Quechua. Main products: natural gas, zinc, tin, gold.

Brazil Area: 8 511 965 sq km. Population: 165 158 000. Capital: Brasília. Language: Portuguese. Main products: coffee, sugar, cattle, textiles.

Chile Area: 756 945 sq km. Population: 14 824 000. Capital: Santiago. Language: Spanish. Main products: copper, fruit, fish meal, paper.

Colombia Area: 1 141 748 sq km. Population: 37 685 000. Capital: Bogotá. Language: Spanish. Main products: coffee, bananas, minerals.

Ecuador Area: 269 178 sq km. Population: 12 175 000. Capital: Quito. Language: Spanish. Main products: petroleum, shrimps, bananas.

Guyana Area: 215 083 sq km. Population: 856 000. Capital: Georgetown. Language: English, Hindi, Urdu. Main products: bauxite, sugar, rice.

Paraguay Area: 406 752 sq km. Population: 5 222 000. Capital: Asunción. Language: Spanish. Main products: cotton soya beans, meat, coffee, timber.

Peru Area: 1 285 216 sq km. Population: 24 797 000. Capital: Lima. Languages: Spanish, Aymara, Quechua. Main products: coffee, sugar, minerals.

Surinam Area: 163 265 sq km. Population: 442 000. Capital: Paramaribo. Language: Dutch. Main products: aluminium, shrimps, rice.

Uruguay Area: 176 215 sq km. Population: 3 239 000. Capital: Montevideo. Language: Spanish. Main products: textiles, meat, animal hides.

Venezuela Area: 912 050 sq km. Population: 23 242 000. Capital: Caracas. Language: Spanish. Main products: petroleum, natural gas.

Europe

In political terms, Russia is a European nation and on this map the whole country is included in Europe. However, geographically, the area to the east of the Ural Mountains is regarded as being in Asia.

Albania Area: 28 748 sq km. Population: 3 445 000. Capital: Tirana. Language: Albanian. Main products: minerals, foods.

Andorra Area: 468 sq km. Population: 64 000. Capital: Andorra la Vella. Languages: Catalan, French, Spanish. Main products: tourism, consumer goods.

Austria Area: 83 856 sq km. Population: 8 210 000. Capital: Vienna. Language: German. Main products: machinery, consumer goods, tourism.

Belarus Area: 207 600 sq km. Population: 10 323 000. Capital: Minsk. Languages: Byelorussian, Russian. Main products: livestock, timber.

Belgium Area: 30 518 sq km. Population: 10 213 000. Capital: Brussels. Languages: Flemish, French. Main products: metals, textiles, chemicals, ceramics.

Bosnia-Herzegovina Area: 51 129 sq km. Population: 3 994 000. Capital: Sarajevo. Language: Serbo-Croatian. Main products: agriculture, chemicals, machinery.

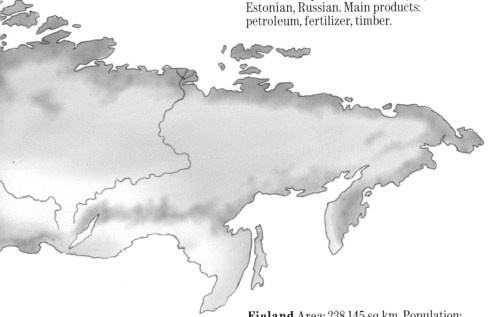

◁ The flag of the European Union (EU). The EU consists of fifteen member countries: Austria, Belgium, Denmark, Finland, France, Germany, Greece, Ireland, Italy, Luxembourg, the Netherlands, Portugal, Spain, Sweden and the United Kingdom.

Denmark Area: 40 093 sq km. Population: 5 258 000. Capital: Copenhagen. Language: Danish. Main products: dairy foods, beer, chemicals.

Estonia Area: 45 100 sq km. Population: 1 442 000. Capital: Tallinn. Languages: Estonian, Russian. Main products: petroleum, fertilizer, timber.

Finland Area: 338 145 sq km. Population: 5 156 000. Capital: Helsinki. Language: Finnish. Main products: wood products, engineering, fish.

Bulgaria Area: 110 994 sq km. Population: 8 387 000. Capital: Sofia. Languages: Bulgarian, Turkish. Main products: foods, wine, tobacco.

France Area: 543 965 sq km. Population: 58 733 000. Capital: Paris. Language: French. Main products: foods, wine, engineering, consumer goods.

Croatia Area: 56 538 sq km. Population: 4 494 000. Capital: Zagreb. Language: Serbo-Croatian. Main products: agriculture, machinery, clothing, textiles.

Georgia Area: 69 700 sq km. Population: 5 428 000. Capital: Tbilisi. Languages: Georgian, Russian. Main products: mining, agriculture.

Czech Republic Area: 78 865 sq km. Population: 10 223 000. Capital: Prague. Language: Czech. Main products: machinery, vehicles, consumer goods.

Germany Area: 357 050 sq km. Population: 82 401 000. Capital: Berlin. Language: German. Main products: engineering, chemicals, textiles, vehicles.

Greece Area: 131 944 sq km. Population: 10 551 000. Capital: Athens. Language: Greek. Main products: foods, clothing, petroleum products.

Hungary Area: 93 030 sq km. Population: 9 930 000. Capital: Budapest. Language: Hungarian. Main products: machinery, foods, consumer goods.

Iceland Area: 102 819 sq km. Population: 277 000. Capital: Reykjavik. Language: Icelandic. Main product: fish.

Ireland Area: 70 285 sq km. Population: 3 564 000. Capital: Dublin. Languages: Irish, English. Main products: manufactured goods, foods.

Italy Area: 301 277 sq km. Population: 57 244 000. Capital: Rome. Language: Italian. Main products: foods, wine, textiles, engineering, vehicles.

△ Farmworkers in Poland. Many countries in Eastern Europe were ruled from 1945 to 1989 by Communist governments. During that time their farms and factories were badly run and relied on out-of-date equipment.

Latvia Area: 64 500 sq km. Population: 2 447 000. Capital: Riga. Languages: Latvian, Russian. Main products: machinery, electrical equipment, foods.

Liechtenstein Area: 160 sq km. Population: 28 000. Capital: Vaduz. Language: German. Main products: tourism, banking, engineering.

Lithuania Area: 65 200 sq km. Population: 3 710 000. Capital: Vilnius. Languages: Lithuanian, Russian. Main products: chemicals, metal goods, electrical equipment.

Luxembourg Area: 2856 sq km. Population: 421 000. Capital: Luxembourg. Languages: Letzeburgish, French. Main products: iron, steel.

Macedonia Area: 25 715 sq km. Population: 2 205 000. Capital: Skopje. Language: Serbo-Croatian. Main product: foods.

Malta Area: 316 sq km. Population: 374 000. Capital: Valletta. Languages: Maltese, English. Main products: ship repair, tourism.

Moldova Area: 33 700 sq km. Population: 4 451 000. Capital: Kishinev. Languages: Moldovian, Russian. Main products: agriculture, foods, chemicals.

Monaco Area: 1.9 sq km. Population: 30 000. Capital: Monaco. Languages: French, Monegasque. Main products: property, banking, tourism.

Netherlands Area: 41 863 sq km. Population: 15 739 000. Capital: Amsterdam. Language: Dutch. Main products: foods, flowers, manufacturing, natural gas.

Norway Area: 323 878 sq km. Population: 4 379 000. Capital: Oslo. Language: Norwegian (two types). Main products: natural gas, petroleum, timber, fish.

Poland Area: 312 677 sq km. Population: 38 664 000. Capital: Warsaw. Language: Polish. Main products: machinery, chemicals, foods, textiles.

Portugal Area: 92 389 sq km. Population: 9 798 000. Capital: Lisbon. Language: Portuguese. Main products: foods, fish, cork, textiles, manufacturing.

Romania Area: 237 500 sq km. Population: 22 573 000. Capital: Bucharest. Languages: Romanian, Hungarian. Main products: minerals, manufacturing, timber.

Russia Area: 17 075 400 sq km. Population: 147 231 000. Capital: Moscow. Language: Russian. Main products: manufacturing, tourism.

San Marino Area: 61 sq km. Population: 25 000. Capital: San Marino. Language: Italian. Main products: maize, pigs, steel, factory goods.

Slovakia Area: 49 035 sq km. Population: 5 360 000. Capital: Bratislava. Language: Slovak. Main products: agriculture, foods, wood products.

Slovenia Area: 20 251 sq km. Population: 1 919 000. Capital: Ljubljana. Language: Slovenian. Main products: grains.

Spain Area: 504 783 sq km. Population: 39 754 000. Capital: Madrid. Languages: Spanish, Catalan. Main products: foods, wine, manufacturing, banking, tourism.

Sweden Area: 449 964 sq km. Population: 8 863 000. Capital: Stockholm. Language: Swedish. Main products: uranium, iron, timber, wood pulp, engineering.

Switzerland Area: 41 293 sq km. Population: 7 325 000. Capital: Bern. Languages: German, French, Italian, Romansch. Main products: manufactured goods, engineering, banking.

Ukraine Area: 603 700 sq km. Population: 51 218 000. Capital: Kiev. Languages: Ukrainian, Russian. Main products: engineering, agriculture.

United Kingdom Area: 244 110 sq km. Population: 58 249 000. Capital: London. Language: English. Main products: manufacturing, petroleum, financial services, tourism.

Vatican City Area: 0.44 sq km. Population: 1,000. Capital: Vatican City. Languages: Italian, Latin. Main products: none.

Yugoslavia Area: 95 493 sq km. Population: 10 410 000. Capital: Belgrade. Language: Serbo-Croatian. Main products: agriculture, clothing, textiles.

The Arctic

The Arctic region lies to the north of an imaginary line called the Arctic Circle. It contains the most northerly parts of North America, Europe and Asia. The central area of the Arctic, surrounding the North Pole, consists of an ice cap, about 6 metres thick, floating on the Arctic Ocean. The size of the ice cap depends on the season. On the map (left) the dark blue area shows the ice in summer when it is at its smallest extent; the pale blue areas show how far it extends during the coldest winters.

Africa

Algeria Area: 2 381 714 sq km. Population: 30 175 000. Capital: Algiers. Languages: Arabic, French. Main products: petroleum, processed foods.

Angola Area: 1 246 700 sq km. Population: 11 967 000. Capital: Luanda. Language: Portuguese. Main products: petroleum, vegetable and animal products.

Benin Area: 112 600 sq km. Population: 5 881 000. Capital: Porto-Novo. Language: French. Main products: petroleum, palm products.

Botswana Area: 581 730 sq km. Population: 1 551 000. Capital: Gaborone. Languages: Tswana, English. Main products: minerals, livestock products.

Burkina Faso Area: 274 200 sq km. Population: 11 402 000. Capital: Ouagadougou. Language: French. Main products: gold, manganese, millet, peanuts.

Burundi Area: 27 834 sq km. Population: 6 589 000. Capital: Bujumbura. Languages: Kirundi, French. Main products: coffee, tea, cotton.

Cameroon Area: 475 442 sq km. Population: 14 323 000. Capital: Yaoundé. Languages: French, English. Main products: petroleum, coffee, cocoa, aluminium.

Cape Verde Area: 4033 sq km. Population: 417 000. Capital: Praia. Language: Portuguese. Main products: bananas, coffee, fish.

Central African Republic Area: 622 984 sq km. Population: 3 489 000. Capital: Bangui. Language: French. Main products: coffee, diamonds, wood, cotton.

Chad Area: 1 284 000 sq km. Population: 6 892 000. Capital: N'Djamena. Languages: Arabic, French. Main products: cotton, uranium.

Comoros Area: 1862 sq km. Population: 672 000. Capital: Moroni. Languages: Arabic, French. Main products: vanilla, copra, perfume.

Congo Area: 342 000 sq km. Population: 2 822 000. Capital: Brazzaville. Language: French. Main products: petroleum, wood, diamonds.

Côte d'Ivoire Area: 320 763 sq km. Population: 14 567 000. Capital: Abidjan. Language: French. Main products: coffee, cocoa, diamonds.

Djibouti Area: 22 000 sq km. Population: 651 000. Capital: Djibouti. Languages: Arabic, French. Main products: camels, food.

◁ Few people live in the Sahara Desert in North Africa. Those who do are mostly nomads who move from place to place in search of water and grazing land for their livestock. Others live at oases where springs or wells provide water.

Egypt Area: 997 739 sq km.
Population: 65 675 000. Capital:
Cairo. Languages: Arabic,
French. Main products:
petroleum, cotton, textiles.

Equatorial Guinea Area:
28 050 sq km. Population:
430 000. Capital: Malabo.
Language: Spanish. Main products:
cocoa, timber.

Eritrea Area: 117 600 sq km.
Population: 3 548 000. Capital:
Asmara. Language: Amharic. Main
products: coffee, salt.

Ethiopia Area: 1 104 400 sq km.
Population: 62 111 000. Capital: Addis
Ababa. Language: Amharic. Main
products: coffee, animal hides,
livestock, pulses.

Gabon Area: 267 667 sq
km. Population: 1 170 000.
Capital: Libreville.
Language: French. Main products:
petroleum, timber, manganese.

Gambia Area: 10 689 sq km. Population:
1 194 000. Capital: Banjul. Language:
English. Main products: peanut products,
fish, tourism.

Ghana Area: 238 533 sq km. Population: 18 857 000. Capital: Accra. Language: English. Main products: cocoa, gold, timber.

Guinea Area: 245 857 sq km. Population: 7 673 000. Capital: Conakry. Language: French. Main products: bauxite, diamonds, gold.

Guinea-Bissau Area: 36 125 sq km. Population: 1 134 000. Capital: Bissau. Language: Portuguese. Main products: cashew nuts, peanuts.

Kenya Area: 582 646 sq km. Population: 29 020 000. Capital: Nairobi. Languages: Swahili, English. Main products: coffee, tea, petroleum products, tourism.

Lesotho Area: 30 355 sq km. Population: 2 184 000. Capital: Maseru. Languages: Sesotho, English. Main products: wool, foods, manufactured goods.

Liberia Area: 111 370 sq km. Population: 2 748 000. Capital: Monrovia. Language: English. Main products: iron ore, rubber, timber.

Libya Area: 1 759 540 sq km. Population: 5 980 000. Capital: Tripoli. Language: Arabic. Main product: petroleum.

Madagascar Area: 587 041 sq km. Population: 16 348 000. Capital: Antananarivo. Languages: Malagasy, French. Main products: coffee, vanilla, cloves.

Malawi Area: 118 484 sq km. Population: 10 377 000. Capital: Lilongwe. Languages: Chichewa, English. Main products: tobacco, tea, sugar.

Mali Area: 1 240 192 sq km. Population: 11 832 000. Capital: Bamako. Language: French. Main products: cotton, livestock, nuts.

Mauritania Area: 1 030 700 sq km. Population: 2 453 000. Capital: Nouakchott. Languages: Arabic, French. Main products: fish, iron ore.

Mauritius Area: 2040 sq km. Population: 1 154 000. Capital: Port Louis. Language: English. Main products: textiles, sugar, diamonds, fish.

Morocco Area: 458 730 sq km. Population: 28 012 000. Capital: Rabat. Language: Arabic. Main products: foods, phosphates, fertilizer.

Mozambique Area: 799 380 sq km. Population: 18 691 000. Capital: Maputo. Language: Portuguese. Main products: shrimps, cashews, cotton, sugar.

◁ The grasslands of Africa are home to vast numbers of animals, and some areas have been made into National Parks. Countries such as Kenya and Tanzania benefit from tourists who go there to see the animals.

◁ Diamonds and other minerals are very important exports for countries such as Namibia, South Africa and Swaziland.

Namibia Area: 823 144 sq km. Population: 1 653 000. Capital: Windhoek. Languages: Afrikaans, English. Main products: diamonds, cattle, animal hides.

Niger Area: 1 267 sq km. Population: 10 119 000. Capital: Niamey. Languages: French, Hausa. Main products: uranium, minerals, livestock, vegetables.

Nigeria Area: 923 768 sq km. Population: 121 773 000. Capital: Abuja. Language: English. Main products: petroleum, palm products.

Rwanda Area: 26 338 sq km. Population: 6 528 000. Capital: Kigali. Languages: Kinyarwanda, French. Main products: coffee, tea.

São Tomé & Príncipe Area: 1001 sq km. Population: 127 000. Capital: São Tomé. Language: Portuguese. Main products: cocoa, copra.

Senegal Area: 196 772 sq km. Population: 9 001 000. Capital: Dakar. Language: French. Main products: peanut oil, shellfish, phosphates.

Seychelles Area: 453 sq km. Population: 76 000. Capital: Victoria. Languages: Creole, English, French. Main products: petroleum, fish, tourism.

Sierra Leone Area: 71 740 sq km. Population: 4 577 000. Capital: Freetown. Language: English. Main products: titanium, diamonds, bauxite, coffee.

Somalia Area: 637 657 sq km. Population: 10 653 000. Capital: Mogadishu. Languages: Somali, Arabic. Main products: livestock, bananas, animal hides, fish.

South Africa Area: 1 240 167 sq km. Population: 44 295 000. Capital: Pretoria. Languages: Afrikaans, English. Main products: gold, minerals, foods, manufactured goods.

Sudan Area: 2 508 813 sq km. Population: 28 526 000. Capital: Khartoum. Language: Arabic. Main products: cotton, gum arabic, sesame, sheep.

Swaziland Area: 17 364 sq km. Population: 931 000. Capital: Mbabane. Languages: Swazi, English. Main products: sugar, timber, coal, diamonds.

Tanzania Area: 945 087 sq km. Population: 32 189 000. Capital: Dodoma. Languages: Swahili, English. Main products: coffee, cotton.

Togo Area: 56 785 sq km. Population: 4 434 000. Capital: Lomé. Language: French. Main products: fertilizer, coffee, tea, cocoa.

Tunisia Area: 154 530 sq km. Population: 9 497 000. Capital: Tunis. Language: Arabic. Main products: clothing, petroleum, phosphates.

Uganda Area: 236 036 sq km. Population: 21 318 000. Capital: Kampala. Languages: Swahili, English. Main product: coffee.

Zaire (Democratic Republic of the Congo) Area: 2 345 409 sq km. Population: 49 208 000. Capital: Kinshasa. Language: French. Main products: copper, coffee, diamonds, petroleum.

Zambia Area: 752 614 sq km. Population: 8 690 000. Capital: Lusaka. Language: English. Main products: copper, zinc, cobalt.

Zimbabwe Area: 390 759 sq km. Population: 11 924 000. Capital: Harare. Language: English. Main products: tobacco, gold.

◁ Uluru (formerly known as Ayers Rock), in central Australia, is the largest single rock in the world. It stands 348 m high and measures 10 km around its base. The rock is a sacred place for the Aboriginal people who live in the region and its caves contain pictures that were painted by their ancestors many centuries ago.

Australia and Oceania

Australia Area: 7 682 000 sq km. Population: 18 445 000. Capital: Canberra. Language: English. Main products: minerals, machinery, foods, wool.

Fiji Area: 18 274 sq km. Population: 822 000. Capital: Suva. Languages: English, Fijian, Hindi. Main products: sugar, copra, fish, timber.

Kiribati Area: 728 sq km. Population: 77 000. Capital: Bairiki. Languages: English, I-Kiribati. Main products: copra, fish.

Marshall Islands Area: 181 sq km. Population: 63 000. Capital: Majuro. Languages: English, Marshallese. Main products: copra, cocunut oil.

Micronesia Area: 2900 sq km. Population: 106 000. Capital: Kolonia. Languages: English, Mortlockese, Trukese, Pohnpeian and others. Main products: fish, copra.

HAWAII

MARSHALL ISLANDS

MICRONESIA

NAURU

KIRIBATI

SOLOMON ISLANDS

PAPUA NEW GUINEA

TUVALU

WESTERN SAMOA

VANUATU

FIJI

TONGA

AUSTRALIA

NEW ZEALAND

Nauru Area: 21 sq km. Population: 10 400. Main town: Yaren. Languages: Nauruan, English. Main products: phosphates, coconuts, financial services.

New Zealand Area: 268 676 sq km. Population: 3 680 000. Capital: Wellington. Language: English. Main products: dairy foods, lamb, wool, fish.

Palau Area: 497 sq km. Population: 17 000. Capital: Koror. Languages: Palauan, English and others. Main products: coconuts, cassava.

Papua New Guinea Area: 461 691 sq km. Population: 4 602 000. Capital: Port Moresby. Languages: English, local languages. Main products: copper, coffee, timber.

Solomon Islands Area: 28 370 sq km. Population: 417 000. Capital: Honiara. Languages: English, Pidgin. Main products: copra, cocoa, coconuts.

Tonga Area: 699 sq km. Population: 97 000. Capital: Nuku'alofa. Languages: Tongan, English. Main products: vanilla, vegetables, fish, coconuts.

Tuvalu Area: 24 sq km. Population: 10 300. Capital: Fongafale. Languages: Tuvaluan, English. Main product: copra.

Vanuatu Area: 12 190 sq km. Population: 183 000. Capital: Vila. Languages: Bislama, English, French. Main products: copra, meat, cocoa, timber.

Western Samoa Area: 2831 sq km. Population: 170 000. Capital: Apia. Languages: Samoan, English. Main products: coconut products, taro, timber.

▽ Wool is a major export in New Zealand and sheep shearing is an important job. Shearers are often paid according to the number of sheep they shear, rather than by the hour, and a good shearer can remove the fleece from a sheep in less than a minute.

Asia

Afghanistan Area: 652 225 sq km. Population: 23 364 000. Capital: Kabul. Languages: Pushto, Dari. Main products: cereals, dried fruit, wool, cotton.

Armenia Area: 29 800 sq km. Population: 3 646 000. Capital: Yerevan. Languages: Armenian, Russian. Main products: chemicals, agriculture, machinery.

Azerbaijan Area: 86 600 sq km. Population: 7 714 000. Capital: Baku. Languages: Azerbaijani, Russian. Main products: oil, iron, steel, textiles.

Bahrain Area: 692 sq km. Population: 594 000. Capital: Manama. Language: Arabic. Main products: petroleum, natural gas.

Bangladesh Area: 143 998 sq km. Population: 124 043 000. Capital: Dhaka. Language: Bengali. Main products: rice, jute, tea.

Bhutan Area: 47 000 sq km. Population: 1 917 000. Capital: Thimphu. Language: Dzongkha. Main products: foods, timber.

Brunei Area: 5765 sq km. Population: 313 000. Capital: Bandar Seri Begawan. Language: Malay. Main products: natural gas, petroleum.

Cambodia Area: 181 916 sq km. Population: 10 751 000. Capital: Phnom Penh. Languages: Khmer, French. Main product: rice.

China Area: 9 572 900 sq km. Population: 1 255 091 000. Capital: Beijing. Language: Mandarin Chinese. Main products: rice, minerals, fish, manufactured goods.

Cyprus Area: 9251 sq km. Population: 775 000. Capital: Nicosia. Languages: Greek, Turkish. Main products: foods, wine, tourism.

KAZAKHSTAN
UZBEKISTAN
KYRGYZSTAN
TURKMENISTAN
TADZHIKISTAN
AZERBAIJAN
ARMENIA
TURKEY
AFGHANISTAN
CYPRUS
SYRIA
LEBANON
IRAQ
IRAN
NEPAL
ISRAEL
JORDAN
KUWAIT
PAKISTAN
BAHRAIN
QATAR
SAUDI ARABIA
UNITED ARAB EMIRATES
INDIA
OMAN
YEMEN
MALDIVES
SRI LANKA

▽ Oil provides more than half of the world's energy. Sixty per cent of the known reserves of oil are in the Middle East, and some Middle Eastern countries have become extremely rich because of their oil deposits. Natural gas, which is often pumped out of the ground along with oil, is burned off in huge flares.

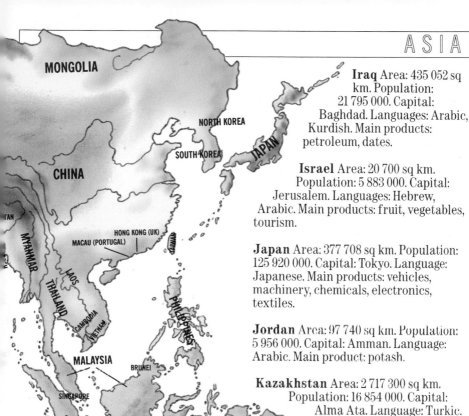

MONGOLIA

NORTH KOREA

SOUTH KOREA

JAPAN

CHINA

HONG KONG (UK)
MACAU (PORTUGAL)

MYANMAR

LAOS

THAILAND

CAMBODIA

VIETNAM

PHILIPPINES

MALAYSIA

BRUNEI

SINGAPORE

INDONESIA

Iraq Area: 435 052 sq km. Population: 21 795 000. Capital: Baghdad. Languages: Arabic, Kurdish. Main products: petroleum, dates.

Israel Area: 20 700 sq km. Population: 5 883 000. Capital: Jerusalem. Languages: Hebrew, Arabic. Main products: fruit, vegetables, tourism.

Japan Area: 377 708 sq km. Population: 125 920 000. Capital: Tokyo. Language: Japanese. Main products: vehicles, machinery, chemicals, electronics, textiles.

Jordan Area: 97 740 sq km. Population: 5 956 000. Capital: Amman. Language: Arabic. Main product: potash.

Kazakhstan Area: 2 717 300 sq km. Population: 16 854 000. Capital: Alma Ata. Language: Turkic. Main products: cereals, cotton, petroleum.

Korea, North Area: 122 370 sq km. Population: 23 206 000. Capital: Pyongyang. Language: Korean. Main products: minerals, foods, textiles.

Korea, South Area: 98 484 sq km. Population: 46 115 000. Capital: Seoul. Language: Korean. Main products: vehicles, textiles, ships, steel, fish.

India Area: 3 166 414 sq km. Population: 975 772 000. Capital: New Delhi. Languages: Hindi, English and others. Main products: tea, cotton, sugar, jute, coal, manufactured goods.

Indonesia Area: 1 904 000 sq km. Population: 206 522 000. Capital: Jakarta. Language: Bahasa Indonesia. Main products: petroleum, natural gas.

Iran Area: 1 648 196 sq km. Population: 73 057 000. Capital: Tehran. Languages: Farsi, Azerbaijani. Main products: petroleum, textiles, carpets.

Kuwait Area: 17 818 sq km. Population: 1 809 000. Capital: Kuwait City. Language: Arabic. Main products: petroleum, chemicals, fertilizer.

Kyrgyzstan Area: 198 500 sq km. Population: 4 497 000. Capital: Bishek. Language: Turkic. Main product: cotton.

△ Sumo wrestling is the national sport in Japan. Two wrestlers try to push each other out of a small ring using their strength and their weight.

Laos Area: 236 800 sq km. Population: 5 358 000. Capital: Vientiane. Language: Lao. Main products: agriculture, timber, coffee, tin.

Lebanon Area: 10 230 sq km. Population: 3 194 000. Capital: Beirut. Language: Arabic. Main products: jewellery, clothes, pharmaceuticals.

Malaysia Area: 329 749 sq km. Population: 21 450 000. Capital: Kuala Lumpur. Language: Bahasa Malaysia. Main products: manufactured goods, palm oil, petroleum, rubber, tin.

Maldives Area: 298 sq km. Population: 282 000. Capital: Malé. Language: Divehi. Main products: fish, clothing.

Mongolia Area: 1 565 000 sq km. Population: 2 624 000. Capital: Ulan Bator. Language: Mongolian. Main products: coal, metals, agriculture.

Myanmar (Burma) Area: 676 552 sq km. Population: 47 625 000. Capital: Yangon. Language: Burmese. Main products: timber, rice.

Nepal Area: 147 181 sq km. Population: 23 168 000. Capital: Kathmandu. Language: Nepali. Main products: foods, manufactured goods.

Oman Area: 212 457 sq km. Population: 2 504 000. Capital: Muscat. Language: Arabic. Main products: petroleum.

Pakistan Area: 796 095 sq km. Population: 147 811 000. Capital: Islamabad. Language: Urdu. Main products: cotton, textiles, foods, chemicals.

Philippines Area: 300 000 sq km. Population: 72 164 000. Capital: Manila. Languages: Filipino, English. Main products: electronics, clothing, agriculture, wood.

Qatar Area: 11 427 sq km. Population: 579 000. Capital: Doha. Language: Arabic. Main products: petroleum, chemicals.

Saudi Arabia Area: 2 149 690 sq km. Population: 20 207 000. Capital: Riyadh. Language: Arabic. Main product: petroleum.

Singapore Area: 581 sq km. Population: 3 491 000. Capital: Singapore City. Languages: Chinese, English, Malay, Tamil. Main products: electronics, clothing, petroleum.

Sri Lanka Area: 65 610 sq km. Population: 18 450 000. Capital: Colombo. Languages: Sinhalese, Tamil. Main products: tea, rubber, gemstones.

Syria Area: 185 180 sq km. Population: 15 335 000. Capital: Damascus. Language: Arabic. Main products: petroleum, chemicals, textiles.

Tadzhikistan Area: 143 100 sq km. Population: 6 161 000. Capital: Dushanbe. Language: Tadzhik. Main product: cotton.

Taiwan Area: 36 000 sq km. Population: 21 700 000. Capital: Taipei. Language: Chinese. Main products: electronics, clothes, plastic goods.

Thailand Area: 514 000 sq km. Population: 59 612 000. Capital: Bangkok. Language: Thai. Main products: textiles, rice, rubber, tapioca, timber.

Turkey Area: 777 452 sq km (23 764 sq km in Europe). Population: 63 763 000. Capital: Ankara. Language: Turkish. Main products: textiles, foods, metals.

Turkmenistan Area: 488 100 sq km. Population: 4 316 000. Capital: Ashkhabad. Language: Turkic. Main product: cotton.

United Arab Emirates Area: 83 600 sq km. Population: 2 354 000. Capital: Abu Dhabi. Language: Arabic. Main product: petroleum.

Uzbekistan Area: 447 400 sq km. Population: 24 105 000. Capital: Tashkent. Language: Uzbek. Main product: cotton.

Vietnam Area: 329 556 sq km. Population: 77 896 000. Capital: Hanoi. Language: Vietnamese. Main products: coal, agriculture, livestock, fish.

Yemen Area: 531 869 sq km. Population: 16 891 000. Capital: Sana'a. Language: Arabic. Main products: coffee, animal hides, foods.

Antarctica

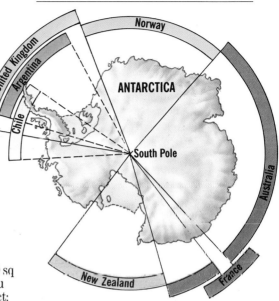

Area: 14 000 000 sq km. No permanent population. Main products: none.

Although 98 per cent of Antarctica is covered by snow and ice, a number of countries have laid claim to part of this vast continent. The reason is that they believe there might be valuable reserves of oil and other minerals buried in the rocks beneath the ice. At present, the continent is protected by an international treaty that prevents any country using it for commercial or military purposes.

The only people who live in Antarctica are scientists who work at scientific research bases there.

◁ An American research base in Antarctica. Scientists at bases like this one study the Earth's climate and atmosphere, including the ozone layer.

Facts and figures

There are no universally agreed estimates for the figures given in this section, as different techniques are used for taking measurements.

The Earth in space
- Light from the Sun takes about 8 minutes to reach the Earth.
  - The Earth orbits the Sun at an average speed of 107 280 km/h.
  - The Earth tilts on its axis at an angle of 23°.

The Earth's surface
- The total surface area is 509 600 000 sq km.
- The area of the land is 148 000 000 sq km.
- The water surface area is 361 600 000 sq km.
- The circumference at the Equator is 40 076 km; at the poles it is 40 000 km.

Cairo

Lake Nasser

River Nile

Khartoum

The longest river systems
(Including river and tributaries that make the longest watercourse)

1. Nile-Kagera-Ruvuvu-Ruvusu-Luvironza   6690 km
2. Amazon-Ucayali-Tambo-Ene-Apurimac 6570 km
3. Chang Jiang (Yangtze) 6380 km
4. Mississippi-Missouri-Jefferson-Beaverhead-Red Rock 6020 km
5. Yenisey-Angara-Selenga-Ider   5870 km

The great oceans
The areas of the main oceans are:

1	Pacific	165 384 000 sq km
2	Atlantic	82 217 000 sq km
3	Indian	73 481 000 sq km
4	Arctic	14 056 000 sq km

Ocean depths
The oceans are most shallow – about 200 m on average – above the continental shelf around the edges of continents. Beyond that, the sea-bed slopes down steeply to about 4 km. The deepest parts of the oceans are long, narrow trenches, which are mostly in the western parts of the main oceans. The deepest of all is the Marianas Trench in the Pacific, which plunges to 11 033 m.

The largest lake
- The world's largest lake is the Caspian Sea, on the borders of Iran, Russia, Turkmenistan, Kazakhstan and Azerbaijan. It covers 371 000 sq km.

Lake Victoria

The highest mountains		4 Lhotse	8511 m	8 Cho Oyu	8153 m
1 Everest	8848 m	5 Makalu 1	8481 m	9 Nanga Parbat	8125 m
2 K2	8611 m	6 Dhaulagiri 1	8172 m	10 Annapurna 1	8091 m
3 Kangchenjunga	8597 m	7 Manaslu	8156 m		

Waterfalls

- The waterfall with the longest single leap is the upper section of the Angel Falls, Venezuela, at 807 m.
- The waterfall with the greatest flow of water is the Boyoma Falls in Zaire, with an average of 17 000 m³ of water per second. A large river in flood can exceed 50 000 m³ per second.

The largest islands

1	Australia	7 892 300 sq km
2	Greenland	2 131 600 sq km
3	New Guinea	790 000 sq km
4	Borneo	737 000 sq km
5	Madagascar	587 000 sq km

Rain and snow

- The highest annual rainfall was 26 460 mm in 1860-61 at Cherrapunji, India.
- The most snow in a year was 31 100 mm in Washington State, USA, in 1971-72.

The largest deserts

1	Sahara	8 600 000 sq km
2	Arabian	2 330 000 sq km
3	Australian	1 550 000 sq km
4	Gobi	1 166 000 sq km

Tsunami

The largest tsunami, or seismic sea waves, were between 35 and 50 m high. They happened in 1883 off Java after the volcano Krakatoa exploded.

The modern world

Population

The world's population is about 5 930 000 000 people, and this number is growing by 81 000 000 each year. The United Nations has estimated that by the year 2050 it will have reached 9 367 000 000.

Most of the growth in population is occurring in the poorer countries of the world. This is partly because people in these countries are now

△ Subsistence farming: in poor countries, farmers have only enough land to grow food for their families.

Rich world, poor world
The world is divided between developed countries, which make most of their money from industry and finance, and poorer developing countries that rely mainly on farming. Most developing nations are in Africa, Asia and South and Central America.

living longer because of better health care, and because more babies are being born, too.

◁ The world's largest cities

▽ This graph shows how the world's population has grown since 8000 BC.

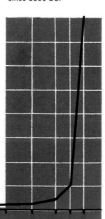

World population (millions)

	World's 10 largest cities – population (see map)	
1	Tokyo-Yokohama, Japan	26 800 000
2	São Paulo, Brazil	16 400 000
3	New York, USA	16 300 000
4	Mexico City, Mexico	15 600 000
5	Bombay, India	15 200 000
6	Shanghai, China	15 100 000
7	Los Angeles, USA	12 500 000
8	Beijing, China	12 400 000
9	Calcutta, India	11 700 000
10	Seoul, South Korea	11 600 000

△ Harvesting wheat in the prairies of North America. The USA is the world's largest wheat producer.

The largest food producers

The countries that produce the most food are the USA, China, Russia and India. Both China and India are developing nations, and although they produce vast amounts of food, they also have very large populations to feed – many of whom are too poor to buy as much food as they need.

Food and famine

The world produces more than enough food to feed its entire population, and yet there are about 1 000 000 000 people who do not have enough to eat. The reason for this is that the world's food is not evenly shared out.

Staple foods

A staple food is the one that people eat most often. Cereals, such as wheat, barley, maize and rice, are the most important food crops. About half of the world's people are totally dependent on rice as their staple food. More than 30 per cent of the world's cereal crops are fed to animals. Most of the meat, milk and eggs produced from the animals is eaten in the developed world.

Rice

The richest countries grow more food than their people need, while poorer countries often can't grow enough. About 70 per cent of the world's grain is eaten by people in the rich, developed countries, which have only 20 per cent of the population.

To earn money, poor countries often grow 'cash crops' – crops such as coffee, bananas, tobacco and cotton which can be sold to richer nations. This leaves less land for poor farmers, and means that even less food can be grown.

The worst situation of all occurs when a poor country suffers wars or drought – a period when not enough rain falls – lasting several years. Crops can't be grown because of the fighting, or the plants die in the fields for lack of water. The result is that the people have even less to eat than usual, and often many thousands of them starve to death.

▽ Food given by developed countries is distributed to people suffering from famine in a developing country in Africa.

Religions

Throughout the world there are many different religions, all trying to give their followers an explanation for the aspects of life that are beyond our control. There are four major religions:

- **Christianity** is the religion with most followers – about 30 per cent of the world's people claim to be Christians.
- **Islam** is the second largest, with about 17 per cent. Its followers are Muslims.
- **Hinduism** is followed by about 14 per cent of the world's population.
- **Buddhism** is the religion of about 6 per cent of people.

Other religions include Judaism, Sikhism, Confucianism, Taoism, Shintoism and Jainism. One of the oldest religions is animism, in which people believe there is a god or spirit in every object, from animals and plants to rocks and rivers.

△ Many of the tasks involved in assembling cars are now carried out by factory robots controlled by computers.

Industry

Industry is mainly about making, building, mining and processing things. Farming, fishing and tourism are now often called industries, too.

Since the Industrial Revolution, which began in eighteenth-century Britain, most industries have come to rely on machines to make their products. At first, the machines were driven by water power and coal-fired steam-engines, and later by electricity and diesel engines. Machines can make things faster and more cheaply than people, and only a few expensive items are still made by hand.

In many wealthy, developed nations, heavy industries, such as mining, shipbuilding and steel-making, are declining. They are being replaced by service industries, including banking, insurance, tourism and leisure, and by light industries, such as electronics.

Another trend is for more and more industrial processes to be controlled by computers and carried out by robots.

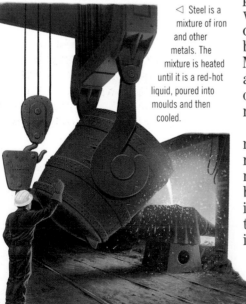

◁ Steel is a mixture of iron and other metals. The mixture is heated until it is a red-hot liquid, poured into moulds and then cooled.

Resources and energy

Resources are things such as fuels, the raw materials from which products are made, and plants and animals that supply such things as food, timber and natural fibres.

The land itself is also a resource. In some places it is being grazed by too many animals and is becoming dry desert where nothing grows.

Energy producers and consumers

- Much of the world's oil comes from the Middle East, especially Saudi Arabia and Iran.
- Although the USA has less than 5 per cent of the world's population, it uses up over 30 per cent of all fossil fuels.
- At present, the developed countries use far more energy than the poorer developing nations. But as the poorer countries become more industrialized, they will consume more and more energy.

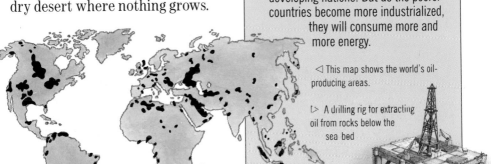

◁ This map shows the world's oil-producing areas.

▷ A drilling rig for extracting oil from rocks below the sea bed

Many resources are now being used up far faster than nature can replace them. This is most true of fossil fuels – oil, gas and coal – from which most of our energy is made.

We can make our resources last longer if we reuse and recycle them, and use renewable energy sources, such as wind and solar power. These actions would also cut down on pollution and reduce the damage caused by mining.

Fish

Some species of fish are disappearing because of overfishing – too many are being caught before they are able to breed. Stocks of cod, herring, haddock and other common fish are now at an all-time low.

Cod

Herring

Haddock

▽ An opencast mine. Huge amounts of rock and soil are removed to expose the minerals below.

The political scene

In 1989, revolutions spread through the countries of Eastern Europe, and the people drove out the Communist leaders who had ruled them since 1945. In 1991, the USSR suffered a similar fate, and that vast country broke up into 15 separate states.

▽ The countries of Eastern Europe in which revolutions took place in 1989 were: Poland (**2**), East Germany (**3**), Czechoslovakia (**5**), Hungary (**6**), Romania (**7**), Albania (**9**) and Bulgaria (**10**). In 1990, East Germany and West Germany (**4**), which had been divided since the end of the Second World War in 1945, were reunified into a single country. In 1990, the republics that made up Yugoslavia (**8**) split up and a fierce civil war followed. The USSR (**1**) was the largest country in the world, with an area of 22 400 000 sq km, until it broke up in 1991.

In the mid-1990s, there were several civil wars in Africa. Among the most brutal was the conflict between the Hutu and Tutsi peoples of Rwanda which began in 1994. It led to the death of more than a million Rwandans and created 1.5 million refugees who fled across the border into Zaire and Tanzania. In 1996, Zaire itself suffered civil war. Rebels overthrew the government and renamed the country the Democratic Republic of the Congo.

At the end of June 1997, Hong Kong was handed back to China. It had been a British colony since 1842. The nearby Portuguese province of Macao returned to China in 1999.

◁ In 1994, Nelson Mandela became President of South Africa in the first elections in which all South Africans could vote. Until then, South Africa was run according to the apartheid system, in which white people held most of the power and money while black people had few rights. The African National Congress, or ANC, had fought to change this but was banned by the government and its leader Nelson Mandela was imprisoned for 27 years. He was finally released in 1990 and the ban on the ANC was lifted.

The United Nations

The United Nations (UN) was set up in 1945 with the aim of preventing wars. It now has more than 150 members. When wars do break out, the UN is sometimes asked to send in peacekeeping forces. This happened after civil war broke out in the former Yugoslavia.

▷ The United Nations symbol – a world map with olive branches, representing peace.

GENERAL KNOWLEDGE

In this section you will find a wide range of useful information on all sorts of subjects.

Famous sevens and twelves

Have you ever noticed how many famous things come in groups of seven or twelve? Here are a few of them:
- **The Seven Seas** – the Arctic, Antarctic, North and South Pacific, North and South Atlantic, and Indian Oceans.
- **The twelve apostles of Jesus** – Peter, Matthew, Andrew, John, James the Less, James the Greater, Philip, Bartholomew, Thomas, Simon, Thaddaeus and Judas.
- **The seven deadly sins** – covetousness, pride, lust, envy, gluttony, anger and sloth.
- **The Twelve Labours of Hercules** – to kill the Nemean lion, kill the Lernean hydra, capture the hind of Ceryneia, capture the boar of Erymanthus, clean the Augean stables, shoot the birds of Stymphalus, capture the Cretan bull, capture the horses of Diomedes, steal Hippolyta's girdle, capture the oxen of Geryon the giant, steal the apples from the garden of the Hesperides, and capture Cerberus, the guardian of Hades.
- **The seven hills of Rome**, on which the city was built – Capitoline, Palatine, Quirinal, Caelian, Aventine, Esquiline and Viminal.
- **The twelve signs of the zodiac** – Aries

Signs of the zodiac

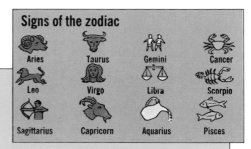

Aries — Taurus — Gemini — Cancer — Leo — Virgo — Libra — Scorpio — Sagittarius — Capricorn — Aquarius — Pisces

(21 March-19 April), Taurus (20 April-20 May), Gemini (21 May-20 June), Cancer (21 June-22 July), Leo (23 July-22 August), Virgo (23 August-22 September), Libra (23 September-22 October), Scorpio (23 October-21 November), Sagittarius (22 November-21 December), Capricorn (22 December-19 January), Aquarius (20 January -18 February) and Pisces (19 February-20 March).

- **The Seven Wonders of the Ancient World** – the pyramids of Egypt, the Hanging Gardens of Babylon, the Pharos of Alexandria, the Temple of Artemis at Ephesus, the tomb of Mausolus at Halicarnassus, the statue of Zeus at Olympia and the Colossus of Rhodes.

The Hanging Gardens of Babylon

Numerals, units and symbols

Arabic, Roman and binary numerals

Arabic	Roman	Binary	Arabic	Roman	Binary
1	I	1	40	XL	101000
2	II	10	50	L	110010
3	III	11	60	LX	111100
4	IV	100	64	LXIV	1000000
5	V	101	90	XC	1011010
6	VI	110	100	C	1100100
7	VII	111	128	CXXVIII	10000000
8	VIII	1000	200	CC	11001000
9	IX	1001	256	CCLVI	100000000
10	X	1010	300	CCC	100101100
11	XI	1011	400	CD	110010000
12	XII	1100	500	D	111110100
13	XIII	1101	512	DXII	1000000000
14	XIV	1110	600	DC	1001011000
15	XV	1111	900	CM	1110000100
16	XVI	10000	1000	M	1111101000
17	XVII	10001	1024	MXXIV	10000000000
18	XVIII	10010	1500	MD	10111011100
19	XIX	10011	1666	MDCLXVI	11010000010
20	XX	10100	2000	MM	11111010000
21	XXI	10101	4000	MV̄	111110100000
25	XXV	11001	5000	V̄	1001110001000
29	XXIX	11101	10 000	X̄	10011100010000
30	XXX	11110	20 000	X̄X̄	100111000100000
32	XXXII	100000	100 000	C̄	11000011010100000

SI units

length: metre (m)
mass: kilogram (kg)
time: second (s)
electric current:
  ampere (A)
thermodynamic
  temperature: kelvin (K)
amount: mole (mol)
luminous intensity:
  candela (cd)

area: square metre (m^2)
volume: cubic metre (m^3)
velocity: metre/second
  ($m\,s^{-1}$)
acceleration:
  metre/second^2 ($m\,s^{-2}$)
density: kilogram/metre^3
  ($kg\,m^{-3}$)
pressure: newton/metre^2
  ($N\,m^{-2}$)

frequency: hertz (Hz)
energy: joule (J)
force: newton (N)
torque: newton metre (N m)
power: watt (W)
electric charge:
  coulomb (C)
potential difference:
  volt (V)
resistance: ohm (Ω)

Mathematical symbols

+	plus
−	minus
±	plus or minus
x	multiplied by (times)
÷	divided by
=	equal to
≠	not equal to
≈	approximately equal to
>	greater than
<	less than
≥	greater than or equal to
≤	less than or equal to
%	per cent
√	square root
π	pi (3.1416)
°	degree
'	minute, foot
"	second, inch
∞	infinity
:	ratio
α	directly proportional to

Multiplication table

To multiply two numbers, first find one of them in the vertical column of **bold** figures on the left side of the table. Then look along the horizontal row of numbers until you find the one in the column under your second number. For example, to multiply 9 x 8, find 9 in the left column and look along the row to the figure below 8. Thus, 9 x 8 = 72.

	2	**3**	**4**	**5**	**6**	**7**	**8**	**9**	**10**	**11**	**12**
2	4	6	8	10	12	14	16	18	20	22	24
3	6	9	12	15	18	21	24	27	30	33	36
4	8	12	16	20	24	28	32	36	40	44	48
5	10	15	20	25	30	35	40	45	50	55	60
6	12	18	24	30	36	42	48	54	60	66	72
7	14	21	28	35	42	49	56	63	70	77	84
8	16	24	32	40	48	56	64	72	80	88	96
9	18	27	36	45	54	63	72	81	90	99	108
10	20	30	40	50	60	70	80	90	100	110	120
11	22	33	44	55	66	77	88	99	110	121	132
12	24	36	48	60	72	84	96	108	120	132	144

Fractions and decimals

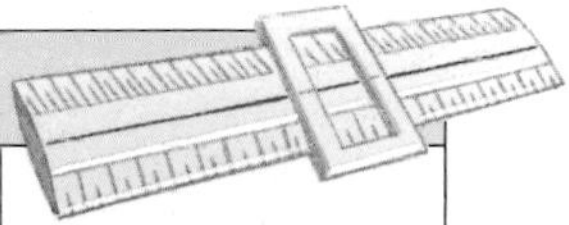

Fraction	Decimal	Fraction	Decimal	Fraction	Decimal	Fraction	Decimal
1/2	0.5000	5/8	0.6250	9/11	0.8181		
1/3	0.3333	7/8	0.8750	10/11	0.9090		
2/3	0.6667	1/9	0.1111	1/12	0.0833	17/20	0.8500
1/4	0.2500	2/9	0.2222	5/12	0.4167	19/20	0.9500
3/4	0.7500	4/9	0.4444	7/12	0.5833	1/32	0.0312
1/5	0.2000	5/9	0.5556	11/12	0.9167	3/32	0.0938
2/5	0.4000	7/9	0.7778	1/16	0.0625	5/32	0.1567
3/5	0.6000	8/9	0.8889	3/16	0.1875	7/32	0.2187
4/5	0.8000	1/10	0.1000	5/16	0.3125	9/32	0.2812
1/6	0.1667	3/10	0.3000	7/16	0.4375	11/32	0.3437
5/6	0.8333	7/10	0.7000	9/16	0.5625	13/32	0.4062
1/7	0.1429	9/10	0.9000	11/16	0.6875	15/32	0.4687
2/7	0.2857	1/11	0.0909	13/16	0.8125	17/32	0.5312
3/7	0.4286	2/11	0.1818	15/16	0.9375	19/32	0.5937
4/7	0.5714	3/11	0.2727	1/20	0.0500	21/32	0.6562
5/7	0.7143	4/11	0.3636	3/20	0.1500	23/32	0.7187
6/7	0.8571	5/11	0.4545	7/20	0.3500	25/32	0.7812
1/8	0.1250	6/11	0.5454	9/20	0.4500	27/32	0.8437
3/8	0.3750	7/11	0.6363	11/20	0.5500	29/32	0.9062
		8/11	0.7272	13/20	0.6500	31/32	0.9687

Metric-Imperial conversions

Metric units into Imperial units

To convert	Into	Multiply by
Length		
centimetres	inches	0.3937
metres	feet	3.2808
kilometres	miles	0.6214
Area		
square centimetres	square inches	0.155
square metres	square feet	10.7639
hectares	acres	2.471
square kilometres	square miles	0.3861
Volume		
cubic centimetres	cubic inches	0.061
litres	pints	1.7598
litres	gallons	0.2199
Mass		
grams	ounces	0.0353
kilograms	pounds	2.2046
tonnes	tons	0.9842

Imperial units into metric units

To convert	Into	Multiply by
Length		
inches	centimetres	2.54
feet	metres	0.3048
miles	kilometres	1.6093
Area		
square inches	square centimetres	6.4516
square feet	square metres	0.0929
acres	hectares	0.4047
square miles	square kilometres	2.5899
Volume		
cubic inches	cubic centimetres	16.3871
pints	litres	0.5682
gallons	litres	4.546
Mass		
ounces	grams	28.3495
pounds	kilograms	0.4536
tons	tonnes	1.016

Time zones and seasons

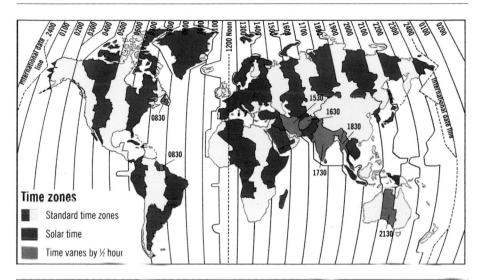

Time zones

■ Standard time zones

■ Solar time

■ Time varies by ½ hour

Day and night

We have day and night because the Earth spins on its axis, making one turn every 23 hours, 56 minutes and 4 seconds. The side of the Earth facing the Sun has day and the other side has night. As the Earth turns, day becomes night and then day again.

We set our clocks so that at 12 noon the Sun is at its highest point in the sky. This occurs at different times all around the world, and so time varies from place to place. That is why the world is divided into different time zones, as shown on the map above.

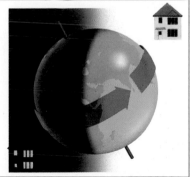

The seasons

We have seasons because the Earth is tilted in space. When the northern half of the world (or hemisphere) is tilted towards the Sun, it is summer there and winter in the southern half. Spring and autumn are the seasons in which winter is changing to summer and summer to winter. The appoximate dates of the seasons are:

• **Northern hemisphere** Spring: 21 March-21 June, Summer: 21 June-23 September, Autumn: 23 September-21 December, Winter: 21 December-21 March

• **Southern hemisphere** Spring: 23 September-21 December, Summer: 21 December-21 March, Autumn: 21 March-21 June, Winter: 21 June-23 September.

Airline Marks and Insignia

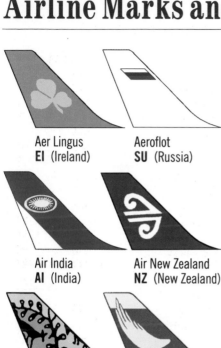

Aer Lingus **EI** (Ireland)	Aeroflot **SU** (Russia)

Air India **AI** (India)	Air New Zealand **NZ** (New Zealand)

British Airways **BA** (UK)	Cathay Pacific Airways **CX** (Hong Kong)

El Al Israel Airlines **LY** (Israel)	Garuda Indonesia **GA** (Indonesia)

Japan Airlines
JL (Japan)

KLM
KL (Netherlands)

Air Canada
AC (Canada)

Air France
AF (France)

Alitalia
AZ (Italy)

American Airlines
AA (USA)

Delta Air Lines
DL (USA)

Egyptair
MS (Egypt)

Gulf Air
GF (Bahrain)

Iberia
IB (Spain)

Lufthansa
LH (Germany)

Malaysian Airlines
MH (Malaysia)

Olympic Airways
OA (Greece)

Pakistan Int. Airlines
PK (Pakistan)

Qantas
QF (Australia)

Sabena Airlines
SN (Belgium)

Scandinavian Airlines
SK (Sweden)

Singapore Airlines
SQ (Singapore)

Swissair
SR (Switzerland)

Thai Airways Int.
TG (Thailand)

United Airlines
UA (USA)

Varig
RG (Brazil)

Distances by air

The distances by air from London to other major cities around the world.

City	Distance km	miles
Amsterdam	372	232
Athens	2416	1501
Baghdad	4929	3063
Berlin	954	593
Bombay	7887	4901
Brussels	351	218
Buenos Aires	11 138	6961
Cairo	3531	2206
Calcutta	7986	4991
Chicago	6641	4127
Colombo	9421	5854
Copenhagen	980	609
Djakarta	13 417	8337
Dublin	449	280
Geneva	753	468
Gibraltar	1746	1085
Hong Kong	13 038	8102
Johannesburg	9093	5683
Karachi	6338	3961
Kuala Lumpur	12 686	7883
Lagos	5473	3401
Lisbon	1565	972
Los Angeles	8758	5442
Madrid	1247	775
Melbourne	19 206	11 934
Mexico City	9178	5703
Montreal	5216	3260
Moscow	2493	1549
Nairobi	7128	4429
New York	5541	3463
Oslo	1162	722
Paris	346	215
Rome	1461	908
San Francisco	9928	6169
Singapore	10 879	6799
Sydney	17 019	10 636
Tokyo	16 200	10 066
Warsaw	1471	914

Currencies

Country	Currency	Country	Currency
Afghanistan	afghani	Djibouti	Djibouti franc
Albania	lek	Dominica	East Caribbean dollar
Algeria	Algerian dinar	Dominican Republic	Dominican peso
Andorra	French franc, Spanish peseta	Ecuador	sucre
Angola	new kwanza	Egypt	Egyptian pound
Antigua & Barbuda	East Carib. dollar	El Salvador	El Salvador colón
Argentina	Argentine peso	Equatorial Guinea	ekwele
Armenia	dram	Eritrea	Ethiopian birr
Australia	Australian dollar	Estonia	kroon
Austria	schilling	Ethiopia	birr
Azerbaijan	manat	Fiji	Fiji dollar
Bahamas	Bahamian dollar	Finland	markka
Bahrain	Bahrain dinar	France	French franc
Bangladesh	taka	Gabon	CFA franc
Barbados	Barbadian dollar	Gambia	dalaisi
Belarus	rouble	Georgia	kupon
Belgium	Belgian franc	Germany	Deutsche mark
Belize	Belize dollar	Ghana	cedi
Benin	CFA franc	Greece	drachma
Bhutan	ngultrum	Grenada	East Caribbean dollar
Bolivia	Boliviano	Guatemala	quetzal
Bosnia-Herzegovina	Bosnian dinar	Guinea	Guinean franc
Botswana	pula	Guinea-Bissau	Guinea-Bissau peso
Brazil	real	Guyana	Guyana dollar
Brunei	Brunei dollar	Haiti	gourde
Bulgaria	lev	Honduras	lempira
Burkina Faso	CFA franc	Hong Kong	Hong Kong dollar
Burundi	Burundi franc	Hungary	forint
Cambodia	riel	Iceland	krónur
Cameroon	CFA franc	India	Indian rupee
Canada	Canadian dollar	Indonesia	rupiah
Cape Verde	escudo	Iran	Iranian rial
Central African Republic	CFA franc	Iraq	Iraqi dinar
Chad	CFA franc	Ireland	Irish pound
Chile	Chilean peso	Israel	shekel
China	yuan	Italy	Italian lira
Colombia	Colombian peso	Jamaica	Jamaican dollar
Comoros	CFA franc	Japan	yen
Congo	CFA franc	Jordan	Jordanian dinar
Costa Rica	Costa Rican colón	Kazakhstan	tenge
Côte d'Ivoire	CFA franc	Kenya	Kenyan shilling
Croatia	Croatian dinar	Kyrgystan	som
Cuba	Cuban peso	Kiribati	Australian dollar
Cyprus	Cypriot pound, Turkish lira	Korea, North	won
Czech Republic	koruna	Korea, South	won
Denmark	Danish krone	Kuwait	Kuwaiti dinar

Country	Currency	Country	Currency
Laos	kip	St Lucia	East Caribbean dollar
Latvia	lats	St Vincent & Grenadines	E. Carib. dollar
Lebanon	Lebanese pound	San Marino	Italian lira
Lesotho	loti	São Tomé & Príncipe	dobra
Liberia	Liberian dollar	Saudi Arabia	Saudi Arabian riyal
Libya	Libyan dinar	Senegal	CFA franc
Liechtenstein	Swiss franc	Seychelles	Seychelles rupee
Lithuania	litas	Sierra Leone	leone
Luxembourg	Luxembourg franc	Singapore	Singapore dollar
Macedonia	denar	Slovakia	koruna
Madagascar	Madagascar franc	Slovenia	tolar
Malawi	Malawi kwacha	Solomon Islands	Solomon Is. dollar
Malaysia	ringgit	Somalia	Somali shilling
Maldives	rufiyaa	South Africa	rand
Mali	CFA franc	Spain	peseta
Malta	Maltese lira	Sri Lanka	Sri Lankan rupee
Marshall Islands	US dollar	Sudan	pound
Mauritania	ougiya	Surinam	Surinam guilder
Mauritius	Mauritian rupee	Swaziland	emalangeni
Mexico	Mexican new peso	Sweden	Swedish krona
Micronesia	US dollar	Switzerland	Swiss franc
Moldova	leu	Syria	Syrian pound
Monaco	French franc	Tadzhikistan	Tadzik rouble
Mongolia	tughrik	Taiwan	new Taiwan dollar
Morocco	Moroccan dirham	Tanzania	Tanzanian shilling
Mozambique	metical	Thailand	baht
Myanmar (Burma)	kyat	Togo	CFA franc
Namibia	Namibian dollar	Tonga	pa'anga
Nauru	Australian dollar	Trinidad & Tobago	Trin. & Tobago dollar
Nepal	Nepalese rupee	Tunisia	Tunisian dinar
Netherlands	Dutch guilder	Turkey	Turkish lira
New Zealand	New Zealand dollar	Turkmenistan	manat
Nicaragua	new córdoba	Tuvalu	Australian dollar
Niger	CFA franc	Uganda	Ugandan shilling
Nigeria	naira	Ukraine	coupons
Norway	Norwegian krone	United Arab Emirates	UAE dirham
Oman	Omani rial	United Kingdom	pound sterling
Pakistan	Pakistan rupee	Uruguay	Uruguayan peso
Palau	US dollar	USA	US dollar
Panama	balboa	Uzbekistan	som
Papua New Guinea	kina	Vanuatu	vatu
Paraguay	guaraní	Vatican City	Italian lira
Peru	sol	Venezuela	bolivar
Philippines	Philippine peso	Vietnam	dông
Poland	zloty	Western Samoa	tala
Portugal	escudo	Yemen	Yemeni riyal
Qatar	Qatar riyal	Yugoslavia	new dinar
Romania	leu	Zaire (Dem. Rep. of the Congo)	new zaïre
Russia	rouble	Zambia	Zambian kwacha
Rwanda	Rwanda franc	Zimbabwe	Zimbabwe dollar
St Kitts-Nevis	East Caribbean dollar		

Foreign Words and Phrases

L – Latin; F – French; G – German; I – Italian; S – Spanish; P – Portuguese.

à bas (F) down with
ad hoc (L) for this purpose
ad infinitum (L) to infinity; for ever
ad nauseam (L) to a disgusting degree
aficionado (S) enthusiast for a sport or hobby
aide-mémoire (F) aid to memory
alter ego (L) one's other self
amour propre (F) self-respect
ancien régime (F) the old order of things
Angst (G) fear, anxiety
à propos (F) to the point
au contraire (F) on the contrary
auf Wiedersehen (G) till we meet again
au naturel (F) in its natural state
au revoir (F) till we meet again
auto-da-fé (P) act of faith

bête noire (F) pet hate
billet doux (F) love letter
bis (F, I, L) twice
bona fide (L) genuine
bon marché (F) a bargain; cheap
bon voyage (F) have a good journey

café au lait (F) coffee with milk
carpe diem (L) enjoy the day
carte blanche (F) full powers
cause célèbre (F) famous law case
caveat emptor (L) let the buyer beware
chacun à son goût (F) each to his or her own taste
chef-d'oeuvre (F) a masterpiece
che sarà sarà (I) what will be, will be
circa (L) about
comme il faut (F) as it should be
compos mentis (L) of sound mind; sane
coup d'état (F) sudden change of government

de facto (L) in fact
déjà vu (F) seen before
de rigueur (F) as etiquette requires
Deus ex machina (L) a solution to a problem in the nick of time
ditto (I) the same; the above
double entendre (F) double meaning

embarras de richesse (F) having too much
éminence grise (F) power behind the throne
en famille (F) with one's family; at home
enfant terrible (F) indiscreet person
en masse (F) in a large group
en route (F) on the way
et cetera (L) and the rest; and others

fait accompli (F) an accomplished fact
faux pas (F) mistake; false step
fiesta (S) festival; holiday

hors-d'œuvre (F) appetizer

ibidem (ibid) (L) in the same place

idée fixe (F) an obsession

in extremis (L) at the point of death

in memoriam (L) in memory (of)

in situ (L) in position

inter alia (L) among other things

in toto (L) entirely

ipso facto (L) from the facts

je ne sais quoi (F) a quality or feature that can't be described

laissez-faire (F) leave alone; policy of non-interference

lèse-majesté (F) treason

locum tenens (L) a substitute

magnum opus (L) a great work; an author's main book

mea culpa (L) it is my fault

modus operandi (L) a way of working

modus vivendi (L) a way of living

nil desperandum (L) despair of nothing

nom de guerre (F) assumed name

nom de plume (F) assumed name of an author

nom de théâtre (F) stage name

non compos mentis (L) of unsound mind

non sequitur (L) it does not follow

opus (L) work of art, literature or music

per annum (L) yearly

per capita (L) for each person

per diem (L) daily

per mensem (L) monthly

persona non grata (L) an unacceptable person

pièce de résistance (F) the main item

post mortem (L) after death

précis (F) summary

prima facie (L) at first sight

prix fixe (F) fixed price

pro rata (L) in proportion

quid pro quo (L) something in return

raison d'être (F) purpose of existence

requiescat in pace (RIP) (L) rest in peace

résumé (F) summary

sans souci (F) carefree

savoir-faire (F) skill; tact

semper fidelis (L) always faithful

sic (L) thus; so

simpatico (I) congenial

sine qua non (L) an indispensable condition

sobriquet (F) nickname

soi-disant (L) self-styled

sotto voce (L) in an undertone or whisper

status quo (L) the present state of things

table d'hôte (F) a set meal

terra firma (L) solid ground

tête-à-tête (F) private talk between two people

versus (L) against

vice versa (L) the order being reversed

vis-à-vis (F) face to face

243

Abbreviations

AA Automobile Association
AB Able-bodied seaman
AC/ac alternating current
a/c account
AD *anno Domini* (in the year of Our Lord)
am *ante meridiem* (before noon)

BA Bachelor of Arts; British Airways
BBC British Broadcasting Corporation
BC before Christ
BMA British Medical Association
BSc Bachelor of Science
BSE bovine spongiform encephalopathy
BSI British Standards Institution
BST British Summer Time

c *circa* (about)
C Centigrade
CAD computer aided design
CAM computer aided manufacture
CAP Common Agricultural Policy
CATV cable television
CB citizen's band (radio)
CCTV closed circuit television
CD-ROM compact disc read-only memory
CE Church of England
CIA Central Intelligence Agency
CID Criminal Investigation Department
CIS Commonwealth of Independent States
CO Commanding Officer

DC/dc direct current
DNA deoxyribonucleic acid
DST daylight saving time
DTP desktop publishing

eg *exempli gratia* (for example)
EC European Community
ECU European Currency Unit
EEC European Economic Community
EFTA European Free Trade Association
ERNIE Electronic Random Number Indicator Equipment

f *forte* (loud) ff *fortissimo* (very loud)
F Fahrenheit
FA Football Association
FBI Federal Bureau of Investigation
FM/fm frequency modulation
FRS Fellow of the Royal Society

GATT General Agreement on Tariffs and Trade
GCSE General Certificate of Secondary Education
GDP gross domestic product
GMT Greenwich Mean Time
GNP gross national product
GP general practitioner

HEP hydro-electric power
HMS Her/His Majesty's Ship
hp horsepower
HQ headquarters

ie *id est* (that is)
IMF International Monetary Fund
IQ intelligence quotient
IRA Irish Republican Army

JP Justice of the Peace

LCD liquid crystal display
LED light-emitting diode
LL B Bachelor of Laws
LL D Doctor of Laws

MA Master of Arts
MP Member of Parliament
MS manuscript; *plural* **MSS**
MSc Master of Science

NATO North Atlantic Treaty Organization
NB *nota bene* (note well)
NHS National Health Service
No number; *plural* **Nos**

OHMS On Her/His Majesty's Service
OPEC Organization of Petroleum Exporting Countries

p *piano* (soft) **pp** *pianissimo* (very soft)
PC personal computer
PhD Doctor of Philosophy
plc public limited company
pm *post meridiem* (after noon)
PO Post Office
POW prisoner of war
PS *postscriptum* (postscript); *plural* **PSS**
PTO please turn over

QC Queen's Counsel

RA Royal Academy
RADA Royal Academy of Dramatic Art
RAF Royal Air Force
RAM random access memory
REM rapid eye movement
RN Royal Navy
ROM read-only memory
RPI retail price index
rpm revolutions per minute

sae stamped addressed envelope
SI Système Internationale d'Unités (International System)

TUC Trades Union Congress

UAE United Arab Emirates
UFO unidentified flying object
UHF ultra high frequency
UK United Kingdom
UN United Nations
USA United States of America

VAT value added tax
VCR video cassette recorder
VHF very high frequency
VHS Video Home Service
VIP very important person
VSO Voluntary Service Overseas

WHO World Health Organization
WRAC Women's Royal Army Corps
WRAF Women's Royal Air Force
WRNS Women's Royal Naval Service
WWF World Wide Fund for Nature

YHA Youth Hostels Association

Sending signals

In an emergency, it may be vital to get help by attracting the attention of other people. There are several ways of sending distress signals, including semaphore, Morse code and international ground-to-air signals. When using a telephone or radio, letters can be misheard. To avoid confusion, follow each letter with its NATO alphabet equivalent.

Semaphore

This method of signalling uses two hand-held flags, or two mechanically operated arms attached to an upright post, and can only be used in daylight. It was widely used for sending messages at sea before the development of electricity led to the invention of other, more reliable, methods that can also be used in the dark.

A and 1   B and 2   C and 3   D and 4   E and 5   F and 6   G and 7

H and 8   I and 9   J   K and 0   L   M   N

O   P   Q   R   S   T   U

V   W   X   Y   Z   Number

Morse code

This was invented by Samuel Morse in 1837. Letters consist of combinations of dots and dashes. Messages can be sent by flashing a light, by sound, or by waving a flag (to your right for a dot, left for a dash).

A ●▬		S ●●●	
B ▬●●●		T ▬	
C ▬●▬●		U ●●▬	
D ▬●●		V ●●●▬	
E ●		W ●▬▬	
F ●●▬●		X ▬●●▬	
G ▬▬●		Y ▬●▬▬	
H ●●●●		Z ▬▬●●	
I ●●		1 ●▬▬▬▬	
J ●▬▬▬		2 ●●▬▬▬	
K ▬●▬		3 ●●●▬▬	
L ●▬●●		4 ●●●●▬	
M ▬▬		5 ●●●●●	
N ▬●		6 ▬●●●●	
O ▬▬▬		7 ▬▬●●●	
P ●▬▬●		8 ▬▬▬●●	
Q ▬▬●▬		9 ▬▬▬▬●	
R ●▬●		0 ▬▬▬▬▬	

I Doctor needed; serious injury

II Medical supplies needed

X Unable to proceed further

F Food and water needed

LL All well with us

△ Safe to land at this spot

K Indicate direction and proceed

↑ I am/we are proceeding in this direction

⊐L Message not understood

N No

Y Yes

□ I/we need map and compass

Ground-to-air signals

These symbols are made using stones, vegetation, clothes, or marks in snow or sand, to be seen by searching aircraft.

NATO alphabet

A	Alpha	J	Juliet	S	Sierra
B	Bravo	K	Kilo	T	Tango
C	Charlie	L	Lima	U	Uniform
D	Delta	M	Mike	V	Victor
E	Echo	N	November	W	Whisky
F	Foxtrot	O	Oscar	X	X-ray
G	Golf	P	Papa	Y	Yankee
H	Hotel	Q	Quebec	Z	Zulu
I	India	R	Romeo		

Braille

Braille is a system of writing and printing for blind people. Each letter consists of a pattern of raised dots, based on the six dots of a domino. People can learn how to 'read' these letters with their fingertips. The alphabet was invented in 1843 by Louis Braille, a Frenchman who had been blinded in an accident in his childhood.

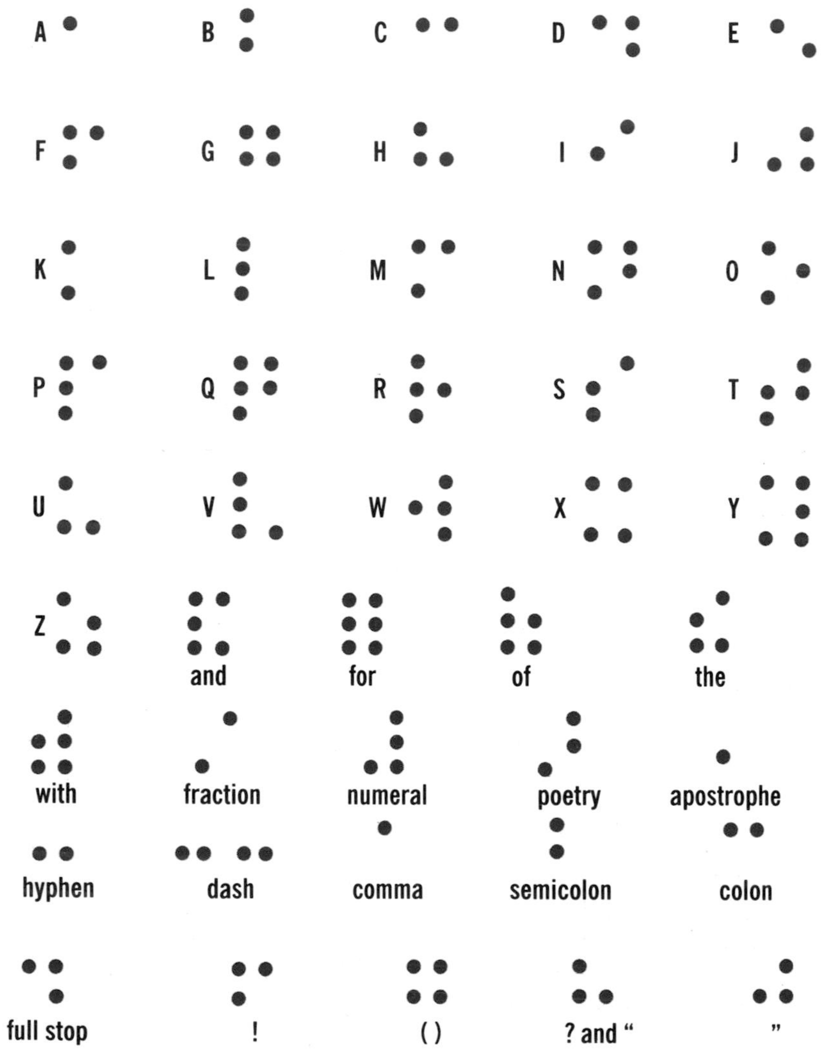

A   B   C   D   E

F   G   H   I   J

K   L   M   N   O

P   Q   R   S   T

U   V   W   X   Y

Z   and   for   of   the

with   fraction   numeral   poetry   apostrophe

hyphen   dash   comma   semicolon   colon

full stop   !   ( )   ? and "   "

Sign language

▽ The sign language alphabet used in Britain. There are a number of other types of sign language which are used in some countries. They are all quite different and a person who knows one type can't necessarily understand any others.

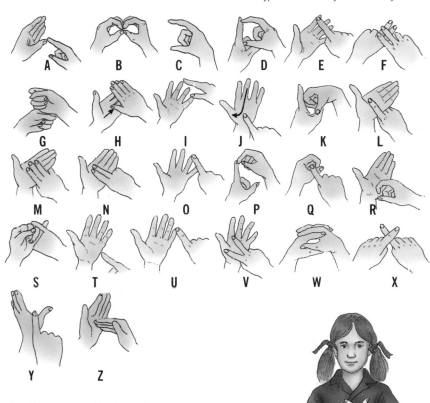

In sign language, the hands are used instead of spoken or written words. It was developed for people who are deaf, dumb or both. The illustration above shows the signs used to make the letters of the alphabet. There are other signs that represent whole words.

The first known sign language for deaf people was developed in 1775 by Abbé Charles Michel de l'Epée for use at a school for the deaf in Paris, France.

▷ This girl is 'signing'. In some television programmes, you may see a person in one corner of the screen using sign language. This helps people who are deaf to enjoy the programme as well as people who are able to hear.

249

First aid

▷ Mouth-to-mouth ventilation.
Between breaths, shout for help.

Accidents can happen at any time, and being able to help an injured person on the spot, before medical attention arrives, could reduce their suffering and anxiety and, in some cases, even save their life.

Below is an introduction to some first aid techniques. The best way to learn is to take a course – contact your local Red Cross for details.

Pulse

The pulse is a throb that passes through the arteries with each beat of the heart. The best places to take a pulse are at the wrist or the neck. At the wrist, place the pads of three fingers firmly on the inside of the arm, just above the wrist. For the neck, place the pads of two or three fingers in the hollow of the neck, just below the ear. Count the number of beats in a minute. A normal pulse is regular and strong, and in adults it averages 60–80 beats a minute; in children it beats up to 100 times a minute.

Unconsciousness

If a person is unconscious, first open their airway (the space between the mouth, nose and throat). Tilt the head back, with the chin pointing upwards. Next, see if the patient is breathing. Put your ear near their mouth and look along the chest.

Listen and feel for breaths and look to see if the chest is moving up and down.

Speed is vital if a patient is not breathing. The best method of getting air into the lungs is mouth-to-mouth ventilation. Keep the patient's head well back, jaw lifted and the mouth open. Run two fingers around the inside of the mouth to check the airway is not blocked by the tongue, broken teeth, mud or vomit. Pinch the nostrils shut with one hand. Take a deep breath, open your mouth wide and seal your lips around the patient's mouth. Blow firmly but gently from your lungs into the patient's mouth. The chest should rise; stop and look to see if it falls as the air comes out again.

▷ **Recovery position**
Once a patient is breathing and the airway is clear, put them in the recovery position.
1 Turn the patient's head towards you and tilt it well back.
2 Pull the patient towards you until they are resting against you.
3 Bend the arm and leg nearest to you to form a right angle to the rest of the body. This will stop the patient rolling on to their face.
4 Straighten the arm furthest from you so it is lying parallel to the patient's body, and slightly bend the leg furthest from you. This will stop the patient rolling on to their back.

Continue this process – blowing into the mouth and then coming away – until the patient starts breathing. Then place them in the recovery position. If breathing does not start, check the pulse in the neck. If there is no pulse, begin chest compression (see below). **Warning: Never practise mouth-to-mouth ventilation on a person who is breathing normally.**

Bleeding

Minor cuts and grazes should be cleaned and dressed. They will then probably heal themselves.

△ Pressing on the wound helps to stop the bleeding.

Serious bleeding must be stopped immediately. First, press on the wound with your thumb and/or fingers, preferably over a clean pad. Lift the injured part above the patient's chest level. Put a sterile dressing on the wound and secure it firmly. In an emergency, use torn-up clothes, handkerchiefs or pillow cases. If blood shows through, don't remove the dressing – put more dressings on top. Watch for signs of shock (see page 252).

Burns

If a person's clothing is on fire, lay them down and douse the flames with water or wrap a blanket or coat around them to smother the flames. A burn should be plunged into cold water immediately and kept there until the pain fades. Dry the area, taking care not to burst any blisters, and cover with a clean, dry dressing. If the burn is severe, get the patient to hospital.

External chest compression

If you cannot feel any pulse in a patient's neck, their heart has stopped beating, cutting off the blood supply to the brain. This technique is intended to restart it.

1 Lay the patient flat on the ground. Place the heel of your hand 4 cm above the bottom of the breast bone. Cover your hand with the heel of your other hand.

2 Kneel upright with your arms straight. Press down about 4.5 cm, then release but do not remove your hands. Do this rapidly 15 times, then give two breaths of mouth-to-mouth. Repeat this, checking the pulse every 3 minutes.

3 When the pulse has returned, stop pumping immediately and continue with mouth-to-mouth ventilation until natural breathing is restored.

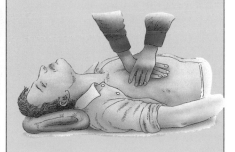

AIDS (acquired immune deficiency syndrome)

This disease can result from direct contact with blood contaminated with the HIV virus. If possible, wear plastic or surgical gloves when treating wounds, cuts or burns.

Fractures and sprains

Broken bones should be supported and the injured part secured to an uninjured part of the body using soft padding and bandages.

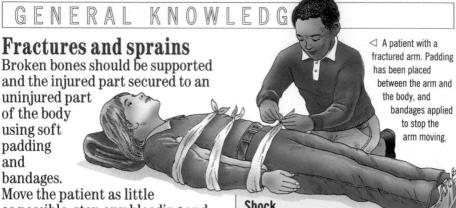

◁ A patient with a fractured arm. Padding has been placed between the arm and the body, and bandages applied to stop the arm moving.

Move the patient as little as possible, stop any bleeding and cover open wounds with sterile bandages. Treat for shock if necessary.

For a sprain, raise the injured part and put on a cold compress – a cloth soaked in cold water and wrung out – or an ice pack. This will reduce the blood flow and swelling. Wrap the sprain with a thick layer of cotton wool and a firm bandage.

Choking

Choking is caused by a blocked windpipe. Tell the patient to bend forward with their head lower than their chest, and to cough. If they can't cough, give four sharp slaps between the shoulder blades with the heel of your hand. Repeat four times, if necessary. Check inside the patient's mouth for any obstructions that you can remove with your fingers. If the patient still can't breathe, stand behind them and place your clenched fist over their stomach. Grasp your fist with the other hand and pull suddenly inward and upward. The obstruction should shoot into and out of the mouth.

Shock

A person with shock looks pale and grey and has a weak, rapid pulse. After any accident, always treat the patient for shock, but treat their injuries and stop any bleeding first. Move the patient as little as possible and give plenty of reassurance.

Lay the patient down with their legs raised – perhaps with a folded coat under their feet – and loosen any tight clothing. Keep them comfortably warm, but don't use artificial heat, such as a hot water bottle. Don't give anything to eat or drink – the patient may have internal bleeding, or might need a general anaesthetic later.

Stings and bites

Most stings and bites cause only temporary discomfort. Insects such as bees leave a small sting in the skin and this should be removed with a pair of tweezers. Apply a cold compress (a damp, cold cloth) and rest the injured part. If there is a severe allergic reaction, get medical attention immediately.

▷ A cold compress or an ice pack will reduce the pain and swelling caused by a sting or bite.

Poisoning

Poisons can enter the body by being swallowed, inhaled, injected or absorbed by the skin. The procedure for first aid treatment is as follows:

1 Call a doctor or ambulance immediately telling them what poison you think has been taken.

2 If the person is unconscious, follow the treatment for an unconscious patient.

3 Get them to hospital as soon as possible, with any tablets or containers found near them and samples of vomit.

▷ **Body temperature** Normal temperature is between 36.9 and 37°C (98.4–98.6°F). A temperature 2°C (3°F) above the normal range usually means there is something wrong but body temperature can vary throughout the day and from person to person. If the temperature drops below 35°C (95°F) then the patient must be kept warm, as hypothermia could develop.

Before using a clinical thermometer (like the one shown here), make sure the silvery thread of mercury has been shaken down into the bulb. In adults, take the temperature by placing the thermometer under the tongue and leaving it for 3 minutes. With very young children, you can use the armpit, which can be kept warm by holding the arm down by the side. Alternatively, use a tape thermometer.

▽ All first aid equipment should be kept in a clean, dry, airtight box which is clearly labelled. Keep the box in a dry place, not in the kitchen or bathroom where its contents could be affected by steam. It must also be kept out of the reach of children.

Variety of dressings and bandages for different injuries

Tweezers to remove splinters

Cotton wool

Adhesive dressings for small cuts and grazes

Pain killing tablets

Scissors to cut bandages

Safety pins and adhesive tape to secure dressings

Eye bath for washing eyes clean of chemicals

Antiseptic cream for minor cuts

Large bandage to support fractures

Elastic bandages to support sprains

Surgical gloves

Emergency checklist

- If there is an uninjured person on hand, send them immediately to get help. The fastest way may be to telephone the emergency services on 999 and ask for an ambulance. If possible, stay with the patient until medical help arrives.
- Treat the patient where they are, if it is safe to do so.
- If the patient is unconscious, open the airway, and check breathing and pulse.
- Stop severe bleeding immediately.
- Immobilize broken bones.
- Reassure the patient and treat for shock, if necessary.
- Keep notes to help the doctor or police, if you have time.
- Look after the patient's property.

INDEX

EQUATORIAL GUINEA
 ERITREA
 ETHIOPIA
 GAMBIA
 GHANA

 GUINEA
 GUINEA-BISSAU
 IVORY COAST
 LIBERIA
 LIBYA

 MALI
 MAURITANIA
 MOROCCO
 NIGER
 NIGERIA

 SÃO TOMÉ & PRINCIPE
 SENEGAL
 SIERRA LEONE
 SOMALI REPUBLIC
 SUDAN

 TOGO
 TUNISIA
 WESTERN SAHARA
 ANGOLA
 BOTSWANA

 BURUNDI
 COMORO ISLANDS
 CONGO
 GABON
 KENYA

 LESOTHO
 MADAGASCAR
 MALAWI
 MAURITIUS
 MOZAMBIQUE

 NAMIBIA
 RWANDA
 SEYCHELLES
 SOUTH AFRICA
 SWAZILAND

 TANZANIA
 UGANDA
 ZAIRE
 ZAMBIA
 ZIMBABWE

 CANADA
UNITED STATES
OF AMERICA
ANTIGUA & BARBUDA
BAHAMAS
BARBADOS